IMAGES
of America

KIOWA COUNTY

KIOWA COUNTY

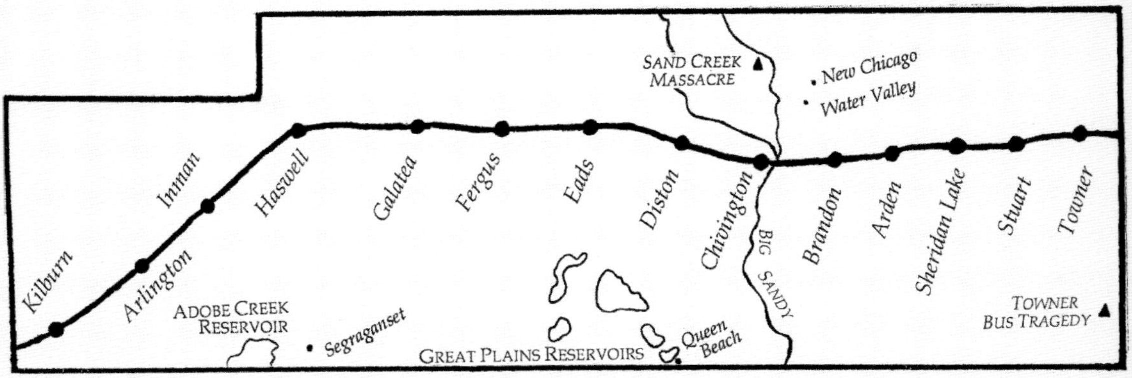

KIOWA COUNTY. Located on the plains of southeastern Colorado, Kiowa County is a rural area with wide-open spaces and an agriculture-based economy. The county measures 78 miles long east to west and 24 miles north to south; the total land area is 1,148,160 acres or 1,794 square miles. This map depicts several sites discussed throughout this book. (Map courtesy Lori Weirich.)

ON THE COVER: Local cowboys Seeley Sherman, Kent France, and Francis Sherman sit on horseback in front of the Kingdon Hotel in Chivington during the town's boom days. Built in the 1887, the hotel was "one of the finest hotels in the west," according to a *Chivington Chief* magazine article. The Queen Anne–style Kingdon Hotel had 60 sleeping rooms, dining rooms, a dance hall, and a 50-foot cupola. The three-story grand hotel was named after Edith Kingdon Gould. (Photograph courtesy Kiowa County Museum.)

IMAGES
of America

KIOWA COUNTY

Eads High School Local History Project
and the Kiowa County Historical Society

ARCADIA
PUBLISHING

ISBN 978-0-7385-8093-7

Published by Arcadia Publishing
Charleston SC, Chicago IL, Portsmouth NH, San Francisco CA

Printed in the United States of America

Library of Congress Control Number: 2010921321

For all general information contact Arcadia Publishing at:
Telephone 843-853-2070
Fax 843-853-0044
E-mail sales@arcadiapublishing.com
For customer service and orders:
Toll-Free 1-888-313-2665

Visit us on the Internet at www.arcadiapublishing.com

To the historians of Kiowa County, past, present, and future,
whose dedication has preserved our local history.

Contents

Acknowledgments

In August 2009, a group of six seniors from the class of 2010 agreed to take on the ambitious project of producing a photographic history of Kiowa County as part of the Local History Project class. Shayla Fagan, Shelby Harris, Ciara Lyon, Jennifer Negley, Garrett Smith, and Lori Weirich worked with their teacher, Kelly Courkamp, to identify and research photographs that represented the county's history. Using a variety of resources to find information about pioneers, schoolhouses, and businesses of yesterday, they learned a great deal about the history of their home county in the process.

The success of this book would not have been possible without the historic research of so many others. Local historians have produced two books about Kiowa County that were invaluable resources to us: *Kiowa County* and *Kiowa County, Colorado: Centennial History*. Additionally, the Kiowa County Public Library had terrific resources on the railroad and historic schools. We would also like to thank Betsy Barnett for finding historic photographs and unpublished information and for reviewing our work; Jeff C. Campbell for sharing his timeline of Kiowa County history and reviewing the text for the book; and Ruthanna Jacobs for her review and comments. Craig Moore, interpreter at the Sand Creek Massacre National Historic Site, found photographs and wrote the captions for the chapter on the Sand Creek Massacre; we truly appreciate his time and expertise. We also would like to extend special thanks to David Adamson for sharing several original photographs taken by Frank Sherman. Adamson's aunt, Martha Adamson Sherman, was married to Francis Sherman, the brother and subject of many of Frank Sherman's images. The photographs David shared with us were given to Martha Sherman by Frank Sherman and were passed down to him. And finally, numerous thanks go to the Kiowa County Museum for the use of the photographs in this book. Unless otherwise noted, all images come from the museum collections. The proceeds of this book will benefit the Kiowa County Museum so that the county's history may continue to be preserved and interpreted into the future.

INTRODUCTION

Located on the high plains of southeastern Colorado, the area now known as Kiowa County has been defined for centuries by its relative isolation. Regardless, Kiowa County has experienced a rich history through Native American and pioneer times, boom and bust, hope and tragedy, and perseverance.

Prior to the 1870s, explorers and pioneers rushed through—rather than to—Colorado's eastern plains. A complex series of interactions between humans and the environment defined the settlement era of Colorado. For centuries, Native Americans occupied what is now Colorado, and many tribes had claimed the region over time. By the late 1700s and into the 1800s, the Cheyenne controlled much of the eastern plains and Front Range of Colorado. The plains supported their horses as well as vast herds of bison, the staple of their existence. By the 1820s, fur trappers lived in the region, marrying, trading, and forging alliances with the Native Americans. Other explorers also crossed through Colorado en route to the West Coast.

By the 1840s, the number of settlers heading west resulted in a demand for military posts to protect travelers, which led to the establishment of forts and small settlements, such as Bent's Fort. In an effort to decrease interactions between Plains Indians and travelers along the Oregon and Santa Fe Trails, the federal government organized the Fort Laramie Council in 1851, designating the eastern plains between the South Platte and Arkansas Rivers as the hunting grounds for the Cheyenne and Arapaho tribes.

The discovery of gold in Cherry Creek in 1858 transformed the course of Colorado history. Prospectors poured into the region, claimed Native American territory as their own, and increasingly expected the federal government to support their actions and eliminate the presence of Native Americans. In 1861, the Treaty of Fort Wise greatly reduced the land of the Cheyenne and Arapaho to a reservation on the southeastern plains between Sand Creek and the Arkansas River. Colorado Territory was created in 1861.

The flood of prospectors and settlers increased tension with the tribes, and the reduction of tribal hunting grounds threatened Native American survival. In spring 1864, the tension reached a crescendo as rebel tribal groups, such as the Dog Soldiers, became more aggressive with their raids on settlers. After several tense and fearful months, the Colorado 1st and 3rd Regiments, led by Col. John M. Chivington, attacked and massacred Cheyenne and Arapaho Indians on the banks of Sand Creek. Immediately controversial, the event also resulted in retaliation by the Dog Soldiers. After three more years of warfare, government representatives met with chiefs from many tribes in Medicine Lodge, Kansas. The Medicine Lodge Treaty of 1867 demanded that tribes move to reservations, learn farming, and attend school. It also confiscated remaining tribal lands and resulted in the removal of many Native Americans from Colorado Territory. In 1876, Colorado became a state.

As settlers continued to populate mountain and Front Range communities, open-range cattlemen grazed hundreds of thousands of cattle on the plains' vast grasslands. While the Front Range developed, the central and southeastern plains of Colorado remained relatively isolated. Enormous cattle ranches claimed large expanses near water sources, as thousands of cattle and a few cowboys defined the landscape rather than bustling communities. Unfortunately, the open-range cattle industry abused the plains' environment by overgrazing, and severe winters and dry summers only escalated the problem.

The transcontinental railroad transformed Colorado's eastern plains. New York financier Jay Gould purchased control of the Missouri Pacific Railroad in the early 1880s and aspired to turn it into a transcontinental railroad by joining it with the Denver and Rio Grande line in Pueblo. In April 1887, the Pueblo and State Line Company was organized to implement Gould's plan. Railroad entrepreneurs formed the Pueblo and State Line Company, which purchased land at each railroad station along the line, platted towns, and advertised for settlers. In what would become Kiowa County, the company platted a town approximately every 7 miles. Eager groups established communities, hoping they would end up on the rail line, but only Sheridan Lake succeeded in Kiowa County.

In April 1889, Prowers, Otero, Crowley, Kiowa, and parts of Cheyenne and Lincoln Counties were formally created from Bent County, leaving the present area of Bent County under the original name. The name "Kiowa" was taken from a watering place on the stage road about 5 miles south of Eads, called Kiowa Springs; the springs were likely named after the Kiowa Indians, who had used southeastern Colorado as summer hunting grounds. Kiowa Springs is also known as Goff Springs after a homesteading family. The Missouri Pacific rail line traversed Kiowa County and provided an economic boost for the establishment of hotels, general stores, post offices, churches, saloons, and other businesses. Homesteaders farmed and ranched in the nearby countryside.

In 1890, the population of Kiowa County was over 1,200 people. Unfortunately, the 1890s also brought drought, which followed the unusually wet years of the 1870s and 1880s, prompting boosters to praise the Colorado "rain belt." The drought shocked many Coloradoans who had become accustomed to the moisture. Discouraged, many abandoned their homesteads. By 1900, the population of Kiowa County dwindled to 700. In less than 10 years, Kiowa County experienced prosperity followed by intense environmental and economic hardship—and an over 30 percent decrease in population.

The aridity of Colorado and the West prompted the federal government to experiment and develop drought-resistant cultivation methods and crops. The Enlarged Homestead Act of 1909 doubled the acreage of a homestead from 160 acres to 320 acres; it also gave Kiowa County a new lease on life as the population rose to 2,899 by 1910.

World War I indirectly contributed to the prosperity of the county. Encouraged to grow crops for the war effort, blessed by fair weather, and aided by new technology and machinery, the citizens of Kiowa County pushed agriculture to commercial proportions. Local farmers began shipping crops out of the county by train. Homesteaders claimed land and established cattle ranches and farms. By 1920, Kiowa County was home to 3,755 people. Unfortunately, war-inflated grain and stock prices dropped in the early 1920s, bringing distress to farmers and ranchers as the population stablized.

The stock market crash of 1929 ushered in the Great Depression, which was worsened in the 1930s by widespread drought, known as the Dust Bowl. Dust storms, intense heat, and dry conditions caused many to flee the eastern plains. A few Kiowa County banks and businesses closed, but residents took advantage of President Roosevelt's "alphabet programs." The Works Progress Administration (WPA) constructed several buildings and bridges, including Weisbrod Hospital, Eads Town Hall, Eads Elementary School, American Legion Hall, Kiowa County Shop (now the firehouse), and Rush Creek Bridge.

The 1930s also brought a calamity of a more personal nature to Kiowa County. On March 26, 1931, a spring blizzard struck the eastern plains. In an attempt to reach safety, a makeshift bus carrying 20 students of Pleasant Hill School near Towner became stuck in a ditch. After being trapped on the bus in subzero weather for over 30 hours, the surviving children were rescued. Five children and the bus driver perished from exposure and hypothermia. Known as the Towner Bus Tragedy, the event garnered national attention and led to reform of school release policies during severe weather.

Kiowa County's population dropped from 3,786 in 1930 to 2,793 in 1940. Since the 1950s, the population has slowly declined and rural schools have consolidated. The bustle of the towns of Arlington, Galatea, Brandon, and Towner has slowly faded into the past. Ironically, innovations such as improved farming equipment, the national highway system, and automobiles have made life easier but also contributed to population decline in rural areas. In a county that once educated hundreds of students in dozens of schools, only two small school districts, Plainview and Eads, still operate.

Through the 20th century, Kiowa County residents changed with the times, experienced hardship and triumph, and sustained visions for a better future. Citizens of Kiowa County value their rich history and their community and family traditions, and many strive to preserve them for the next generation.

One

The Sand Creek Massacre

In late June 1864, territorial governor John Evans issued an invitation for peace to area tribes. Tribal chiefs eventually received the message, but in the meantime, attacks on settlers continued. On August 11, 1864, the War Department gave Governor Evans permission to create a volunteer regiment for 100 days. The Colorado 3rd Volunteer Regiment, under the command of Col. John M. Chivington, was comprised of an assortment of individuals, including miners, farmers, ranchers, shopkeepers, and gamblers. They soon became known as the "Bloodless Third" due to their lack of action against any Native Americans.

In late August, Cheyenne chief Black Kettle sent a message accepting Evans's peace invitation to Fort Lyon, located on the Arkansas River. Under the protection of Maj. Edward Wynkoop, who was convinced of the Native Americans' desire for peace, Cheyenne and Arapaho chiefs traveled to Denver for the governor's meeting, known as the Camp Weld Council. Unfortunately, warrior attacks on white settlements over the summer had already set a military response in motion. Attacks continued as the tribal leaders journeyed to and from Denver to negotiate peace.

By November 1864, Chivington and his unit craved action. Colonel Chivington and his staff left Denver on November 20 and joined most of his command east of Pueblo several days later. They reached Fort Lyon on November 28; by 8:00 p.m., the troops rode toward Sand Creek.

As the sun rose on November 29, 1864, Chivington led approximately 700 men in a surprise attack on about 500 Cheyenne and Arapaho camped along Sand Creek. Over 150 Native Americans were brutally killed in the attack, including many women, children, and elderly. Soldiers chased down the fleeing victims for miles along the creek bed. The following day, some soldiers scalped and mutilated the dead.

The cruelty of the event made the Sand Creek Massacre an instant controversy. In 1865, the federal government conducted one military and two congressional investigations of Sand Creek and determined that Chivington and his troops had deliberately attacked the Cheyenne and Arapaho, which resulted in a senseless massacre. However, by that time, Chivington was no longer serving in the military and could not be prosecuted for his actions.

The National Park Service established the Sand Creek Massacre National Historic Site in 2007 to preserve and protect the cultural landscape of the massacre and educate the public about the event.

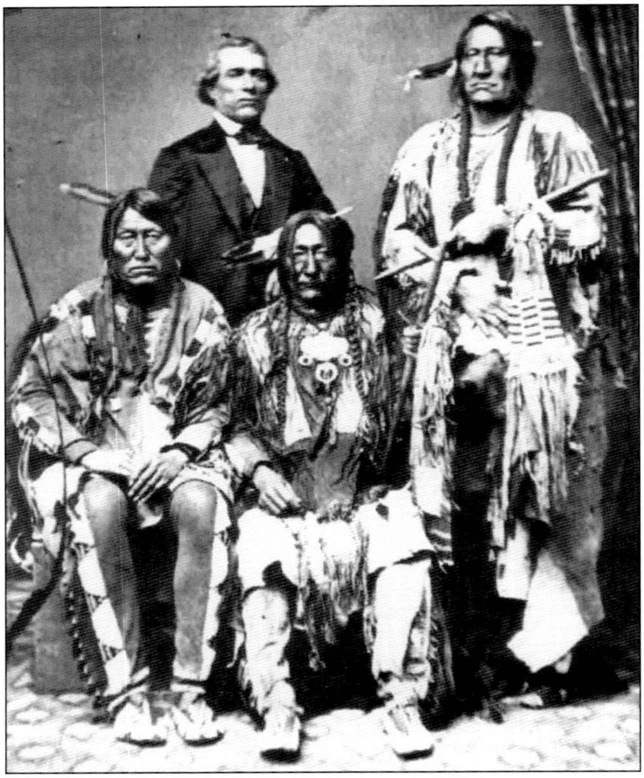

JOHN SMITH AND CHEYENNE LEADERS. In 1863, interpreter John Smith and several Cheyenne leaders visited St. Louis and Washington, D.C. Smith was among a handful of white men in the Cheyenne camp during the Sand Creek Massacre. Cheyenne leader Standing Water sits in front of Smith, and Chiefs War Bonnet and Lean Bear hold pipes. War Bonnet and Standing Water were killed at Sand Creek. (Photograph courtesy Sand Creek Massacre National Historic Site.)

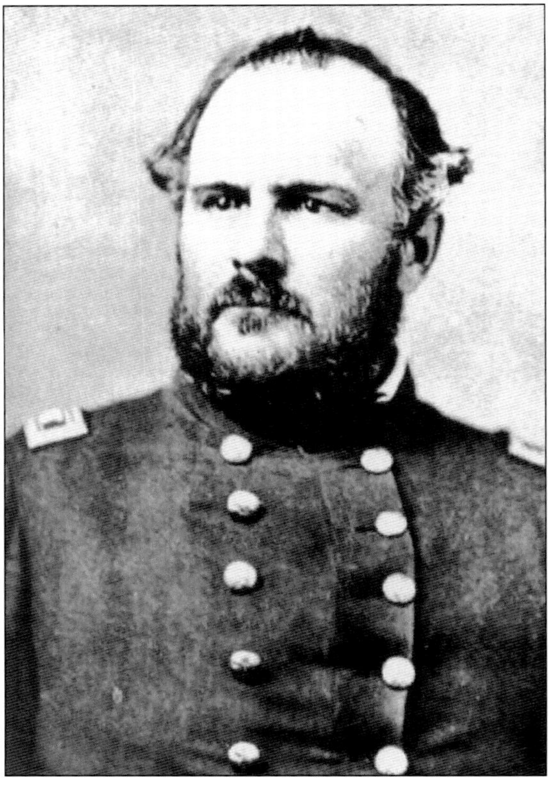

COL. JOHN M. CHIVINGTON. Chivington commanded the troops at the Sand Creek Massacre. A minister, he arrived in Colorado to serve the Rocky Mountain District of the Methodist Church. Commissioned an officer with the 1st Colorado Cavalry, he participated in the 1862 Union victory at Glorieta Pass, New Mexico. After Sand Creek, he was condemned by Congress for his leading role in the controversial attack. Chivington passed away in 1894. (Photograph courtesy Denver Public Library.)

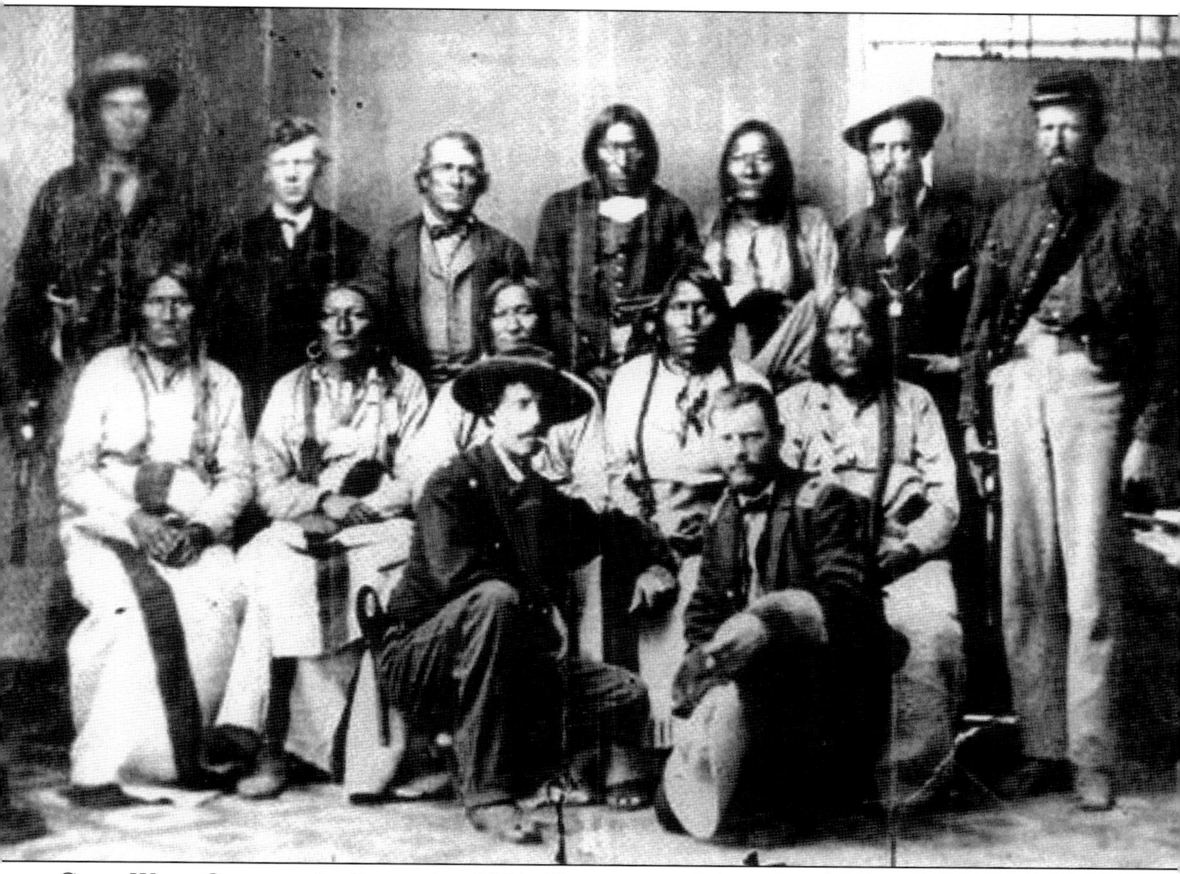

Camp Weld Council. In September 1864, Cheyenne and Arapaho chiefs traveled to Camp Weld near Denver to meet with territorial officials. Talks were given by Cheyenne chiefs Black Kettle (center, second row) and White Antelope (left, second row), Governor Evans, and Colonel Chivington. Maj. Edward Wynkoop (left, kneeling in front) and Capt. Silas Soule (right, kneeling in front) advocated for peace with the tribes in the weeks prior to the Sand Creek Massacre. Evans declined to make a formal peace treaty, but the tribal leaders left Camp Weld believing peace was near. (Photograph courtesy Denver Public Library.)

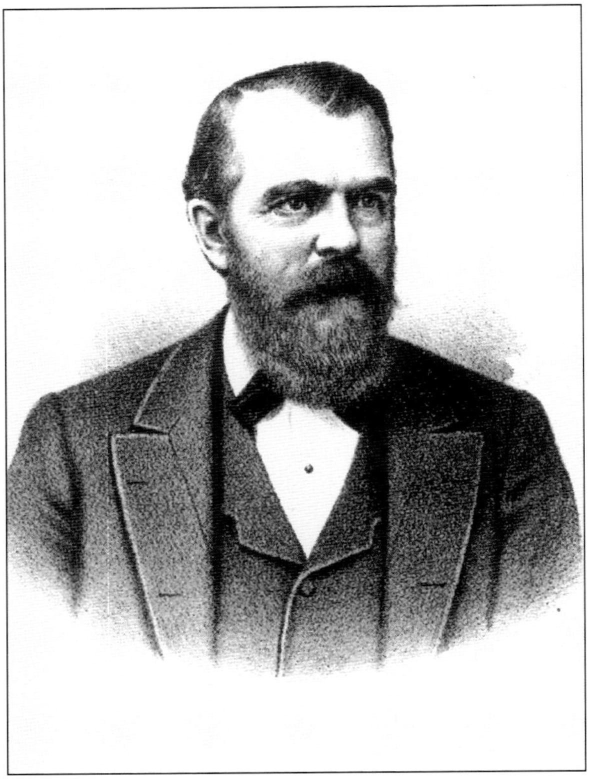

Maj. Jacob Downing. A member of Chivington's staff at the Sand Creek Massacre, Downing arrived in Denver in 1860. A lawyer and an unyielding defender of the attack, he was a member of Chivington's defense team during the Military Court of Inquiry. Downing later became a leading Denver citizen, donating land to the city. In 1911, his widow donated a scalp lock from Sand Creek to the Colorado Historical Society. (Photograph courtesy Denver Public Library.)

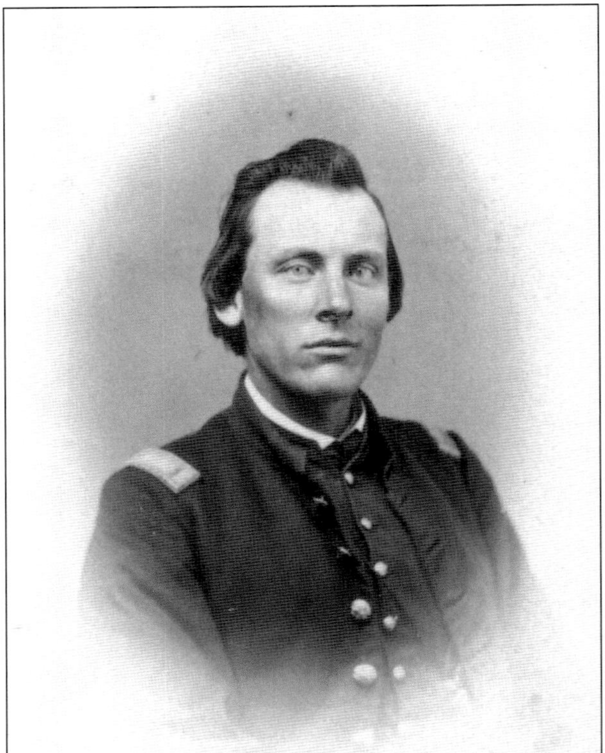

Col. George Shoup. Shoup commanded the 3rd Colorado Regiment at the Sand Creek Massacre. At Sand Creek, he praised the efforts of his three battalions. Detachments of his men chased fleeing Cheyenne and Arapaho for 5 to 10 miles. In addition to soldiering, Shoup's Colorado adventures included mining and merchandising. In 1889, Shoup was appointed the first governor of Idaho. He died in Boise in 1904. (Photograph courtesy Colorado Historical Society.)

LT. HARRY RICHMOND. A member of the 3rd Colorado Cavalry, Richmond was a willing participant in the Sand Creek Massacre. Testimony of Cpl. Amos Miksch, Company E, 1st Colorado Cavalry, identified him as one of the officers allegedly shooting women and children and also engaging in postmortem mutilations. Chivington called Lieutenant Richmond to testify before the Military Commission in May 1865. Richmond also was a professional tragedian/actor. (Photograph courtesy Denver Public Library.)

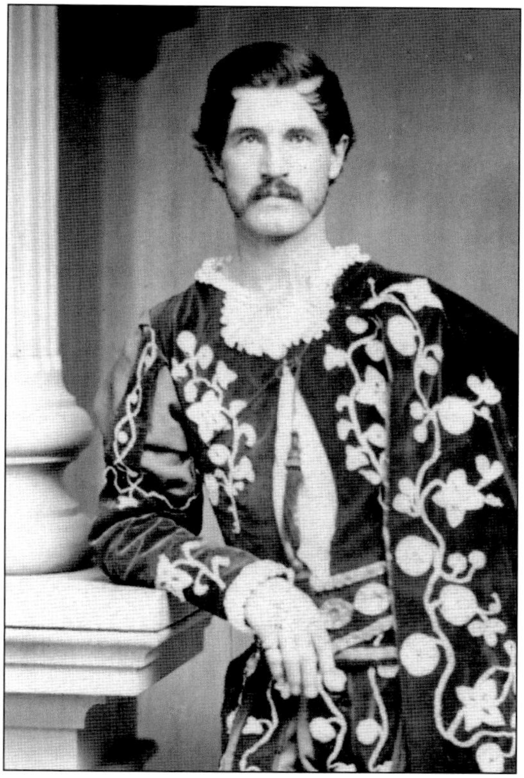

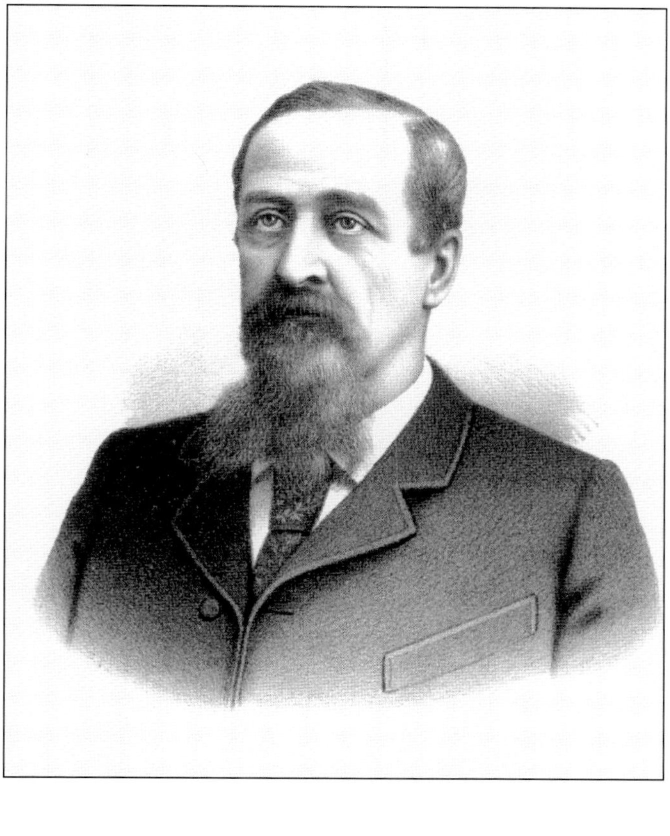

CAPT. OLIVER BAXTER. Baxter left an indelible mark on southeastern Colorado as a rancher, legislator, and civic leader. Part of the 3rd Colorado Calvary, Baxter recalled his Sand Creek action: "At once a line of battle was formed and the Indians were completely surprised, rushed for their tepees and began retreating up the bed of Sand Creek . . . We kept pressing them and killing everything in sight." Baxter passed away in Pueblo in 1910. (Photograph courtesy Denver Public Library.)

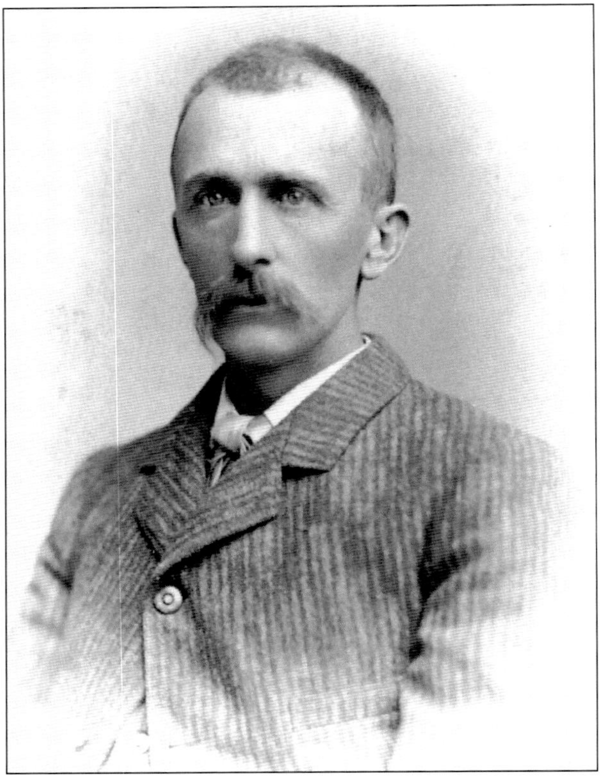

Capt. T. G. Cree. Battalion commander of the 3rd Colorado Calvary at Sand Creek, Cree reported, "As for the bravery displayed by any one in particular, I have no distinctions to make. All I can say for officers and men is that they . . . won for themselves a name that will be remembered for ages to come." Cree, also a veteran of the Vicksburg Campaign, died in 1921. (Photograph courtesy Denver Public Library.)

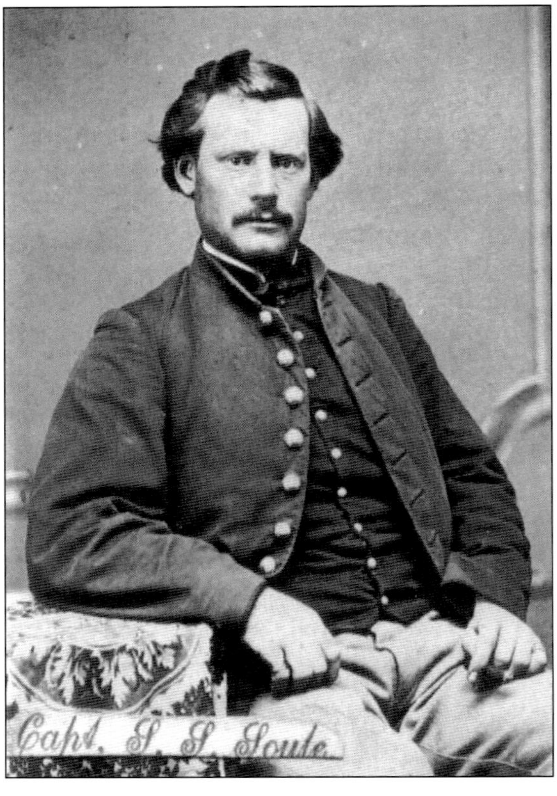

Capt. Silas Soule. A devout abolitionist and Kansas Jayhawker, Soule was with the Fort Lyon Battalion of the 1st Colorado Calvary at the Sand Creek Massacre. Soule's refusal to take part in the massacre resulted in strong criticism from Colonel Chivington. In a letter written by Soule shortly after the attack, he told of the brutality he witnessed. Five months after the massacre, Soule was murdered in Denver. Soule's damaging Sand Creek testimony gave rise to speculation that his death was a revenge killing; however, no direct evidence has been found to support this assumption. (Photograph courtesy Sand Creek Massacre National Historic Site.)

Edmond Guerrier. The son of a Frenchman and Cheyenne mother, Guerrier was in the village at the time of the Sand Creek Massacre. In testimony, he stated, "I could see the soldiers begin to dismount. I thought they were artillerymen and were about to shell the camp . . . I saw . . . there could be no resistance, and I escaped." Guerrier was also married to Julia Bent, the daughter of William Bent and Owl Woman. Guerrier passed away in 1921. (Photograph by Bell; courtesy National Anthropological Archives.)

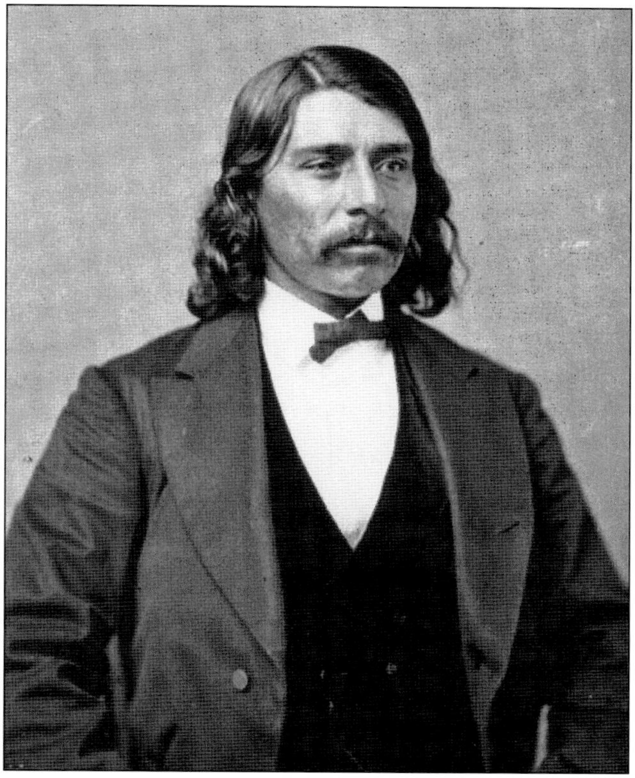

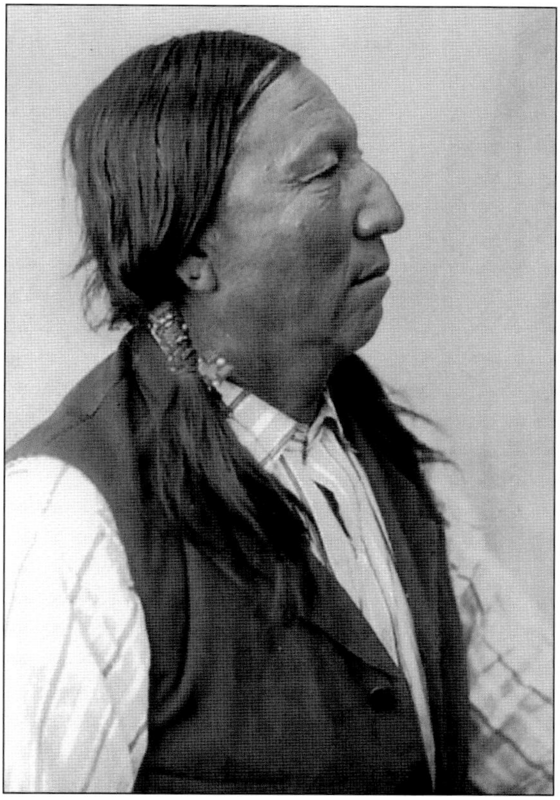

Bull Bear. The Cheyenne Dog Soldiers, and Bull Bear in particular, were regarded by officials as ringleaders in raids on Colorado's isolated ranches and stations prior to the Sand Creek Massacre. Bull Bear was prominent among warrior factions that exacted revenge in the aftermath of the massacre. Bull Bear died in 1892. Two of his children, Richard Davis and Oscar Bull Bear, attended Carlisle Indian School in Pennsylvania. (Photograph by Dorsey; courtesy National Anthropological Archives.)

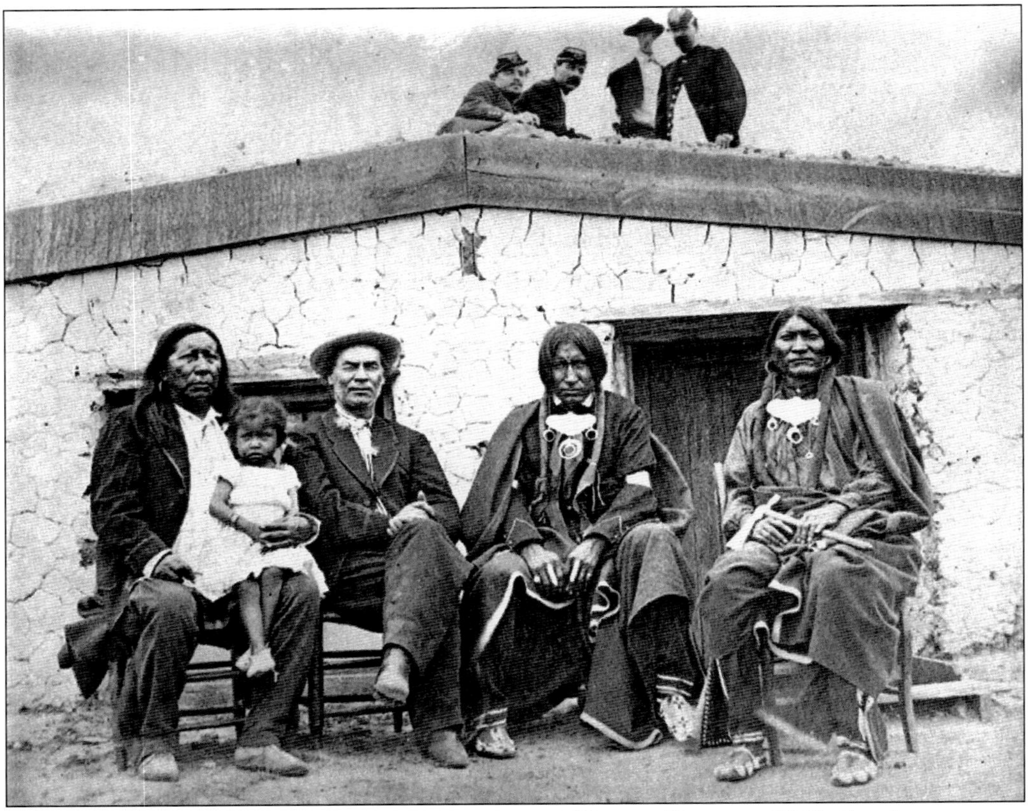

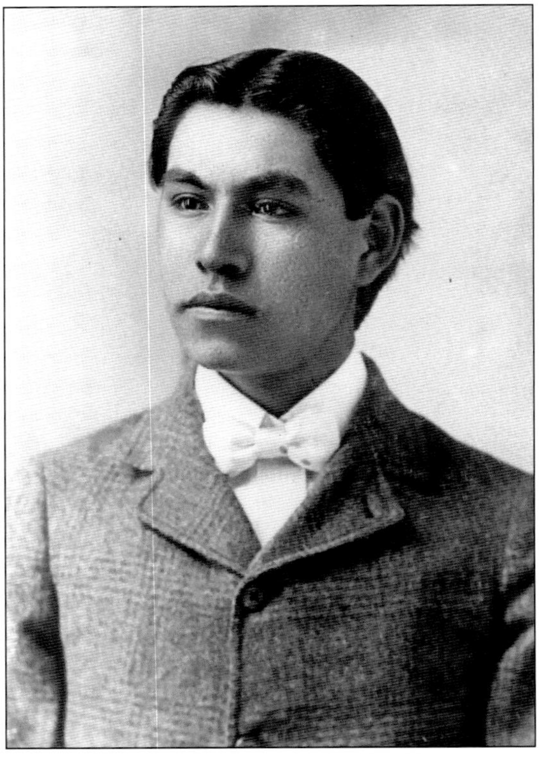

William Bent, c. 1865. Bent's career, which spanned over 35 years in southeastern Colorado, included managing a trading empire, serving briefly as a scout during the Mexican-American War, and acting as an Indian agent for tribes of the Upper Arkansas. Bent and his Cheyenne wives had three sons and a daughter at the Sand Creek Massacre: George, Charles, Robert, and Julia. Bent (second from left) is pictured here with Arapaho chief Little Raven (far left) and family. (Photograph courtesy Sand Creek Massacre National Historic Site.)

Charles Bent. The grandson of William Bent and Owl Woman, Charles Bent was the son of George Bent and his Cheyenne wife, Magpie. His maternal grandfather, Chief Black Wolf, was killed at Sand Creek; his father-in-law, Big Hawk, survived the massacre. Charles attended Carlisle Indian School in Pennsylvania. (Photograph courtesy Cumberland County Historical Society.)

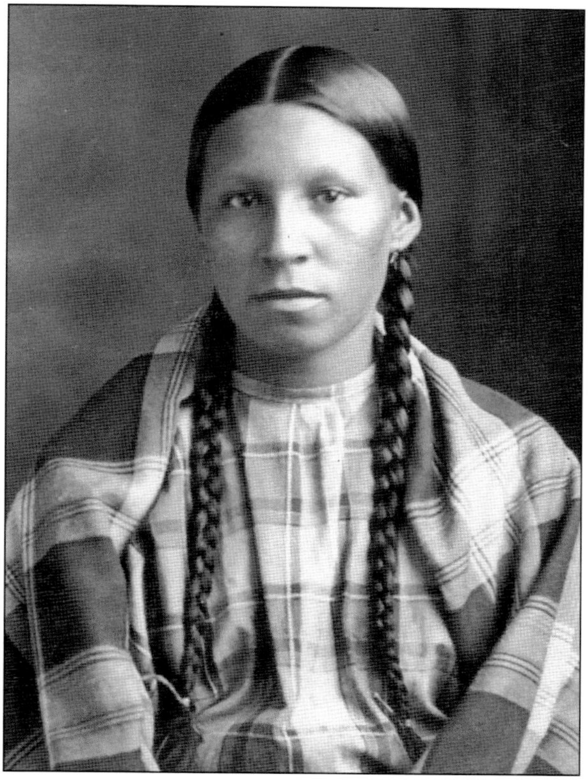

LUCY BENT. Lucy Bent was the daughter of George Bent and Standing Out. Lucy's great-grandfather, John Smith, was in the Cheyenne village during the attack; her in-laws, Littleman Spring, Crooked Woman, and the Standing Bird family, were also Sand Creek people. Lucy became a noted bead worker and Cheyenne matriarch; she passed away in 1988. (Photograph courtesy Sand Creek Massacre National Historic Site.)

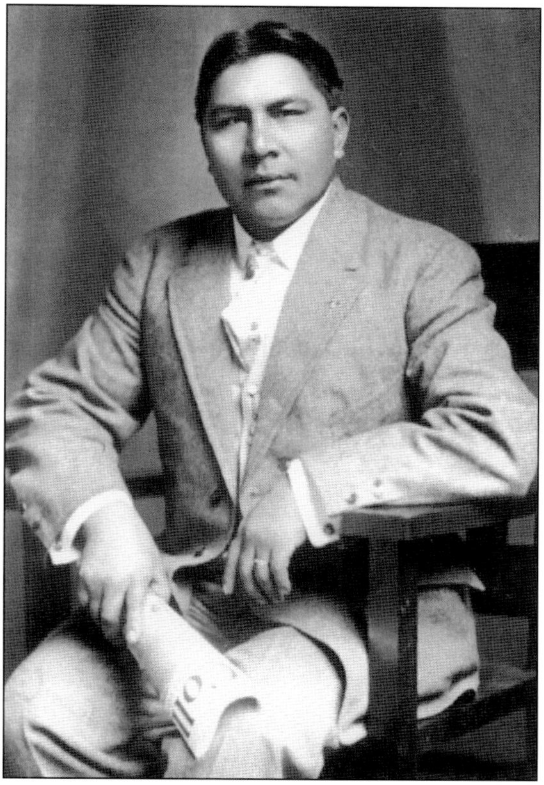

GEORGE BENT JR. The son of George Bent and Kiowa Woman, George Bent Jr. was a half brother to Charles and Lucy Bent. His maternal grandmother, Sage Woman, was killed at Sand Creek. George was a music teacher at Native American schools in Genoa, Nebraska, and Chemawa, Oregon. (Photograph courtesy Sand Creek Massacre National Historic Site.)

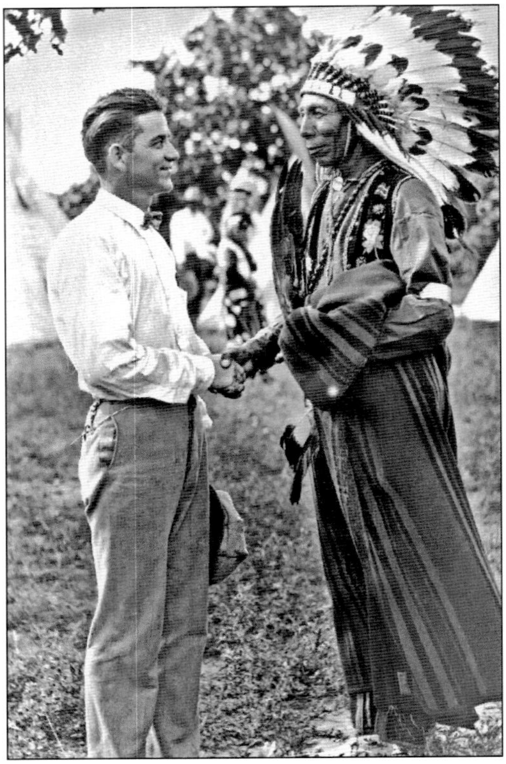

Star Black. A descendant of Black Kettle, Star Black, wearing a headdress, is pictured around 1930. His siblings included Red Bird Black, Ernie Black, May Woman, Malcolm Black, Walking Woman, Jay Black, Jennie Black, and Harry Black. Chief Black Kettle attempted to make peace with military leaders prior to the Sand Creek Massacre. Black Kettle survived but was killed several years later during an attack by George Custer's 7th Cavalry. (Photograph by Brown; courtesy National Anthropological Archives.)

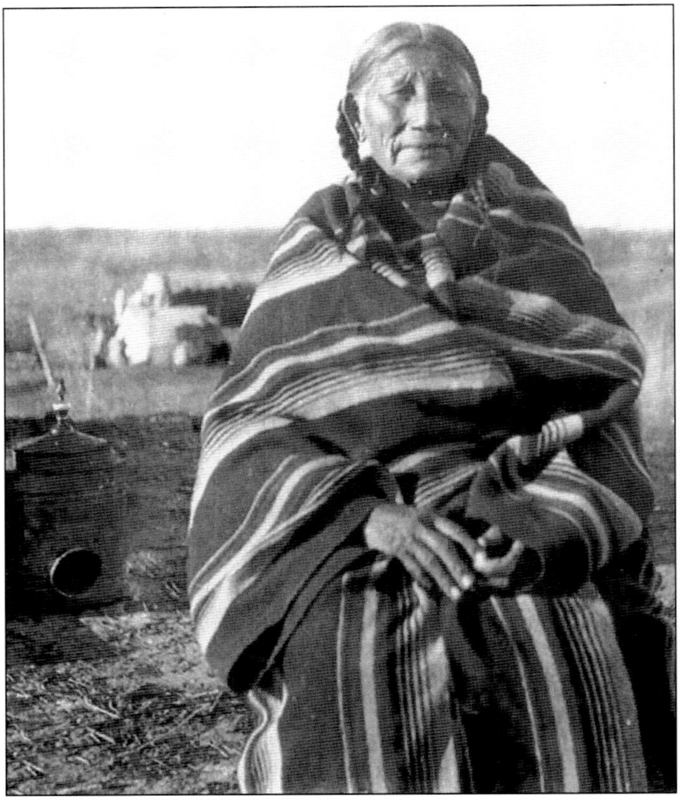

Armama Smith, c. 1906. Daughter of John Smith and a Cheyenne/Sioux woman, Armama's family was in the village during the Sand Creek Massacre. Her brother, Jack Smith, was held as a prisoner during the attack and later shot and killed by a Colorado soldier. Armama, also known as Mrs. Red Eye, was among mixed-blood Cheyennes receiving land claims along the Arkansas Valley in compensation for losses suffered during the massacre. (Photograph by Mooney; courtesy National Anthropological Archives.)

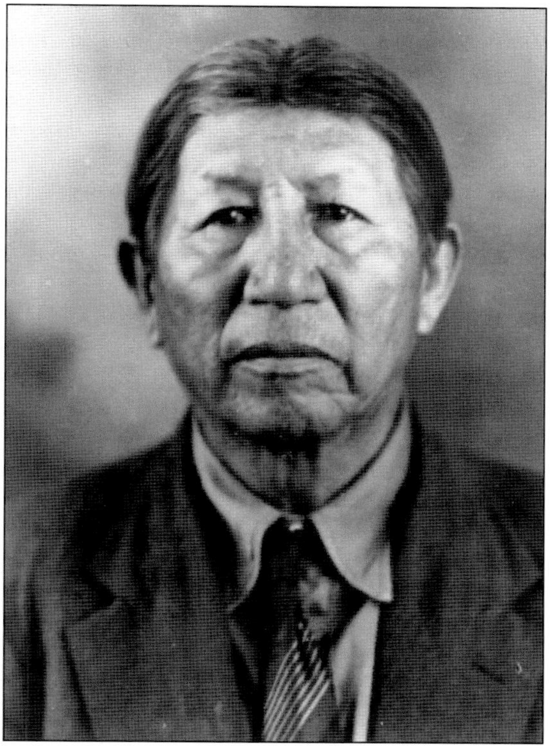

Kish Hawkins. A grandson of White Antelope, a Cheyenne chief killed at the Sand Creek Massacre, Hawkins and Sam Dicke (Shavehead), another descendant of White Antelope, were instrumental in pursuing U.S. reparations stemming from the Sand Creek Massacre. These reparations, per treaty, include securities, goods, provisions, animals, and land. With the death of Hawkins in 1951 and Dicke in 1973, these efforts have passed to current generations. (Photograph courtesy University of Oklahoma Libraries.)

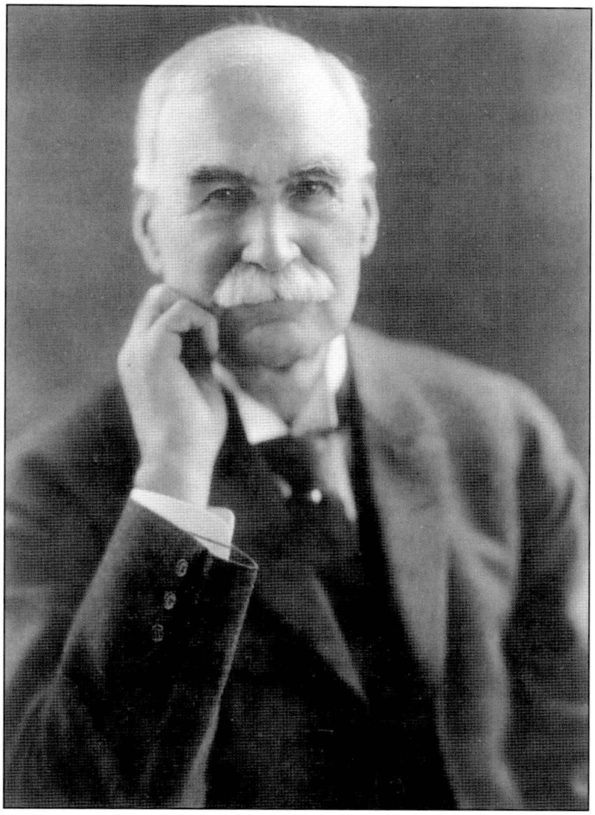

Irving Howbert. Irving Howbert, a noted southern Colorado pioneer, was a young man of 17 when he enlisted with the 3rd Colorado Cavalry and participated in the Sand Creek Massacre. Howbert wrote extensively of the massacre, which he justified. Prior to his passing in 1934, he had served as county clerk, state senator, and bank and railroad president. He was an avid naturalist and historian. (Photograph courtesy Denver Public Library.)

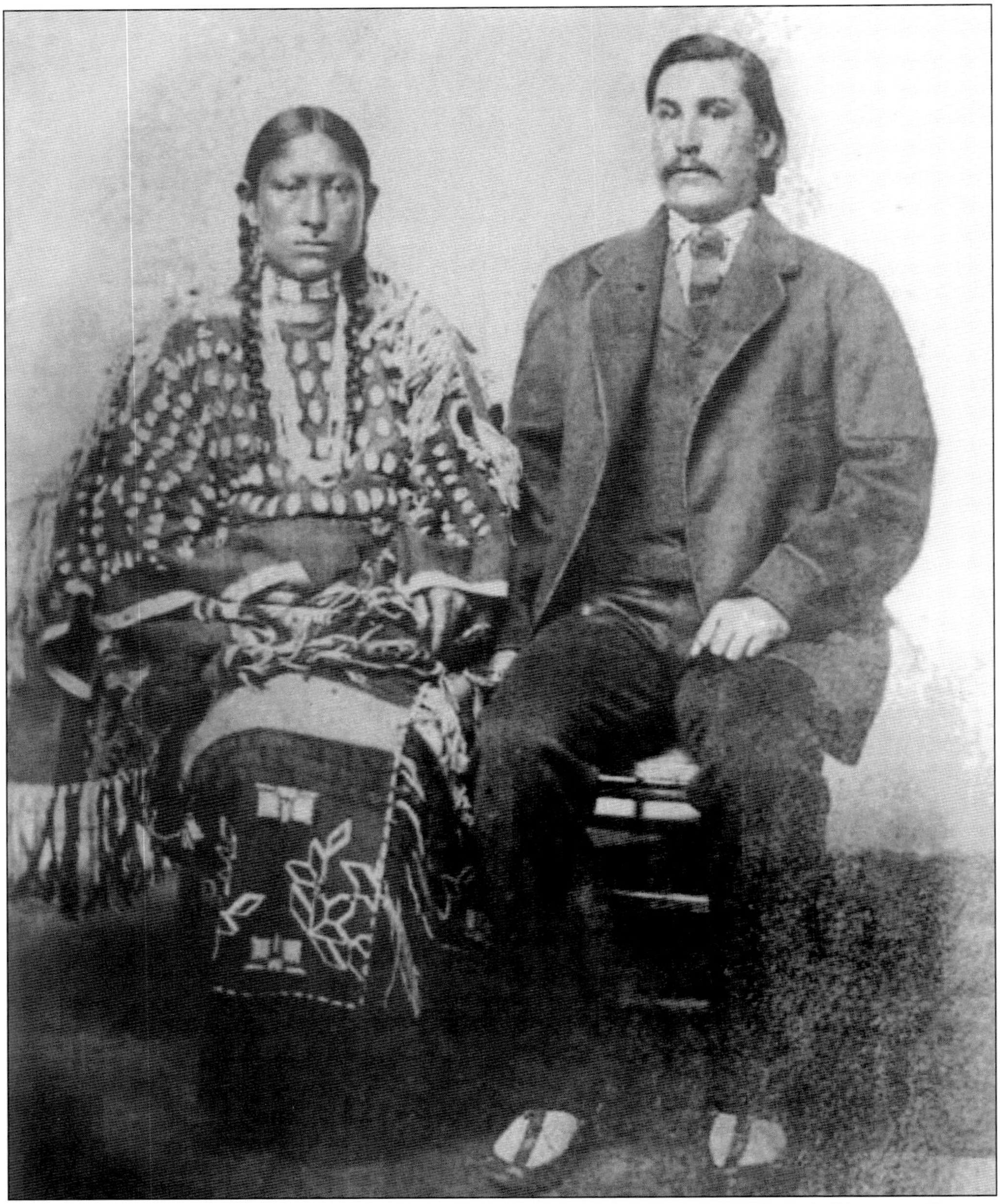

George Bent with Wife Magpie, c. 1869. A son of William Bent and Owl Woman, George Bent was 21 years old at the Sand Creek Massacre. While fleeing the village, he sought safety in pits dug along the creek bed. At some point during the attack he suffered a serious hip wound. Half Cheyenne, Bent participated in nearly all Southern Cheyenne events of the mid- to late 1800s. His knowledge and interest in history, his ability to gather stories from elder Cheyennes, and his fluency in the Cheyenne language prompted correspondence from numerous authors and researchers, including famed naturalist/anthropologist George Grinnell. Bent provided details of the Sand Creek Massacre in many letters. Articles and books, such as *The Fighting Cheyennes*, *Forty Years with the Cheyennes*, *The Life of George Bent*, and *Halfbreed*, were based on his life and letters. George Bent died in Colony, Oklahoma, in 1918. (Photograph courtesy Sand Creek Massacre National Historic Site.)

Two

Agricultural Heritage

Following the Sand Creek Massacre, Colorado Territory became "settled" and achieved statehood in 1876. The eastern plains of Colorado became a haven for open-range cattlemen. One of these "Cattle Kings," Hiram S. Holly, founded the Double S (SS) Ranch in 1871 and claimed 700,000 acres of land on both sides of the Arkansas River. The main ranch headquarters spurred the growth of the town of Holly; the summer ranch was located along Big Sandy Creek near the site of the Sand Creek Massacre. The ranch ran up to 35,000 head of cattle and employed 30 cowboys. Later area cowboys worked for other large fenced ranches, including the Bar Z-O Ranch and the Eads Livestock Company.

With the construction of the Missouri Pacific Railroad in 1881, the area transitioned from open-range ranching to agricultural settlements. However, several smaller ranches still thrived in the area, and the stockyards near railroad depots in several towns linked ranching with the railroad. Farming also became a critical part of the county economy. Early advertisements for settlers boasted about the fertile soil and abundant rainfall, but settlers soon experienced the agony of drought and failed crops. Fortunately, the Enlarged Homestead Act of 1909 doubled the acreage of a homestead from 160 to 320 acres, bringing salvation to farmers and ranchers in Kiowa County and renewing homestead claims. Federal agencies also encouraged dryland farming techniques and developed drought-resistant crop breeds. Despite the arid climate, farmers realized that they could in fact make a living on Colorado's eastern plains.

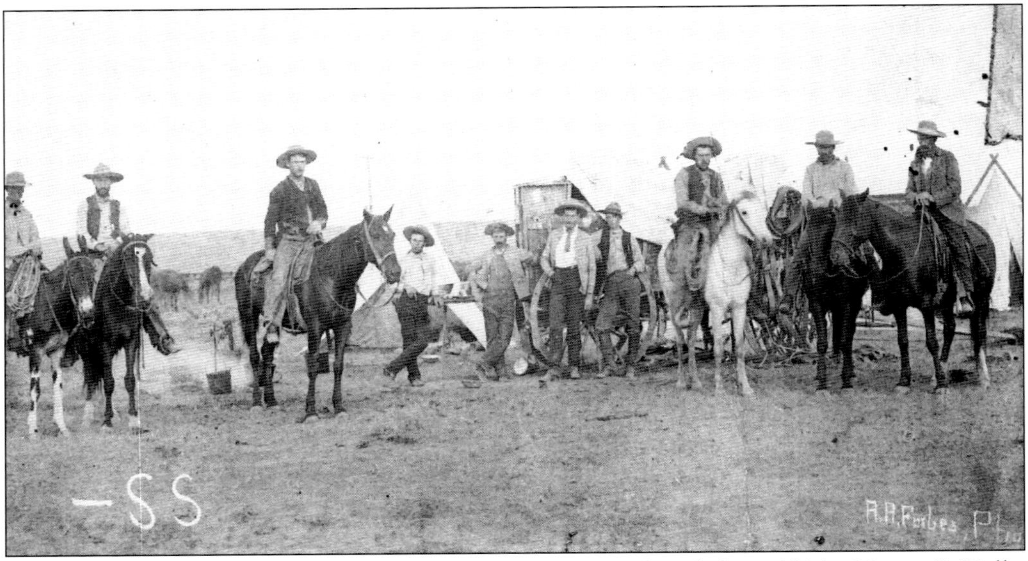

THE DOUBLE S RANCH COWBOYS. This famous ranch was founded in 1871 by Hiram S. Holly. In 1883, Holly sold the ranch to a group of Englishmen, and it became known as the Arkansas Valley Land and Cattle Company. W. J. Wilson bought the ranch in 1896. This photograph of Double S Ranch cowboys was taken prior to 1901.

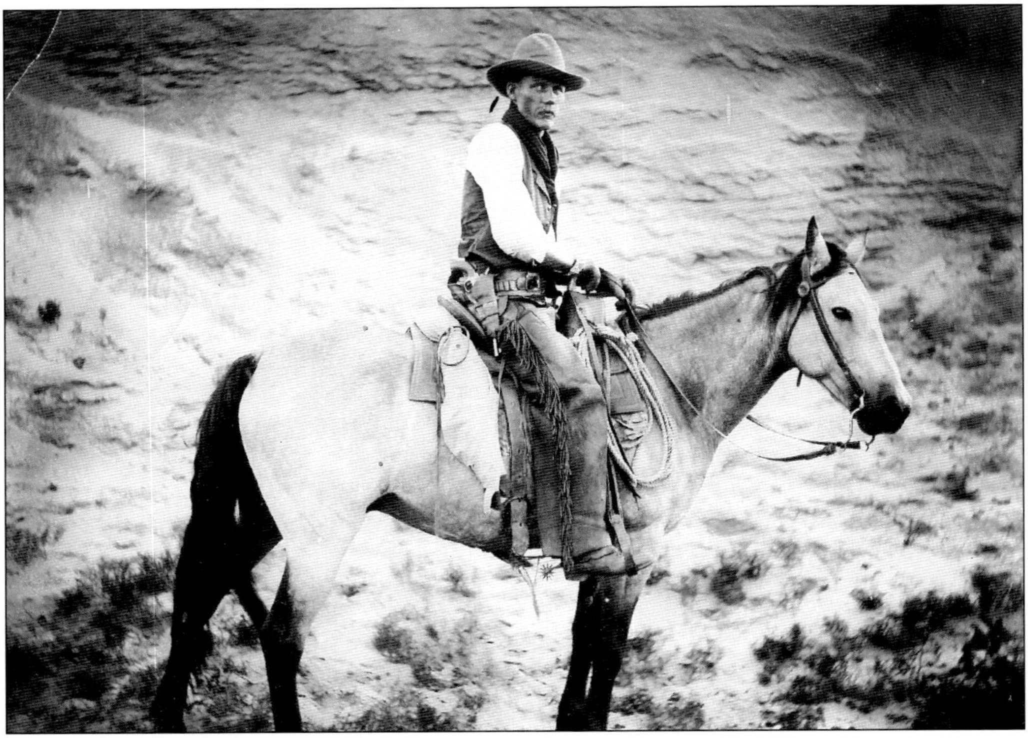

FRANCIS SHERMAN, 1903. Francis C. Sherman was born on January 22, 1876, in Nemaha County, Kansas. In 1887, his parents, J. and Mollie Sherman moved to eastern Colorado by covered wagon with twins Seeley and Stanford and Francis in tow. Their older brother, Frank, stayed in Kansas to finish school. The Shermans proved a homestead 7 miles northwest of Chivington on Rush Creek; they deeded the ranch to Francis in December 1903. (Photograph courtesy David Adamson.)

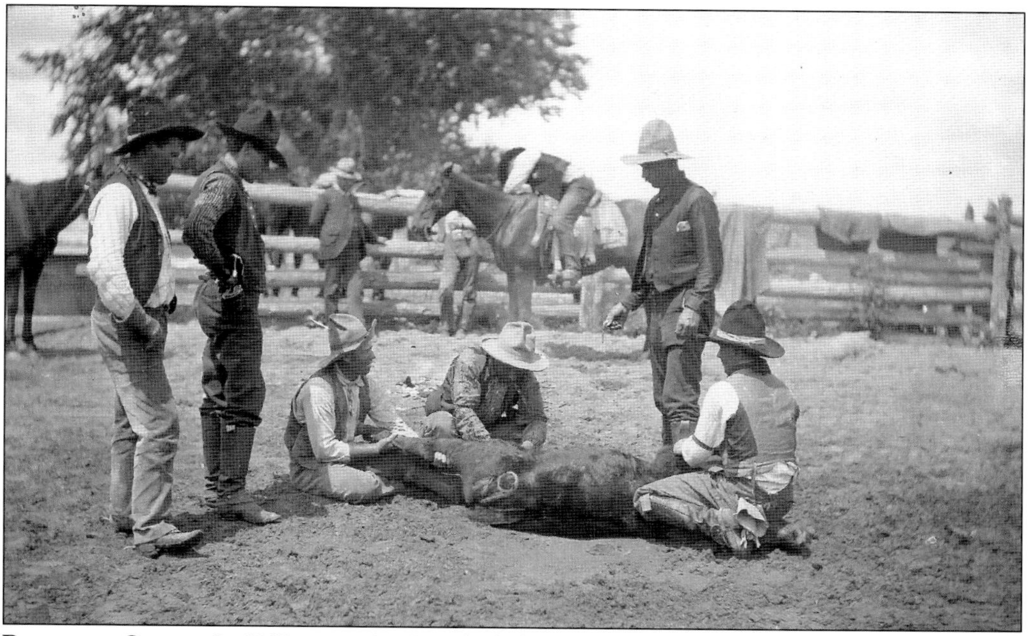

BRANDING CALVES. In 1903, at age 20, Stanford Sherman was the foreman of the Bar Z-O Ranch, which was owned by the Holt Cattle Company and located about 20 miles southwest of Hugo, Colorado. The ranch covered nearly 100 square miles and ran approximately 8,000 head of cattle. (Photograph courtesy David Adamson.)

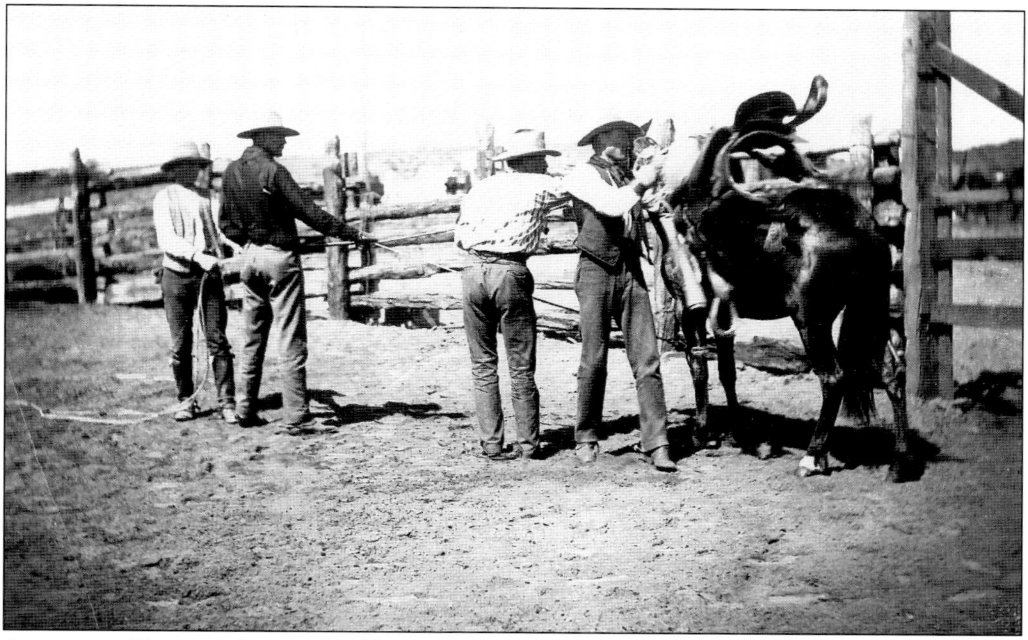

SADDLING A BRONCO. Stanford's older brother, Frank Sherman, was a photographer. Frank joined Stanford and many other cowboys from Kiowa County, including brothers Seeley and Francis, on the ranch's spring roundup in May 1903. Frank took hundreds of pictures that documented the roundup and experiences of the cowboys. Shown in this picture are, from left to right, an unidentified man, Anderson Hickman, Seeley Sherman, and Francis Sherman. (Photograph courtesy David Adamson.)

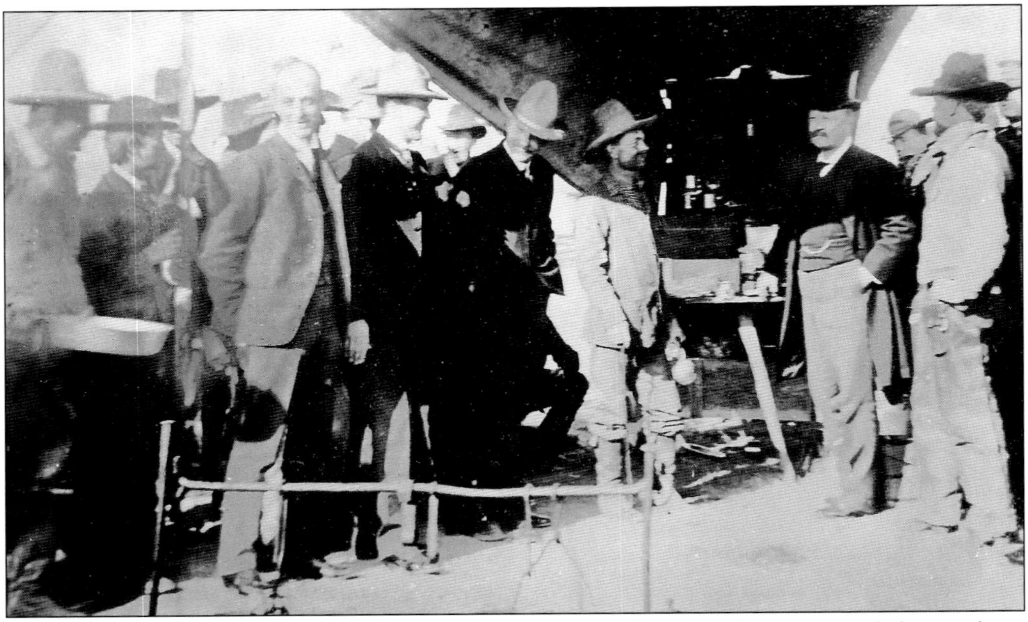

THEODORE ROOSEVELT VISITS THE HUGO COWBOYS. As Stanford Sherman and the cowboys prepared to roundup several hundred head of cattle in May 1903, they received word that Pres. Theodore Roosevelt would be coming through Hugo by train on May 3. They decided to cook the president a chuck wagon breakfast. (Photograph courtesy David Adamson.)

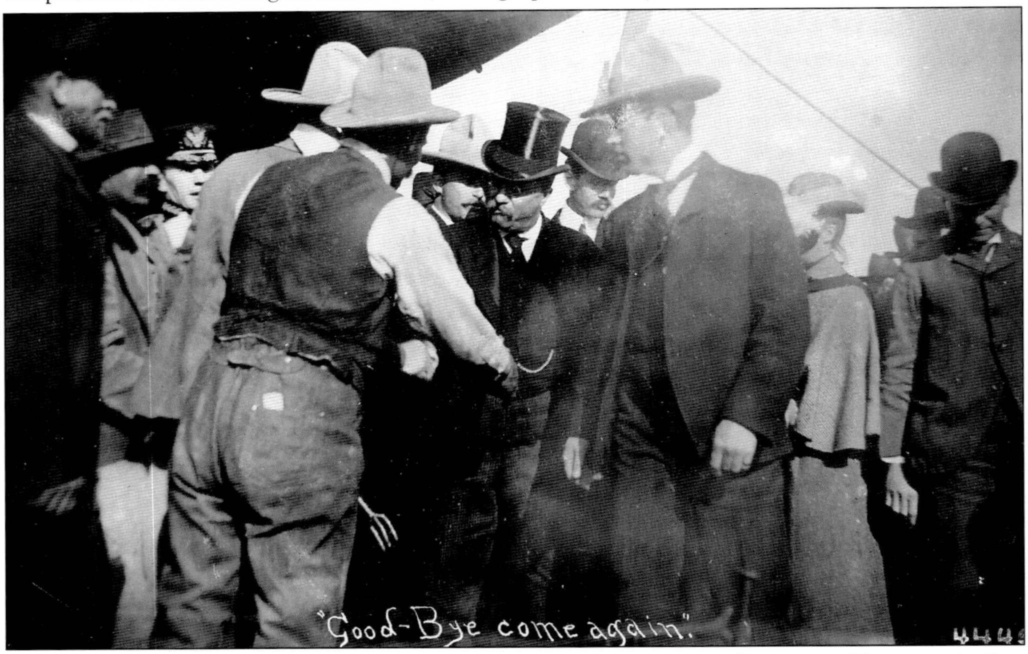

PRESIDENT ROOSEVELT, "GOODBYE, COME AGAIN." President Roosevelt's visit to Hugo resulted in much excitement as well as a great story for the cowboys to tell. In addition to the Sherman brothers, several cowboys from Kiowa County, including Wirt Bailey, Buster Albright, Anderson Hickman, Thomas Hickman, Coral Hickman, Kent France, and Walt France, also had the opportunity to meet the president. Frank Sherman published several photographs of the event in a small booklet titled *President Roosevelt and the Hugo Cowboys.* (Photograph courtesy David Adamson.)

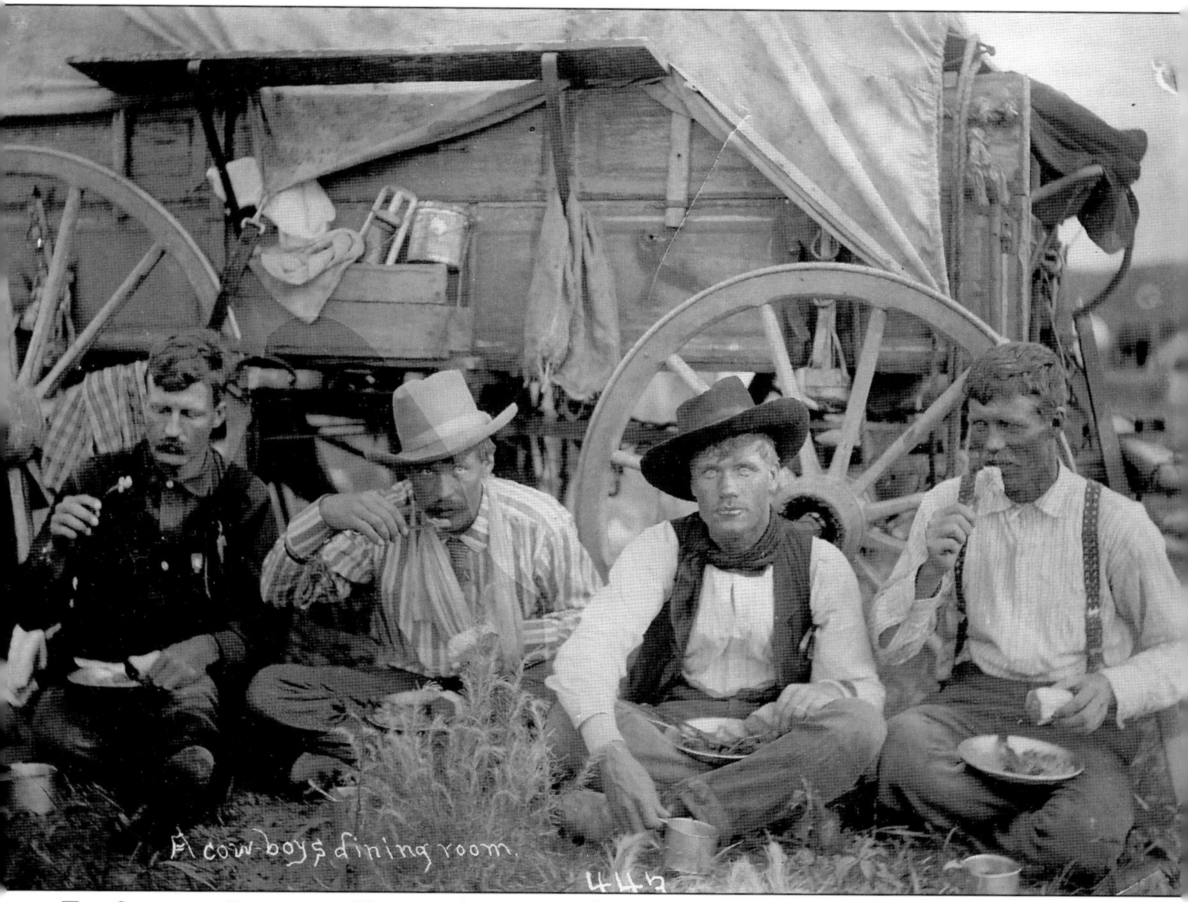

The Sherman Brothers. Photographed eating dinner next to the chuck wagon are, from left to right, the Sherman brothers: Frank, Seeley, Stanford, and Francis. Drawing attention to the absence of table and chairs, Frank called this photograph, "A Cowboy's Dining Room." (Photograph courtesy David Adamson.)

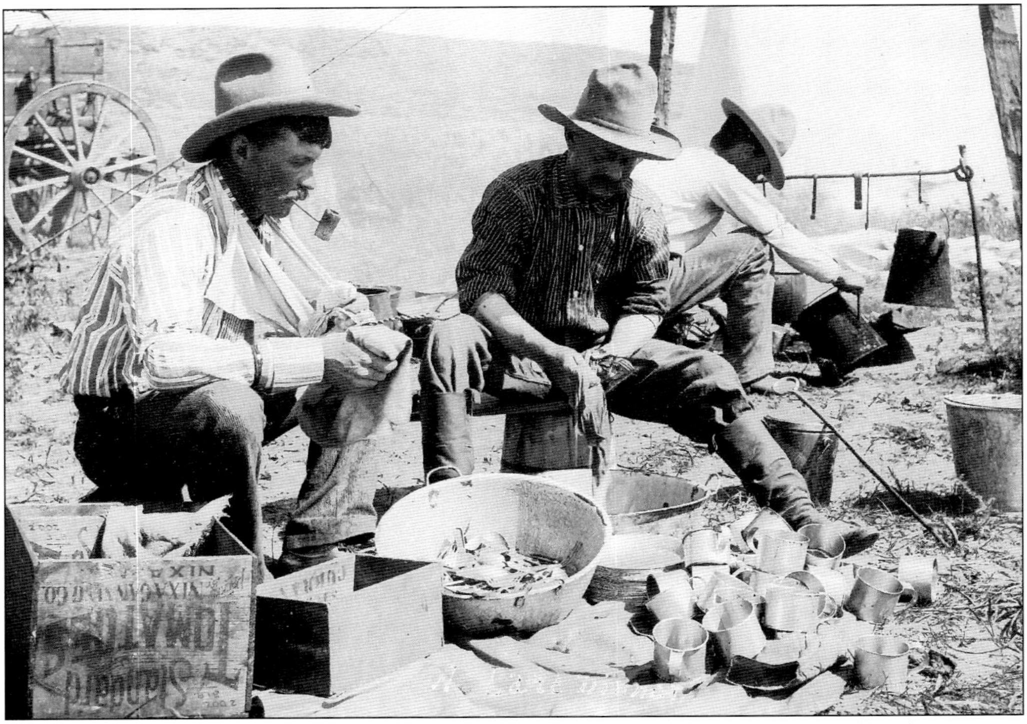

"A LATE DINNER." Seeley Sherman (left) and chuck wagon cook Jack Keppel are shown in this photograph. Keppel was a renowned cook for Bar Z-O Ranch. (Photograph courtesy David Adamson.)

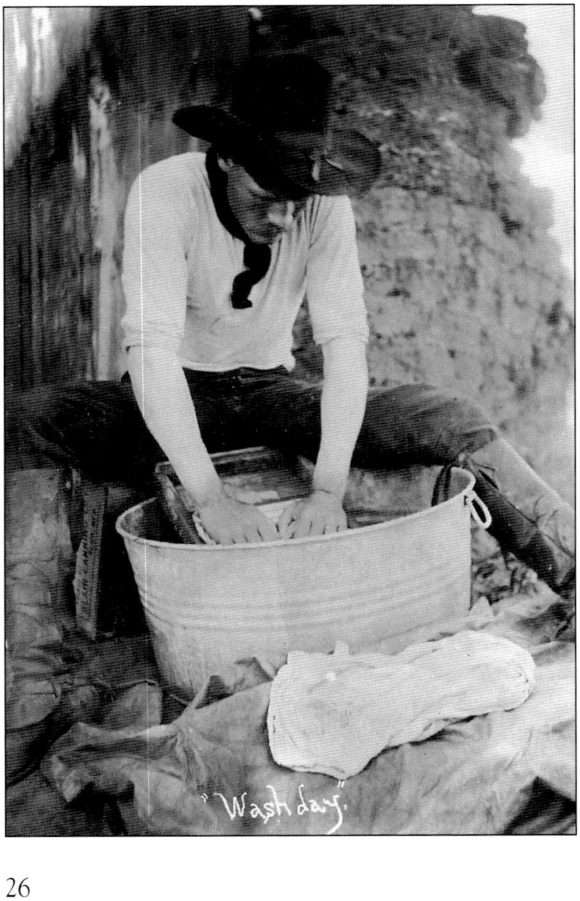

"WASHDAY." Cowboys did not have the luxury of having someone available to do their laundry. Like the other cowboys on the roundup, Stanford Sherman had to scrub his clothes clean using a washboard and tub. The cowboys laid clean clothes out to dry in the sunshine. (Photograph courtesy David Adamson.)

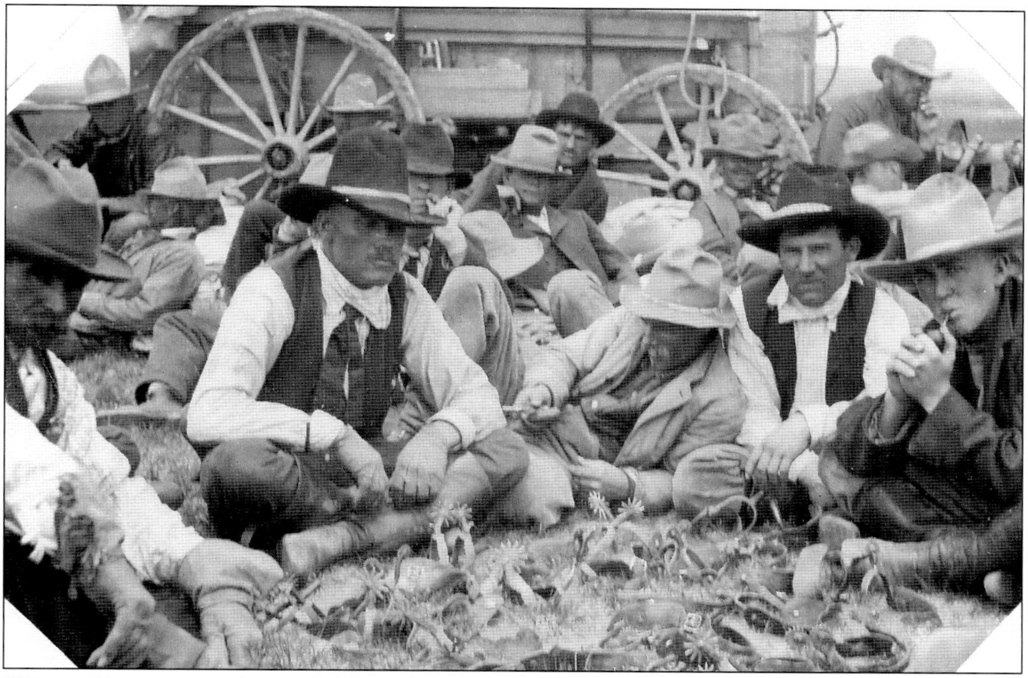

"YOUR CHOICE FOR $3.00." This photograph shows the cowboys relaxing on the prairie. Photographer Frank Sherman alluded that the cowboys were selling the spurs piled in the center to each other for $3. Stanford Sherman is seated second from the left. (Photograph courtesy David Adamson.)

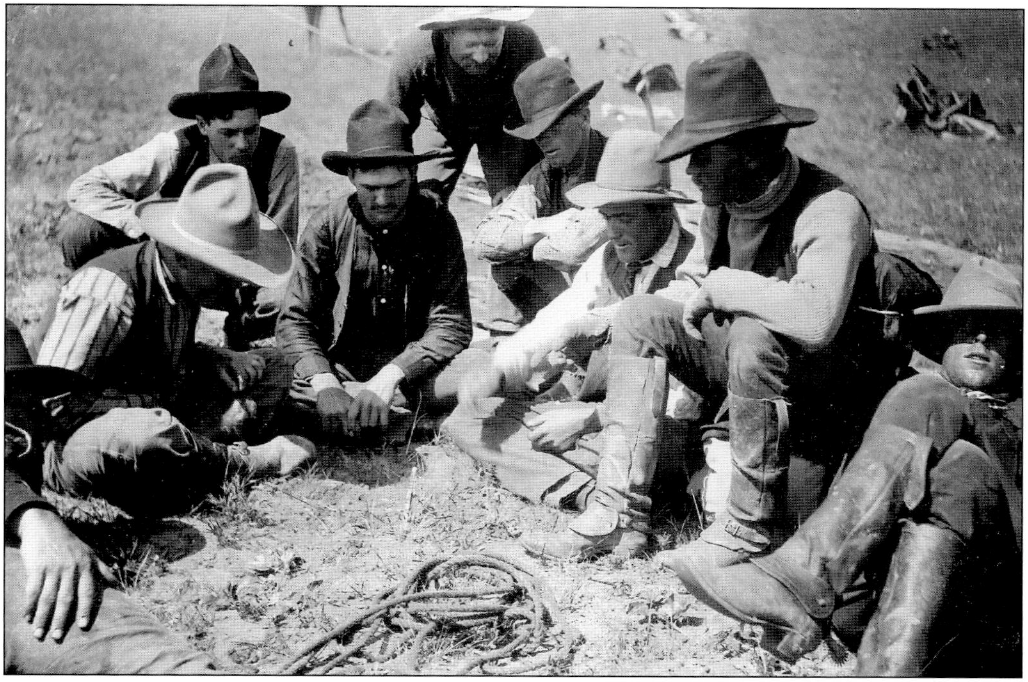

ENTERTAINMENT ON A ROUNDUP. This picture shows several cowboys playing "mumble peg," a game in which the players throw a pocketknife in different ways with the goal of getting the knife to stick in the ground. (Photograph courtesy David Adamson.)

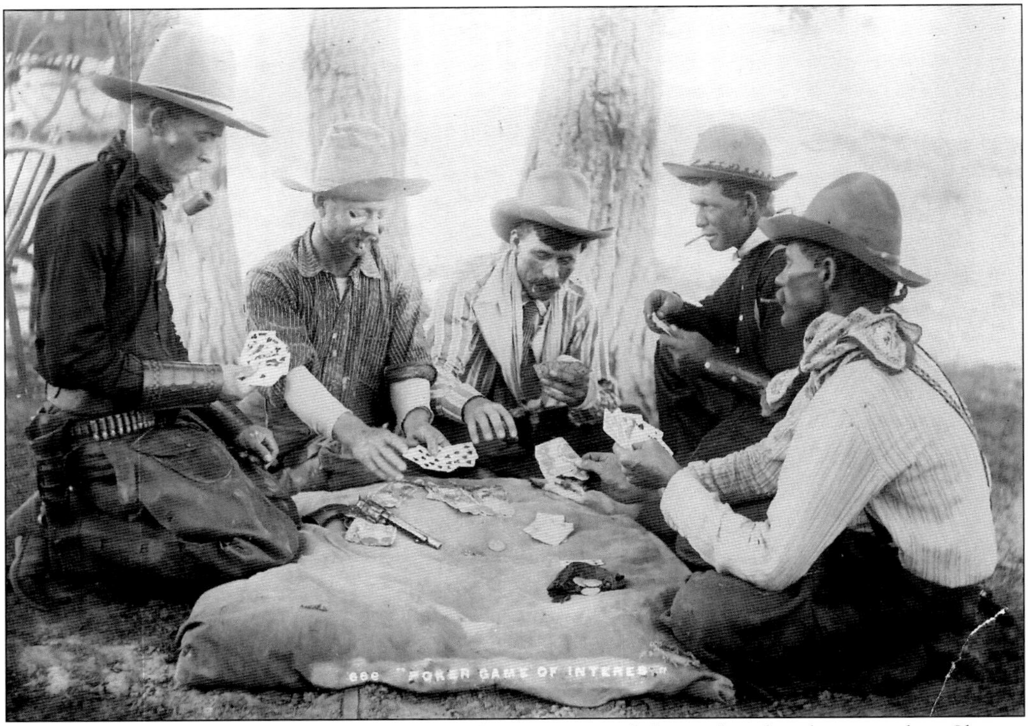

"**Poker Game of Interest.**" The cowboys also entertained themselves by playing poker. Shown here are, from left to right, Kent France, unidentified, Seeley Sherman, unidentified, and Francis Sherman. Kent France was the son of David W. and Mary C. France, who moved to Kiowa County from Ohio in 1886 to claim a homestead. Kent was 24 years old at the time of the 1903 roundup. (Photograph courtesy David Adamson.)

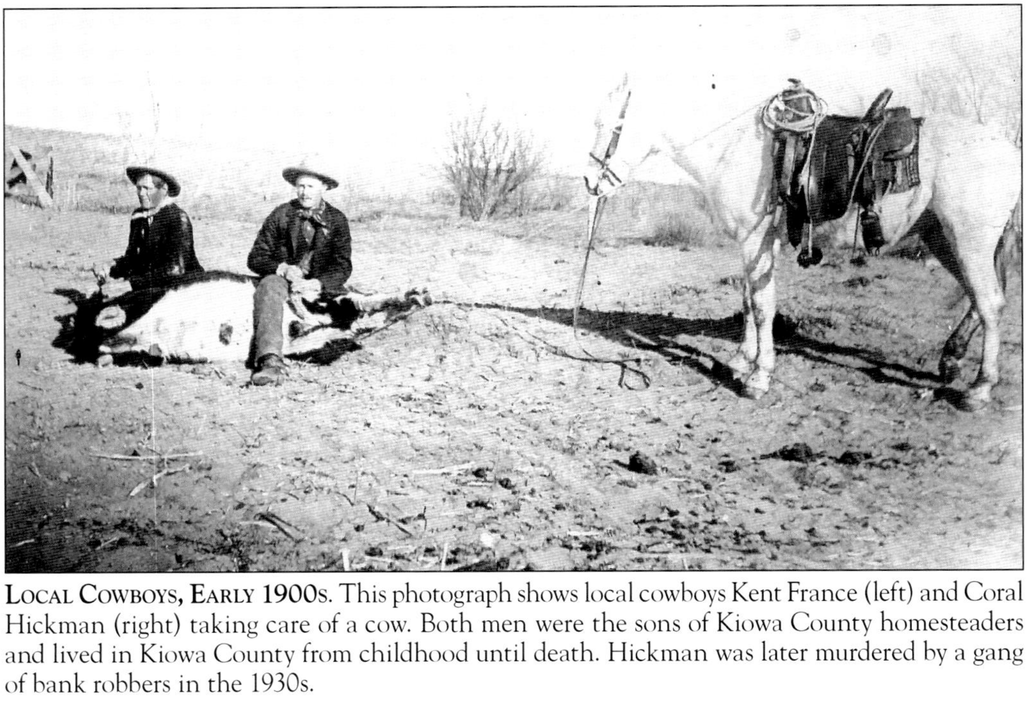

Local Cowboys, Early 1900s. This photograph shows local cowboys Kent France (left) and Coral Hickman (right) taking care of a cow. Both men were the sons of Kiowa County homesteaders and lived in Kiowa County from childhood until death. Hickman was later murdered by a gang of bank robbers in the 1930s.

WALT FRANCE, 1906. Walter France was the son of George and Carrie France, who moved to Kiowa County in 1901 when Walt was 12. He attended school in Eads and lived near the town all his life. In 1903, when Walt was 16, he was the cook's helper on the Bar Z-O Ranch, and he met President Roosevelt in Hugo. Walt later was the foreman of the C. D. Thompson Ranch. In 1919, he became a rural mail carrier, which he continued for 35 years. He also coordinated the Kiowa County Fair Barbeque for many years, beginning in the 1920s. Walt moved into Eads in 1922 and was active in community and church life.

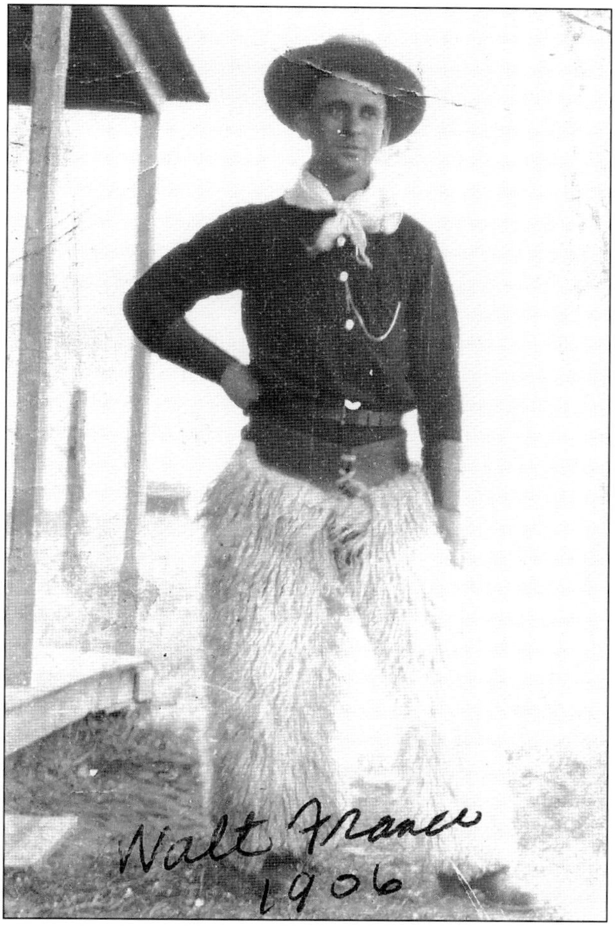

TOWNER HORSE SALE. Interested buyers sit atop corrals and view horses for sale in Towner on November 26, 1912.

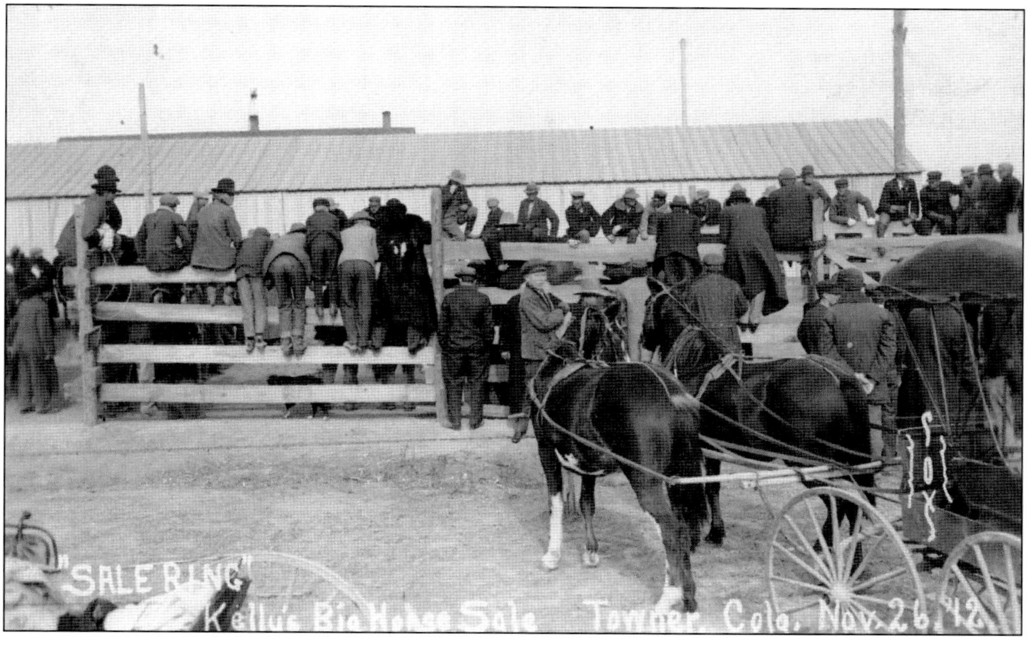

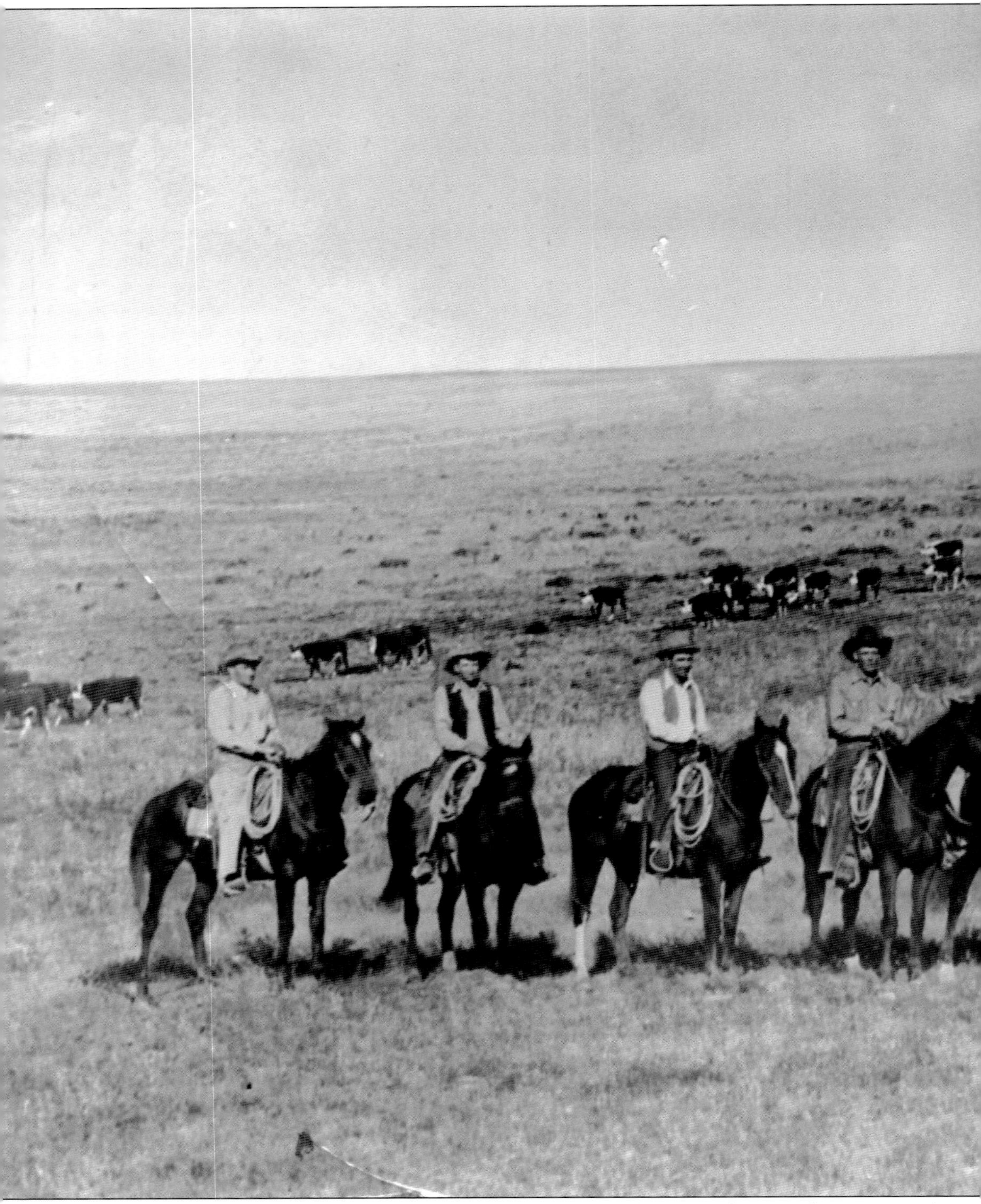

Eads Livestock Company Cattle Drive, 1929. In September 1929, forty cowboys mounted their horses near Sweetwater Lake to continue one of the last great cattle drives of the area. The drive stretched from the foothills of the Front Range to Lakin, Kansas, and took three months to complete. Eads Livestock Company, comprised of 15,000 acres north of Eads, was a subsidiary of

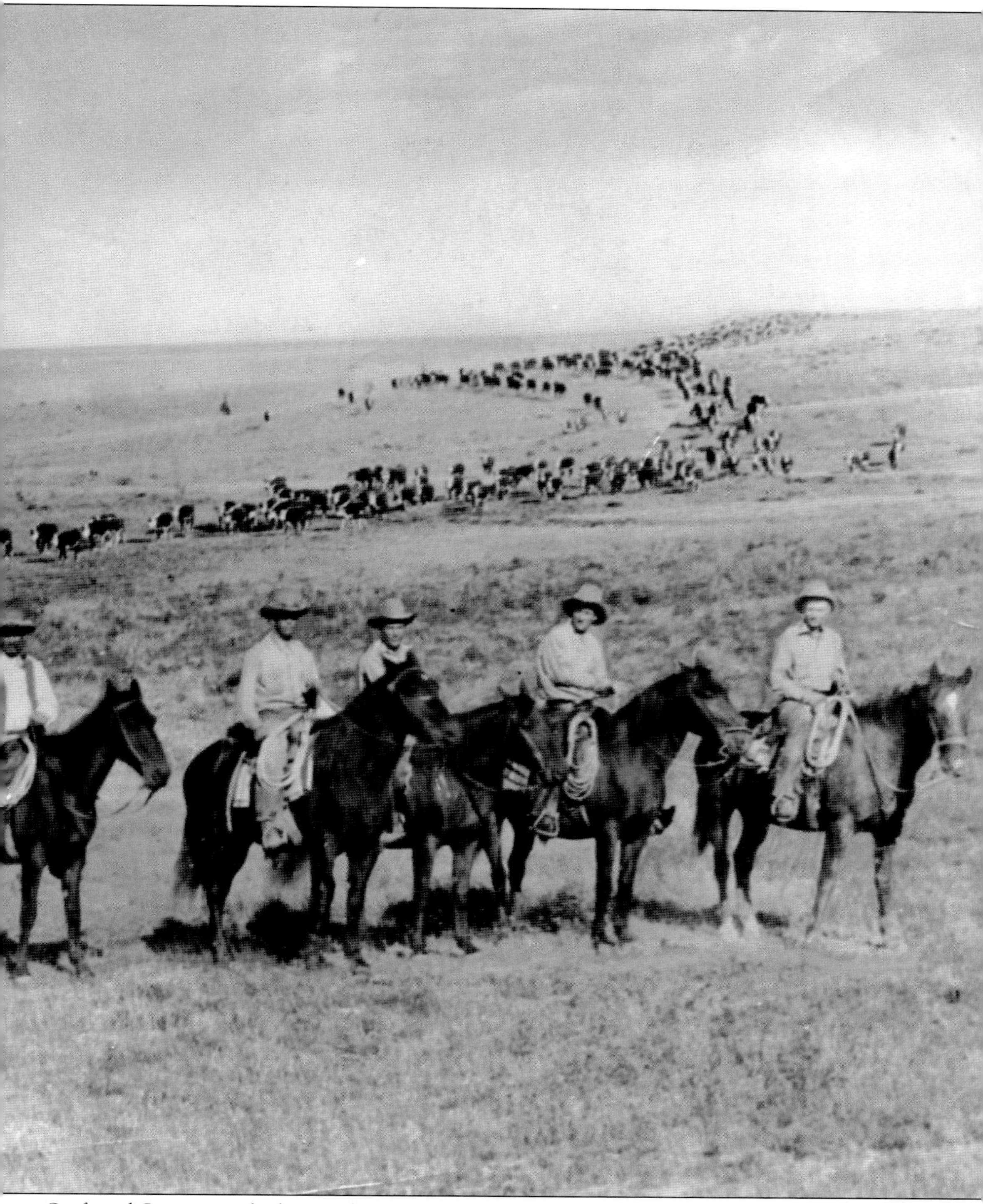

Swift and Company, which owned a string of ranches in eastern Colorado and western Kansas. Matt Jones became the ranch manager in August 1923. In 1928, there were 8,000 steers on the ranch. From late July through fall, the cowboys would drive 100–125 cattle weekly to the stockyards in Kit Carson to be shipped to feedlots.

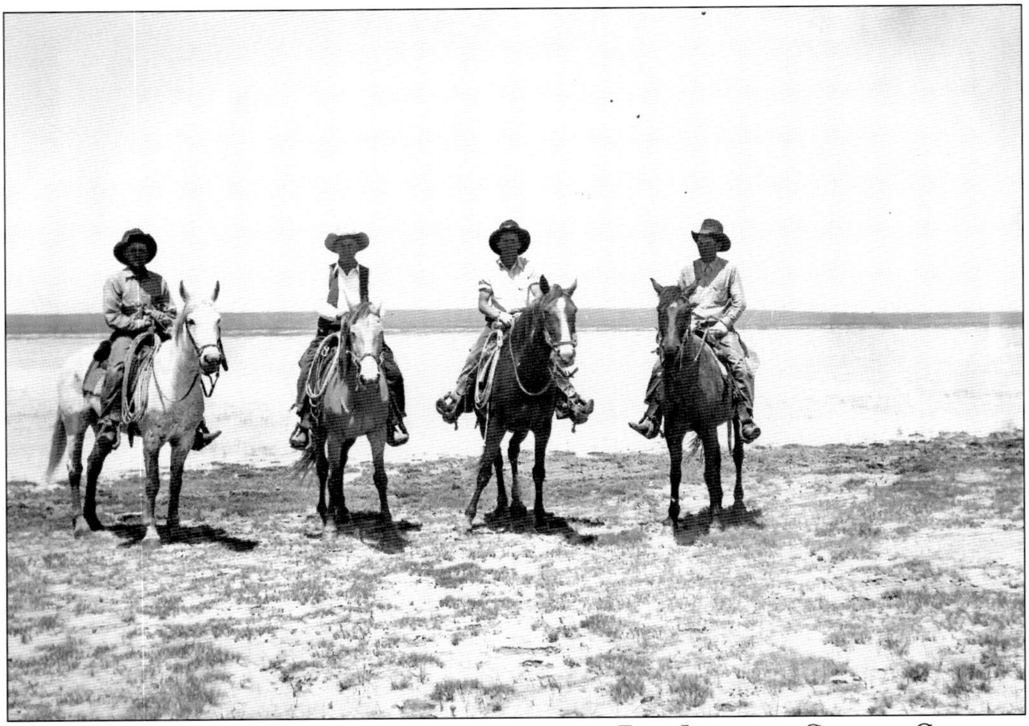

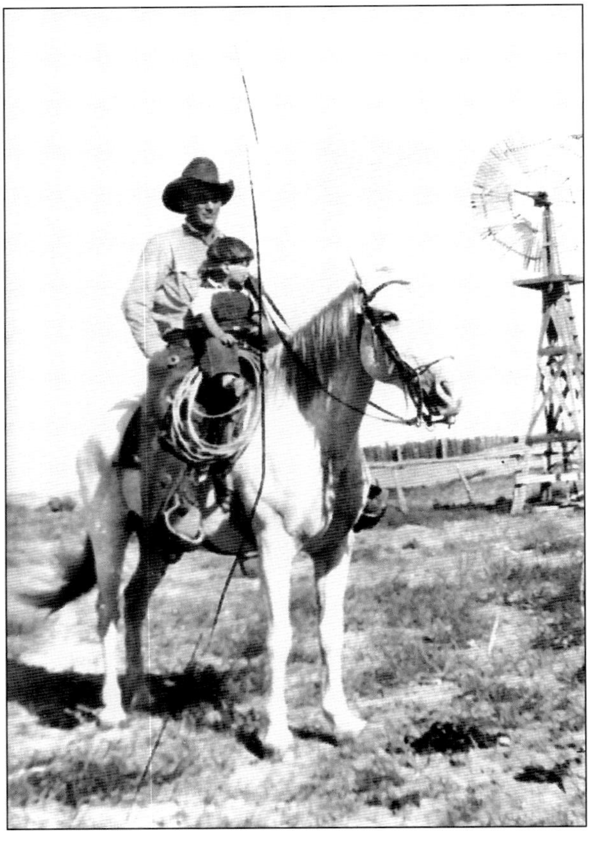

Eads Livestock Company Cowboys, 1929. Photographed at Limestone Lake, Harry Owens, Matt Jones, Joe "Red" Autry, and Cecil Guthrie were just a few cowboys associated with the Eads Livestock Company. Approximately 17 to 20 men worked for the ranch at a time: 15 men were responsible for driving cattle, two kept wells and windmills in repair, and another crew fixed fence. The cowboys would ride an average of 35–40 miles a day.

Harry Owen and Son, Clifford Owen. Harry Owen moved to Eads from the Las Animas area in 1928 to work for the Eads Livestock Company. A true cowboy, Owen had worked on ranches from an early age. He bought his own ranch 12 miles northwest of Eads in 1932, and in 1936, he and his wife, Genevieve (Jo), began ranching on their own with their children, Clifford and Julia Mae (Sis). After Harry and Jo passed on, Sis and her husband, Delbert Wilgus, took over the ranch.

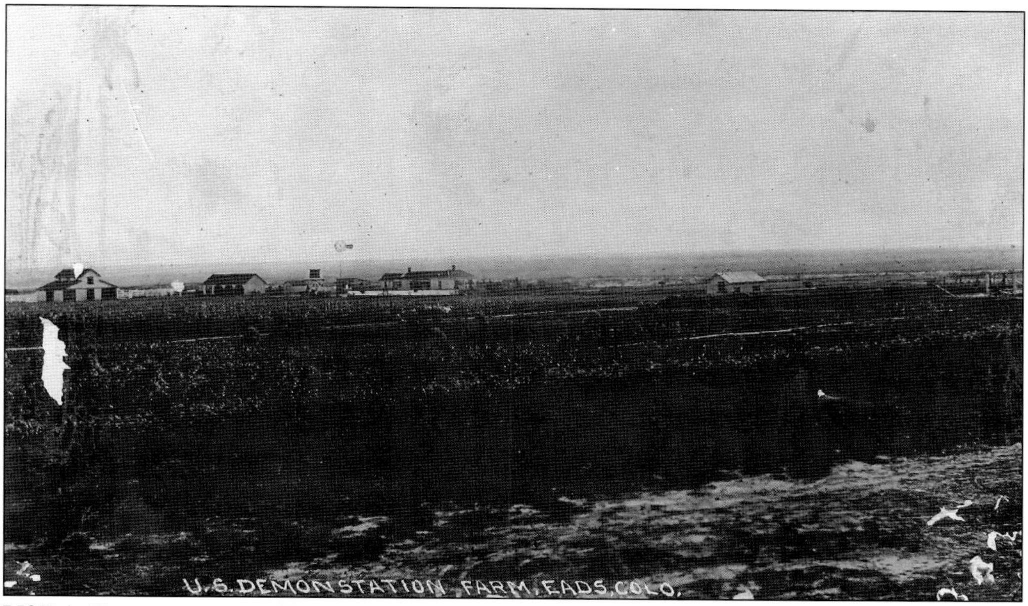

USDA Demonstration Farm, 1907. In 1906, the U.S. Department of Agriculture (USDA) established a demonstration farm on the south side of Eads with the intention of experimenting with water acquisition, storage, and irrigation to benefit area farming practices. The USDA built a barn, remodeled an existing house, drilled wells to determine the best method and cost of obtaining water, and planted 40 acres of crops, both irrigated and dryland.

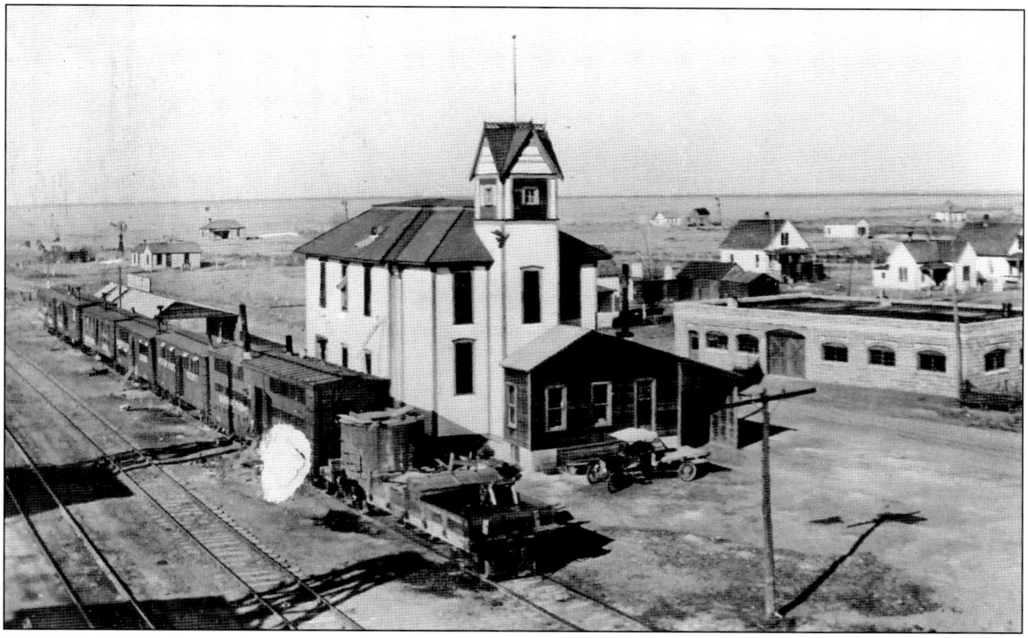

Eads Elevator and Milling Company. The first elevator in Eads was established when A. A. Neiman bought the old Eads schoolhouse and moved it trackside in 1918 to do business as the Eads Elevator and Milling Company. This elevator changed hands several times but continued to do business for years. However, the real impetus to grain shipment was the construction of elevators at Eads, Sheridan Lake, and Towner by J. D. Infield. The Eads elevator held 18,000 bushels of grain and was equipped with wagon dumps and all modern conveniences.

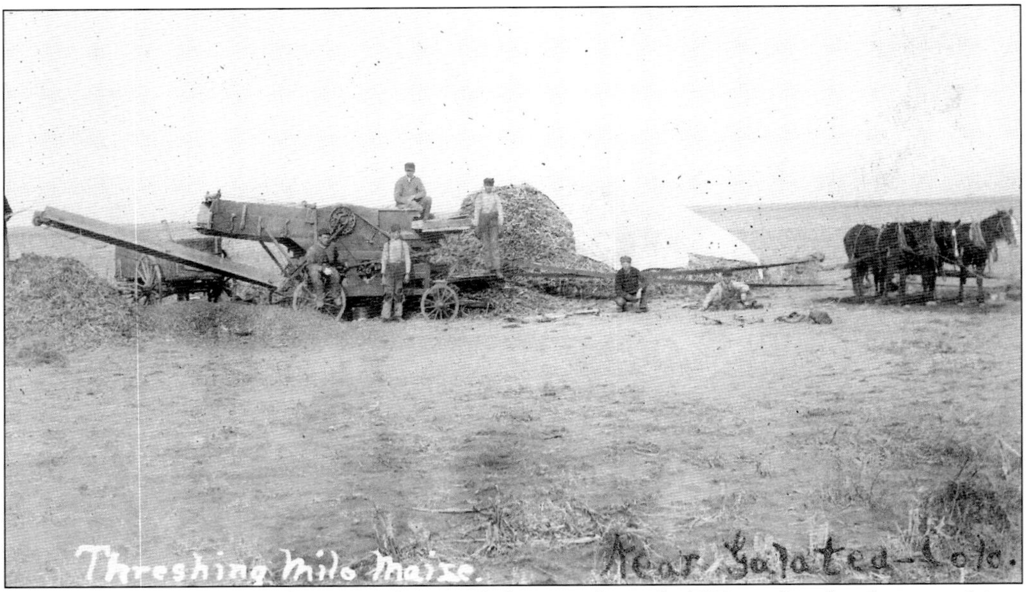

THRESHING MILO. Farmers harvest milo near Galatea in the early 1900s with a threshing machine, the predecessor to modern combines. The threshing process removed the grain from the stalks, but the process still required a great deal of human labor, including hauling bundles of grain to the machine and then pitching them into the thresher.

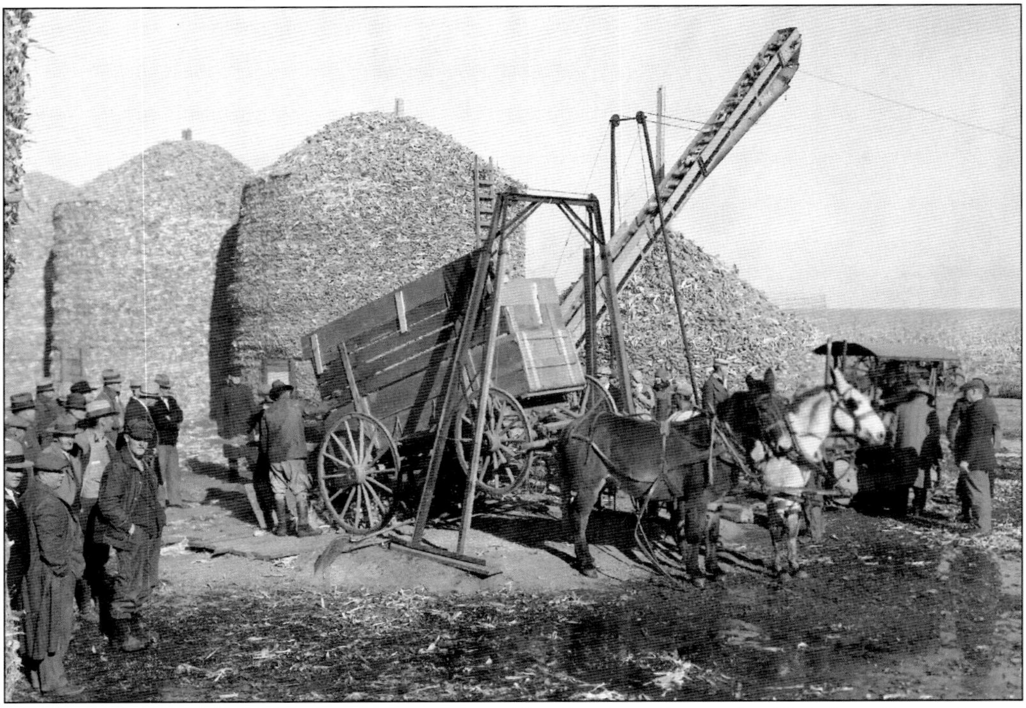

CORN HARVEST, 1931. Adam Aaron Neiman and his family had moved to Eads from Pennsylvania in 1917. After an initial disappointment with dryland farming, Neiman established the first elevator in Eads and was also involved in banking. In 1931, A. A. Neiman became the "Corn-King of the World." Neiman farmed around 1,200 acres a few miles north of Eads. He raised 83,000 bushels of corn, the largest corn crop ever raised on a single farm in America at that time.

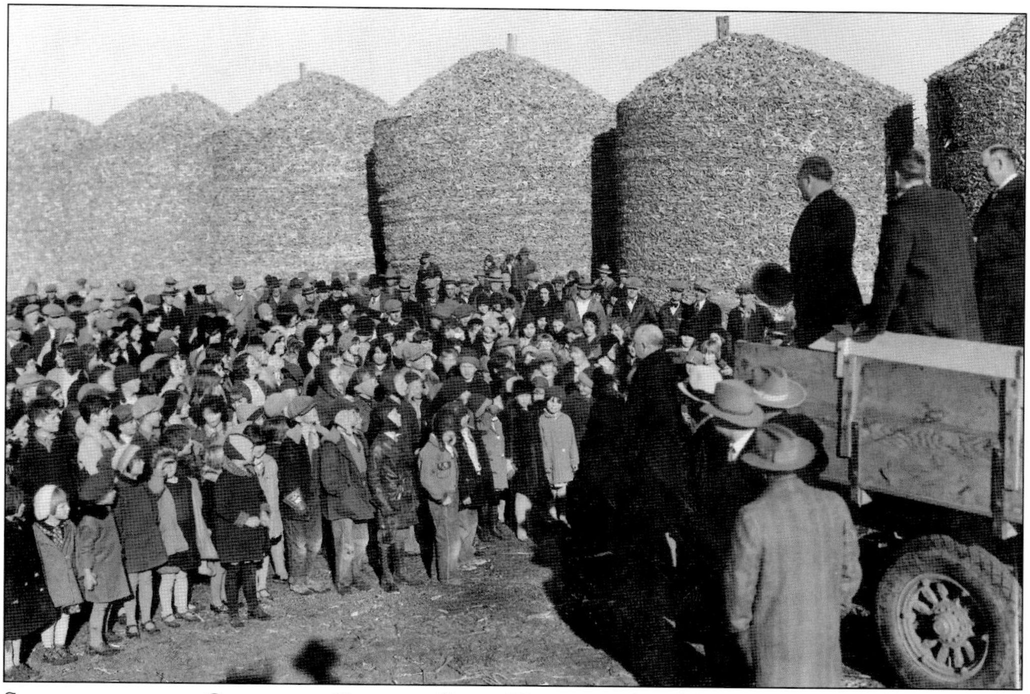

Schoolchildren Celebrate Record Corn Harvest. A celebration was held to recognize Neiman's historic corn harvest, with the governor, businessmen, and busloads of schoolchildren attending. The 1931 corn harvest was very good all over the county, and the tour went on to visit other farms in the eastern part of the county.

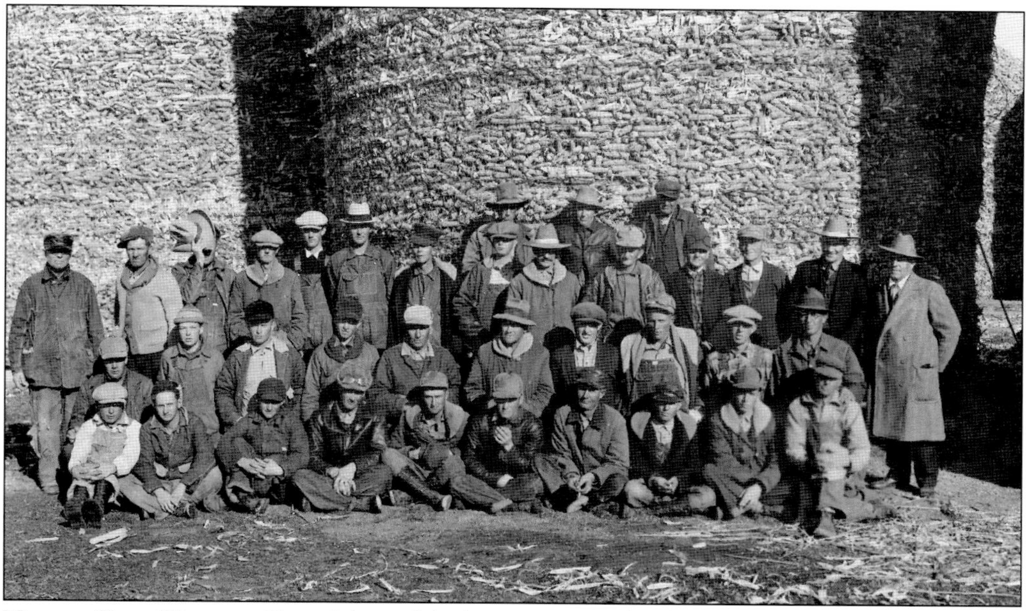

Neiman Corn Harvest Crew. Many of the harvesters were local citizens. The winter of 1930–1931 was cold with a great deal of snow and ice that delayed corn harvest until spring. Neiman finally was able to ship a trainload of corn from Eads to Pennsylvania, but the price of corn had dropped significantly while the corn was in transit. He lost money on his record corn crop because it cost more to ship it than it was worth.

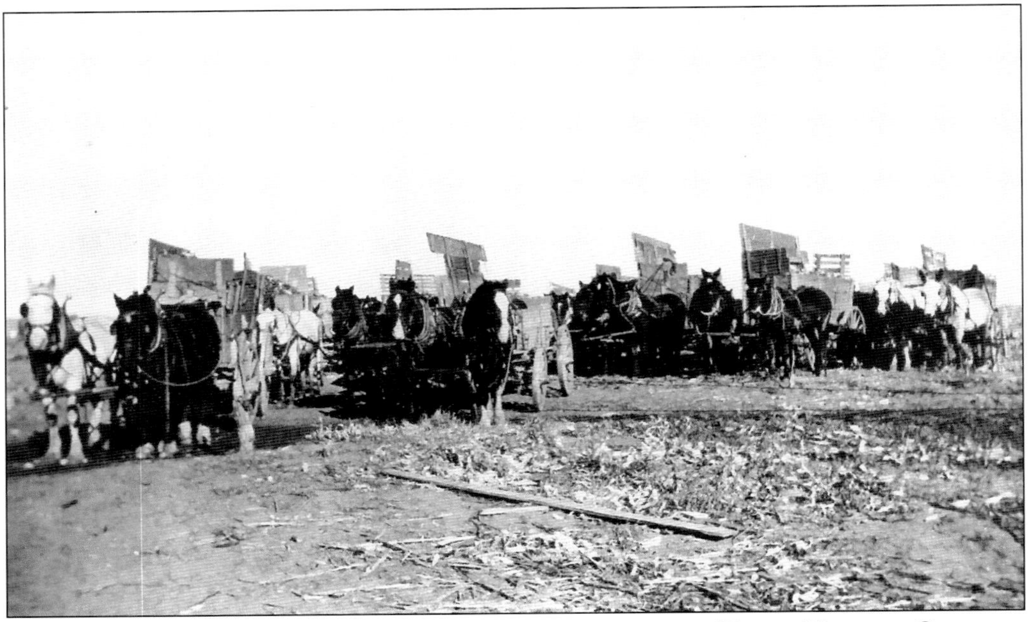

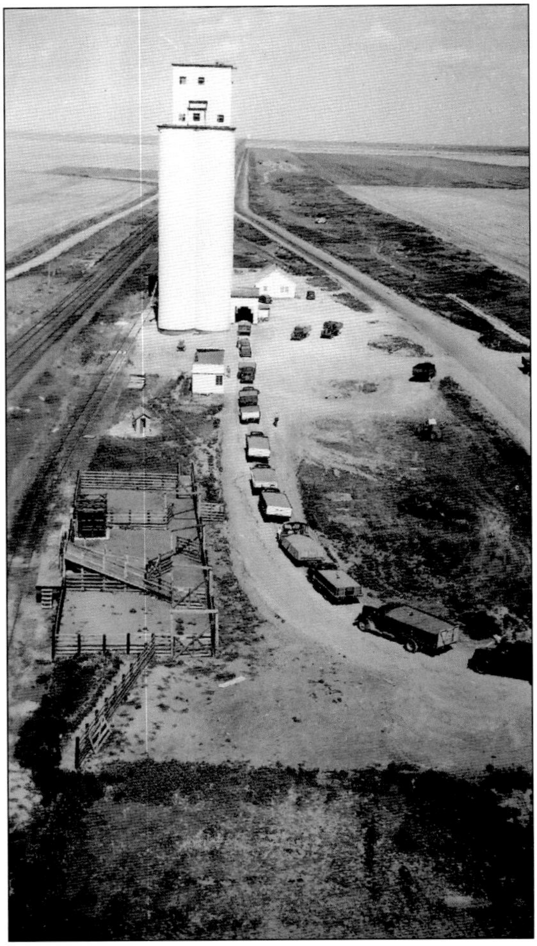

Wagons and Horses Used for Corn Harvest. Prior to the combine, corn in the field was harvested by hand, shucked, and then thrown onto a wagon pulled by horses. It was hauled to the farm and unloaded in the bins shown in this photograph.

Towner Elevator, 1940s. Grain elevators have played an important role in Kiowa County agriculture. Originally developed in 1842, grain elevators prevent the harvested grain crop from being attacked by pests or spoiled by rain. This picture of wheat trucks at the Towner elevator was taken in the 1940s. At one time, Towner had three grain elevators; however, today only one is in use.

Three

The Railroad and Town Development

Born from railroad financier Jay Gould's desire to make the Missouri Pacific Railroad transcontinental, the construction of the Missouri Pacific Railroad through southeastern Colorado in 1887 marked a time of great change. A subsidiary of Missouri Pacific, the Pueblo and State Line Company, constructed 152 miles of railroad line from the Kansas-Colorado border to Pueblo in 106 days, from August 16 to December 2, 1887. Encouraged by a $1,000 bonus if they reached Pueblo by December 1, workers built the railroad at an astonishing pace.

The railroad purchased land, platted town sites, and advertised for settlers. Some sources credit Jessie Mallory Thayer—the daughter of H. S. Mallory, president of the Pueblo and State Line Railroad—with naming the 10 town sites from east to west alphabetically, beginning with Arden, in what would become Kiowa County. Other sources say that Helen Gould and her younger sister—Jay Gould's daughters—had that honor. The railroad established the communities of Towner (called Memphis until 1888), Stewart/Stuart, Arden, Brandon, Chivington, Diston, Eads, Fergus, Galatea, Haswell, Inman, Joliet (later renamed Arlington), and Kilburn. Citizens established several other communities as well.

Without question, the railroad spurred the development of Kiowa County. The success of each community varied: some experienced a booming period of population and business growth, others moved to sites that were thriving, and a few were only occupied by residents for a short time. As the railroad evolved from steam to diesel-fueled engines, the number of stops and jobs required to keep the trains running decreased. Trains stopped traveling through Kiowa County regularly in the late 1990s; however, the rail lines are still used to ship grain from elevators in Haswell, Eads, and Towner.

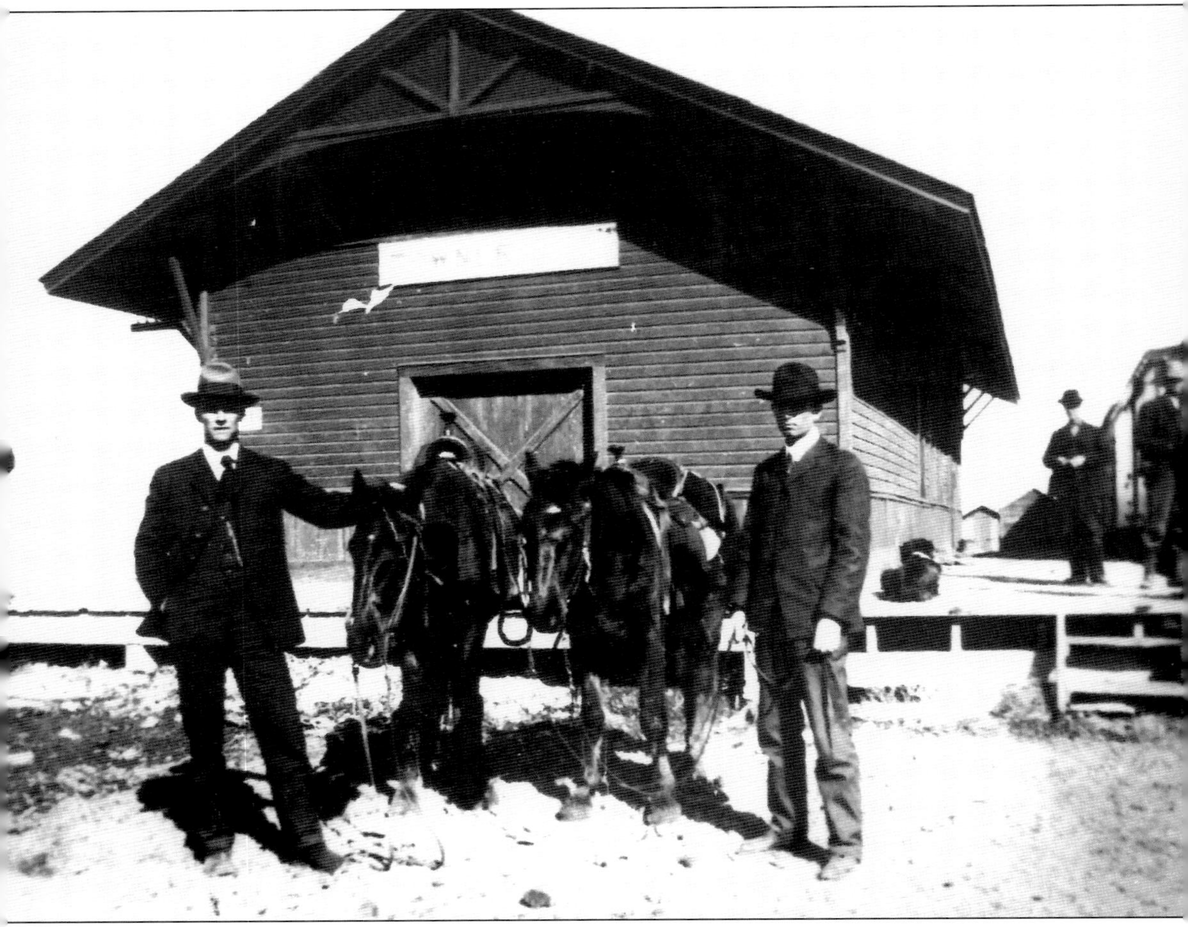

TOWNER DEPOT, EARLY 1900S. In the late 1800s, a passenger train stopped in Towner every morning, and a freight train stopped every evening. As the town's population grew in the early 1900s, so too did the number of businesses. During the 1910s, ranchers drove cattle to the nearby stockyards to ship cattle to Kansas City by rail. A daily passenger train also came through Towner at this time. Brothers Wirt and Carl Bailey are shown in this photograph. Wirt had a homestead near Towner and served as Kiowa County sheriff and a county commissioner.

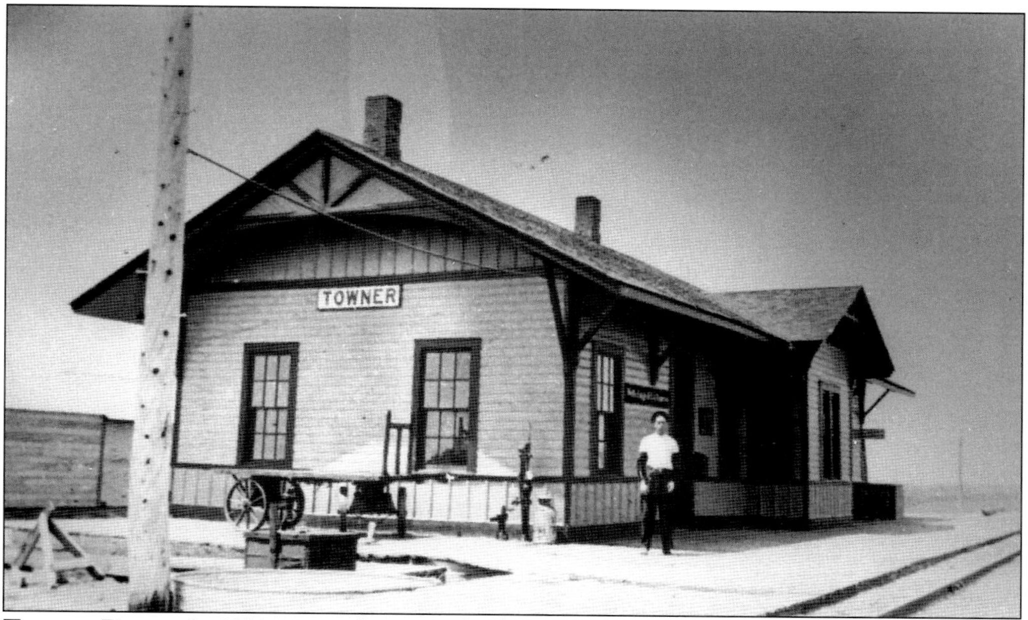

Towner Depot. In 1954, a new depot was built in Towner to replace the one that had been in use since the early 1900s. The depot was destroyed in the 1960s.

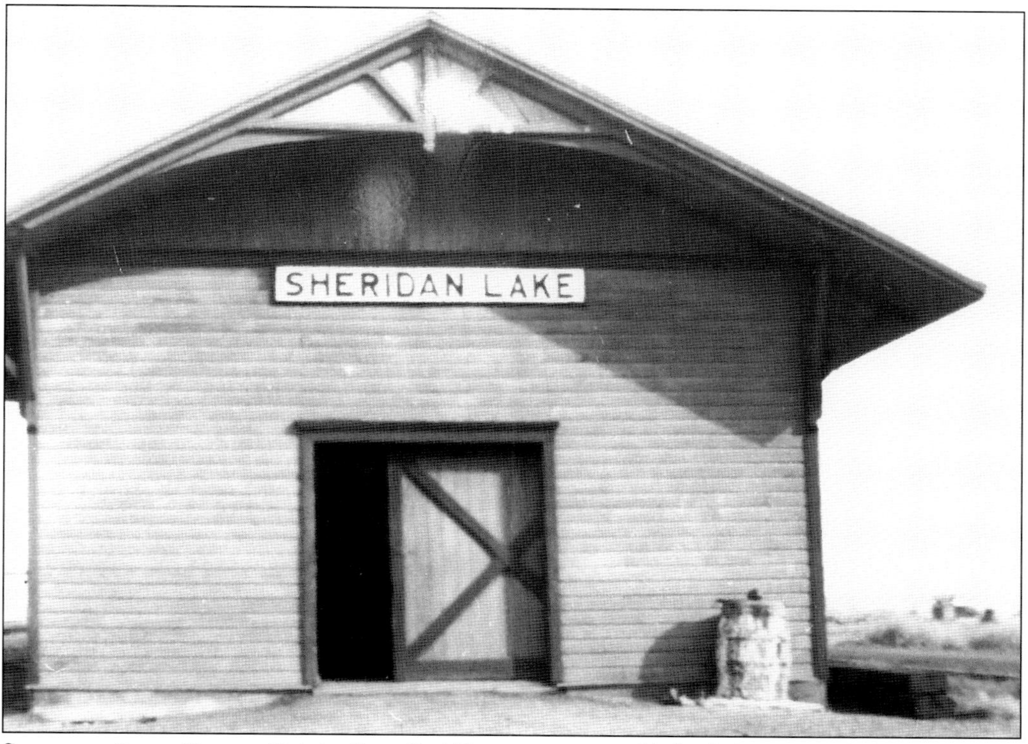

Sheridan Lake Depot. Originally called Bee, citizens established the town of Sheridan Lake, reportedly named after Union general Phil Sheridan, prior to the arrival of the railroad. The railroad refused to make a stop at Sheridan Lake, so the citizens of the town built a depot at their own expense. They then turned the town over to the railroad, and a station stop and telegraph operator were installed. The railroad brought goods and people to and from Sheridan Lake.

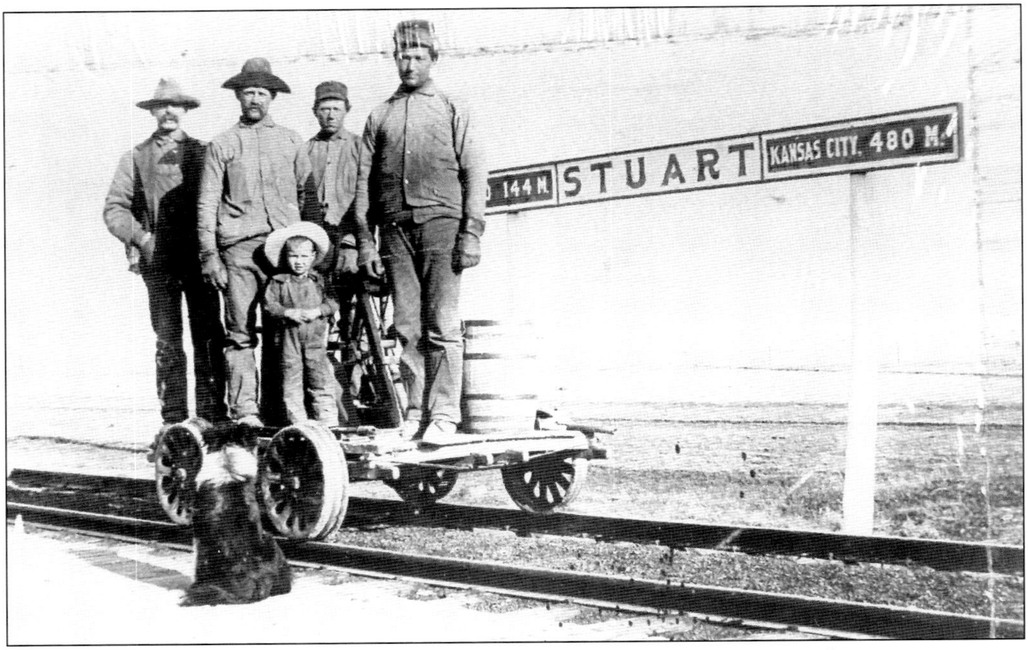

HANDCAR AT STUART, ABOUT 1900. Stuart, located north of the railroad tracks, and Stewart, on the south side, were competitive, booming towns from the construction of the railroad in 1887 through the early 1890s, with a population of 300–400 citizens each. However, as nearby Sheridan Lake grew, it attracted businesses and people away from Stuart; drought also took its toll.

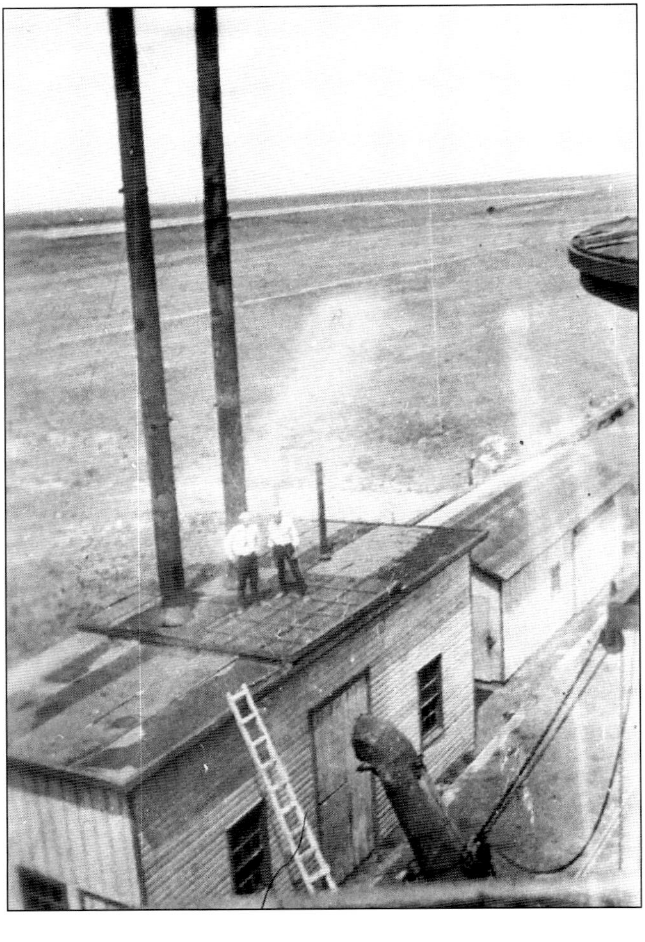

STUART WATER TANKS. As the only water stop between White Law, Kansas, and Pueblo, Colorado, Stuart was a critical stop for trains. Groundwater was pumped into the water tanks, and trains used this water to fill their tanks.

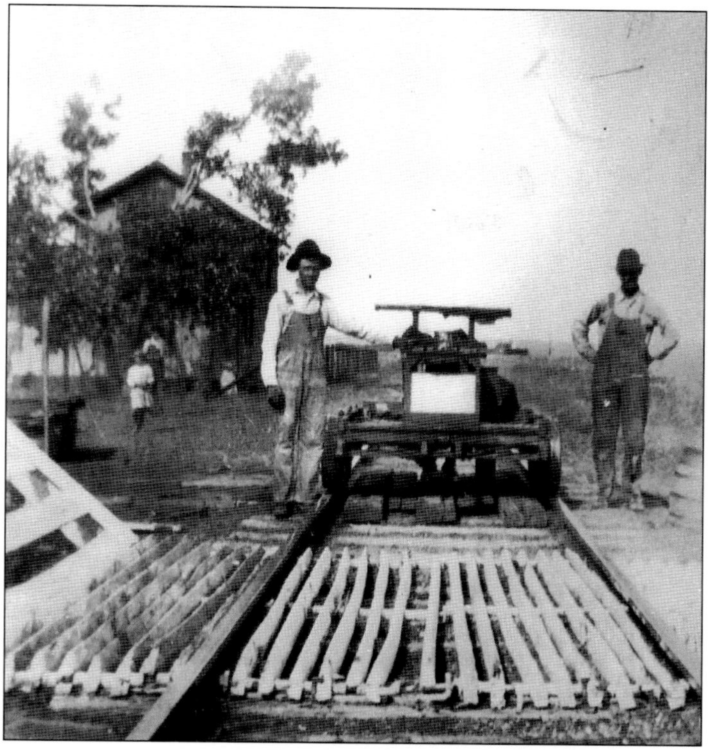

Railroad Track and Handcar at Chivington. In the fall of 1887, the railroad decided to locate its division headquarters in Chivington, which caused the town to grow quickly. Chivington's economy depended on the railroad, its crews, and the businesses that it generated. By 1888, Chivington had a population of 1,500.

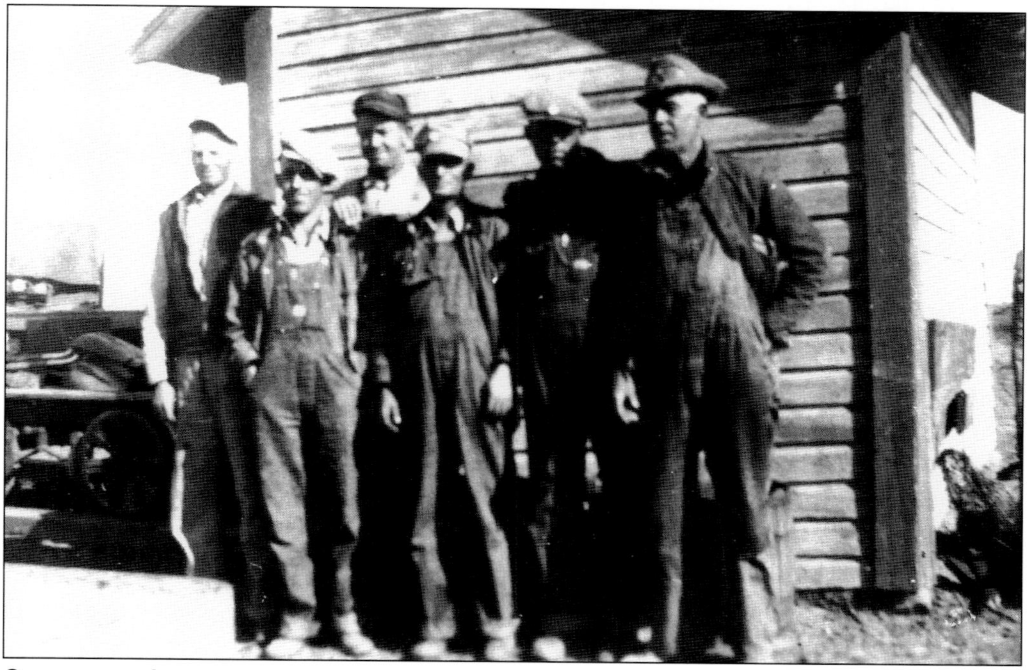

Chivington Section Crew. The railroad divided its track into sections, and each section crew was responsible for the maintenance of the rails and ties in their area. Chivington also had a six-stall roundhouse, repair shops, and several miles of switching in order to service and repair train engines. Because the Chivington water contained alkali, the facilities were soon moved to Horace, Kansas; the population and businesses of Chivington dwindled as a result.

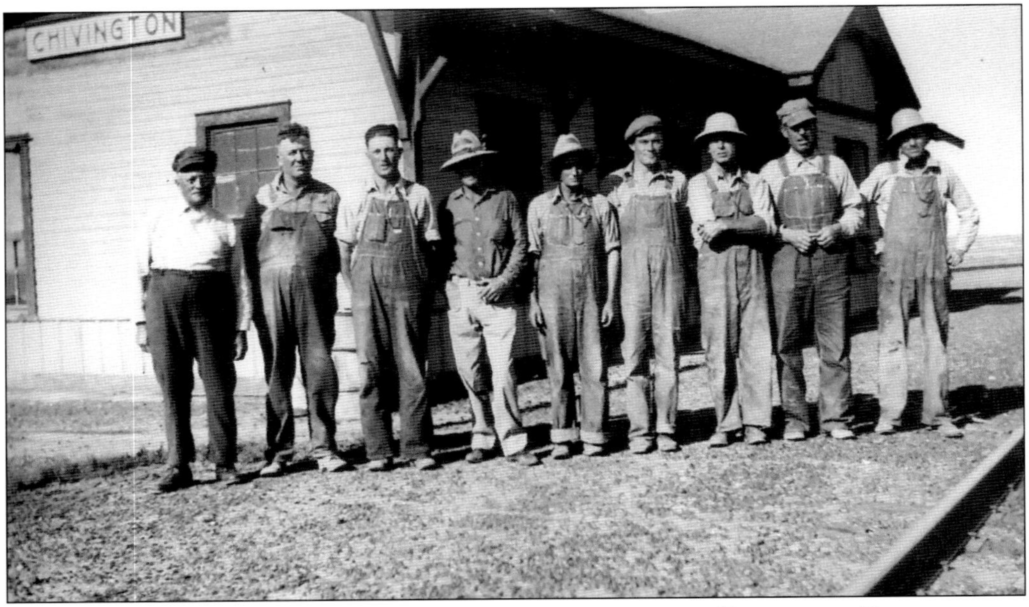

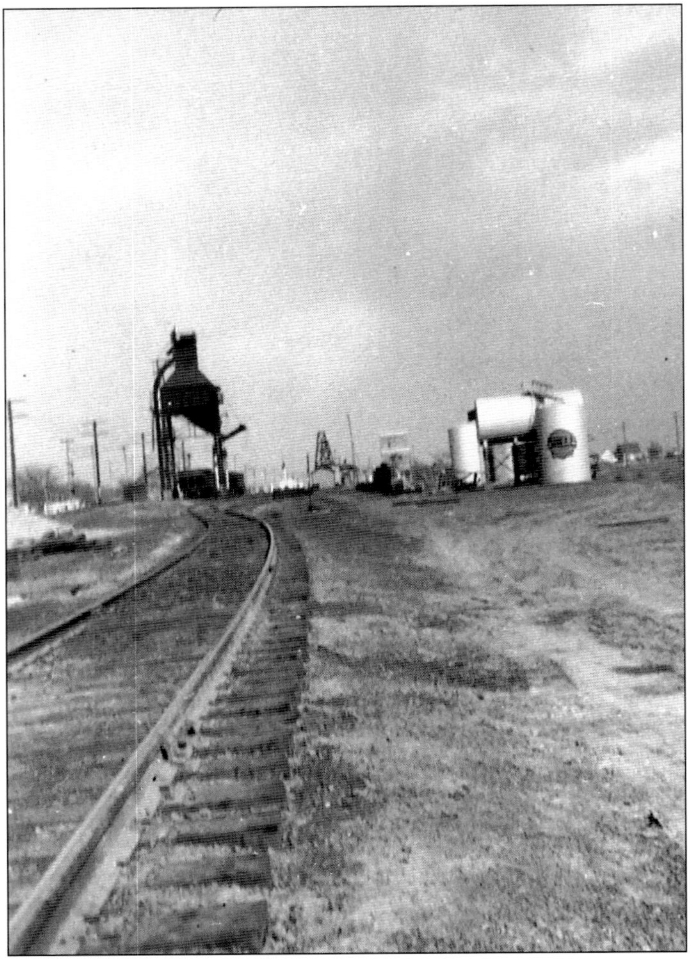

Chivington Depot. Workers on the Chivington section of the railroad are pictured here. John Harmon was the section house boss. Also pictured are John Brown, Jim Richardson, Mike Armstrong, Ray Jennings, Tom ?, Trent Abrams, Bing Newsom, and Walt Thomas. This photograph was likely taken in the late 1920s.

Eads Coal Chutes. In 1923, Missouri Pacific decided to build new coal chutes in Eads, eventually replacing those in Haswell. The railroad had to reduce the number of coaling depots on the line, and officials chose Eads as that location. In 1922, the railroad had replaced the wooden water tanks in Eads with steel tanks that held 200,000 gallons of water; the new water tanks and coal chutes made Eads an ideal stopping point for trains.

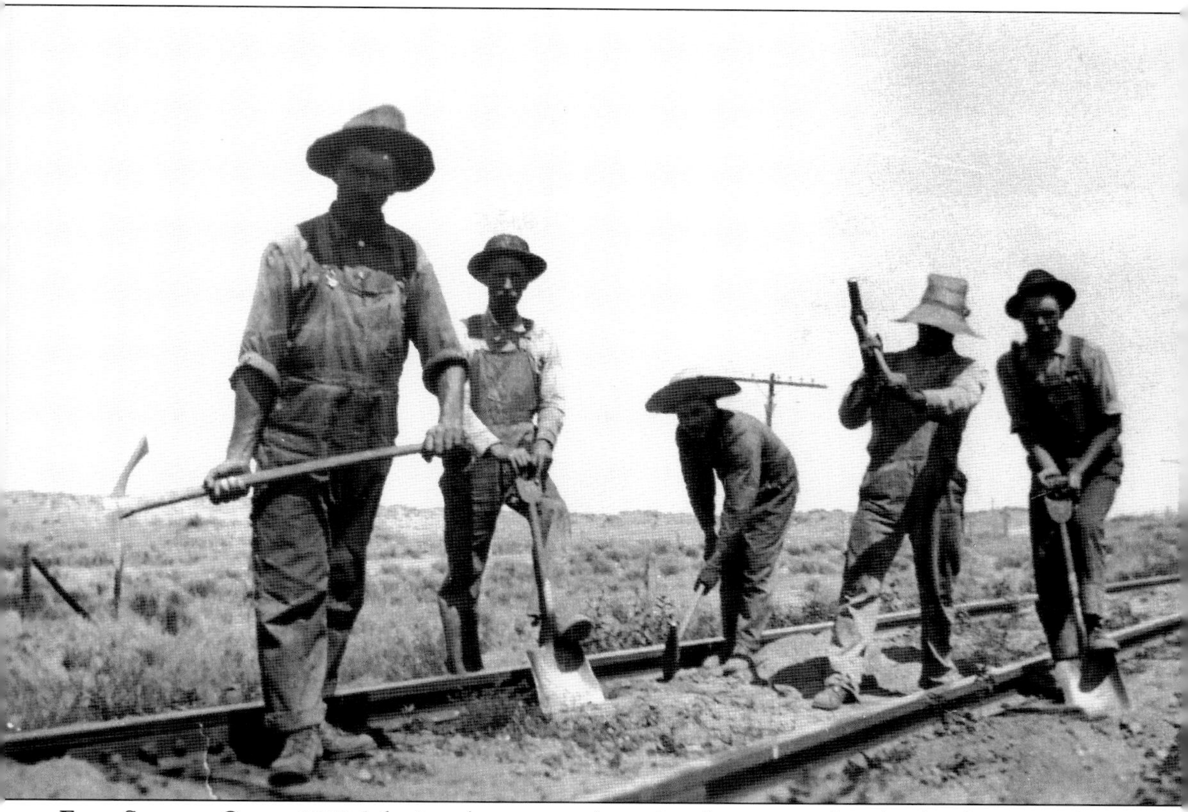

Eads Section Crew, 1917. Like in other towns, the railroad was critical to the development of Eads. The railroad built a water tower, coal chutes, and depot in Eads. Almost all transportation between towns was done on the railroad in the early years of the county; likewise, all coal, lumber, food, and other merchandise was brought in by train. The railroad was also a big employer; in 1887, about 10 of the 67 residents of Eads worked as depot agents, water pumpers, coal-chute shovelers, or members of the section crew.

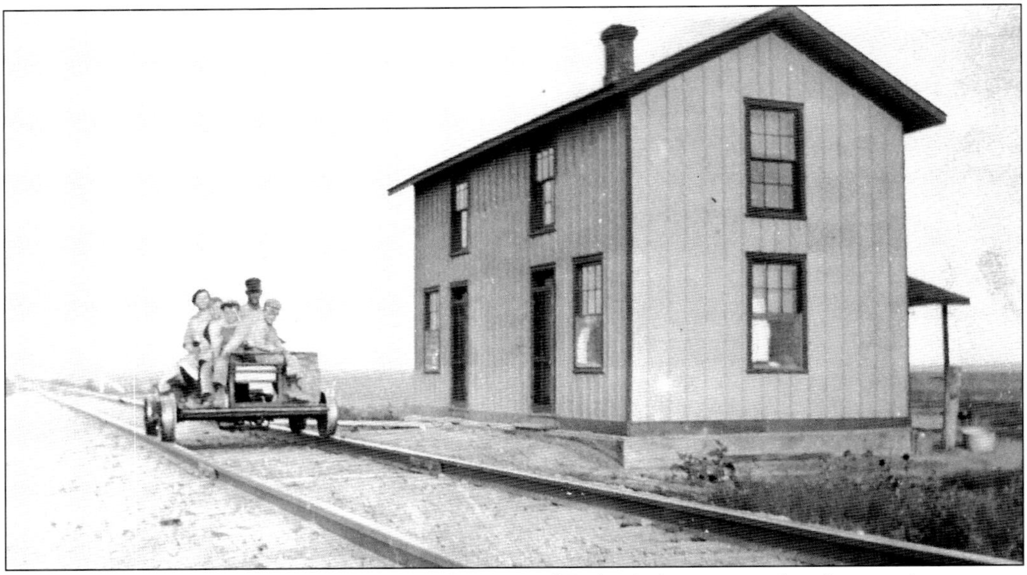

GALATEA SECTION HOUSE. Located 14 miles west of Eads, Galatea was a bustling trading center from the late 1880s into the 1910s. In 1888, the town had a population of 330, two hotels, two general stores, two saloons, a blacksmith shop, an elevator, and a two-room schoolhouse.

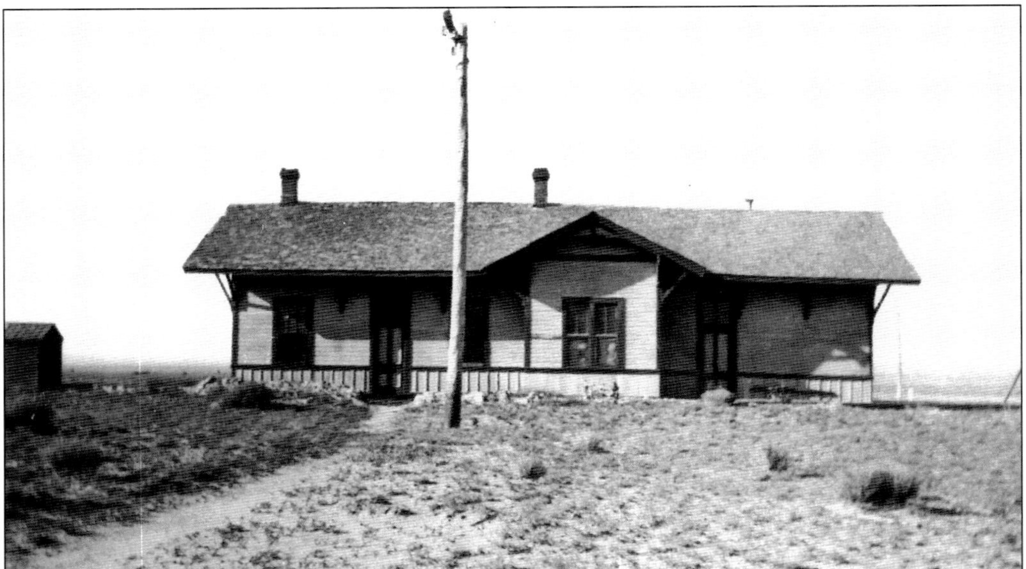

GALATEA DEPOT, 1929. The Missouri Pacific depot in Galatea was the center of commercial activities for many years. Items such as hardware, lumber, and household goods came into Galatea by rail, and livestock and grain left in the same manner. After a fire in 1916, Galatea began to decline.

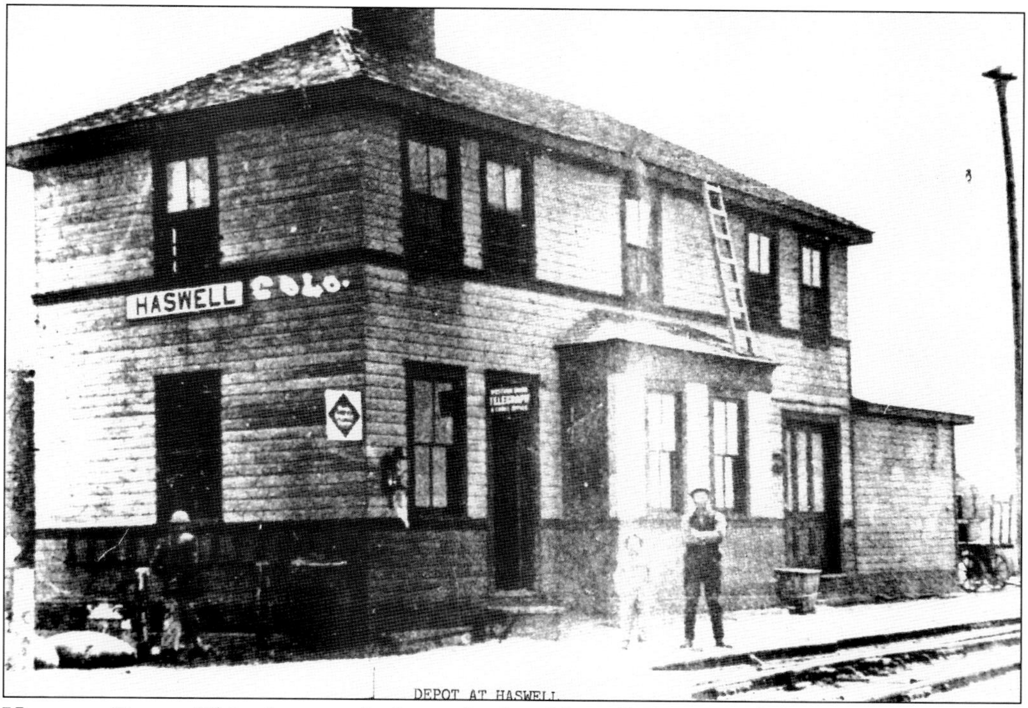

HASWELL DEPOT. This photograph shows the first Haswell Depot, with living quarters located on the top story. Haswell developed more slowly than other communities on the line. In 1887, Haswell had only a section house; 10 years later, a depot, coal chutes, and two cabins had been added to the town.

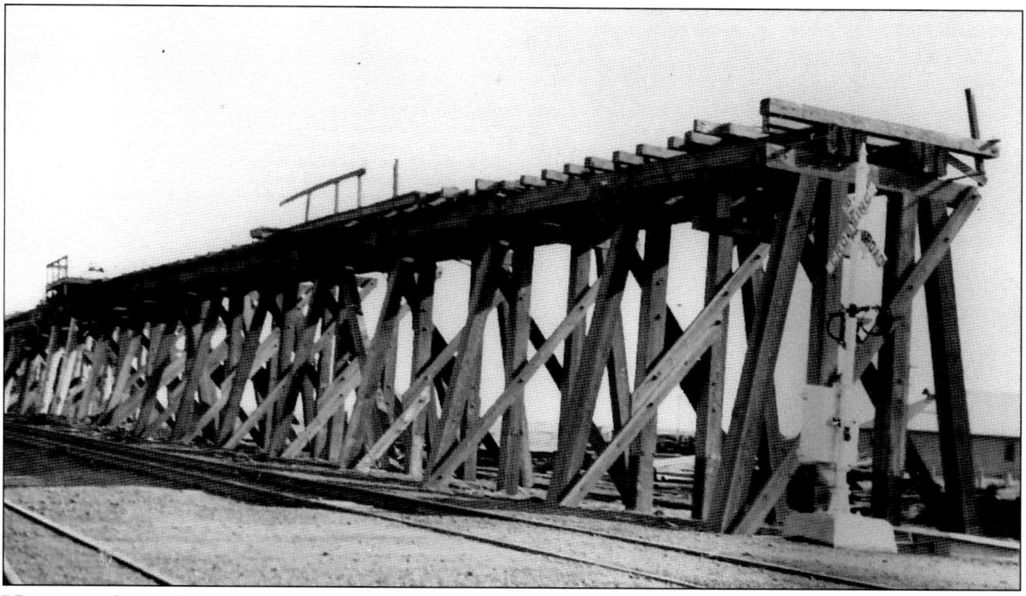

HASWELL COAL CHUTES, 1930S DEMOLITION. The railroad constructed the coal chutes in Haswell in 1901–1902, and a water storage tank was added in 1904. Following the decision to make Eads the location for trains to fill with coal and water, the Haswell coal chutes were torn down in the 1930s.

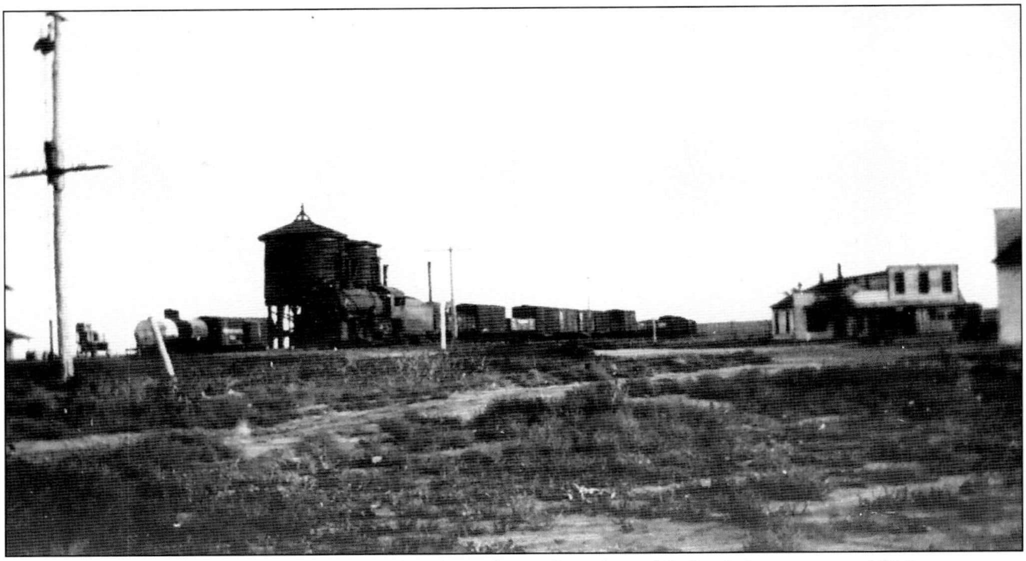

ARLINGTON, 1910S. Originally named Joliet, the railroad established the town in 1887 as a water stop with a depot; the water tanks are shown in the picture. In 1913, the population of Arlington was about 150 people; two years later, it had reached 500. The town had several businesses, including two hotels, a garage, a blacksmith shop, a livery stable, and two general stores. Arlington was also an extremely busy shipping point for livestock, with the largest stockyard from Hoisington, Kansas, to Pueblo, Colorado.

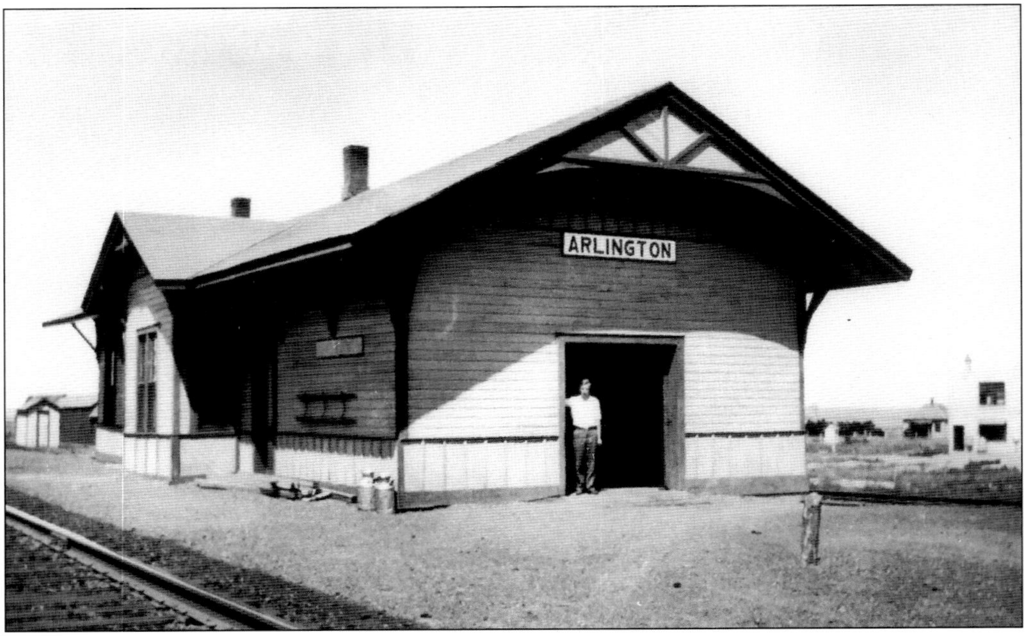

ARLINGTON DEPOT. Joe Barnett (pictured) began working for the Missouri Pacific Railroad in 1925. In 1929, he became the depot agent in Arlington. The Arlington Depot was closed in 1934 and destroyed shortly after. Barnett later worked in Eads from 1935 through the 1950s when the railroad cut jobs in Eads.

Four

Community Legacies

Word spread that a rail line would be built in southeast Colorado. Homesteaders rushed to establish towns, hoping the line would come through their communities. However, the Pueblo and State Line Company purchased land and platted towns roughly every 7 miles along the line, ignoring the homesteaders. On the east end, Memphis started as a camp for the railroad workers and was renamed Towner in 1888. Stewart/Stuart, settlements located on the south and north sides of the tracks, respectively, came next. Arden, Brandon, Chivington, Diston, Eads, Fergus, Galatea, Haswell, Inman, Joliet, and Kilburn followed.

Citizens established other communities, including Bee, Water Valley, New Chicago, Dayton, Segraganset, and Queen Beach. Located north of Brandon, Water Valley had as many as 500 residents and a horseracing track in the summer of 1887. But because the railroad was 5 miles south, the town was abandoned. New Chicago was 2 miles north of Water Valley and only lasted the summer of 1887. Residents of Dayton, near Kiowa Springs, learned their site would be missed by the line, so they moved the buildings. New Dayton relocated near the rail line, but was 3 miles east of Eads, so the railroad would not stop there. Frustrated, the residents of New Dayton again moved everything—to Eads. South of the railroad, communities formed on the Great Plains Reservoirs. Queen Beach, near lower Queens (Nee Skah) Reservoir, and Sweetwater, near Sweetwater (Ne So Pah) Reservoir, fizzled after 1900. Segraganset, a homestead community south of Galatea, contained two schools, a post office, drama club, and Sunday school but dwindled by 1918. Only Bee (renamed Sheridan Lake) was successful, since the rail line came through there.

Some towns fared better than others. Arden, Fergus (also known as Hawkins Switch), Inman, and Kilburn were little more than flag stops. The sites of Stewart/Stuart were actually the result of a disagreement on the spelling. The communities dwindled in the late 1800s, due in part to the success of nearby towns. In 1963, the school districts of Brandon, Sheridan Lake, and Towner consolidated and built Plainview School at the Stuart site. Diston prospered for a few decades then faded. The railroad towns of Towner, Brandon, Chivington, Galatea, Haswell, and Arlington (originally Joliet) prospered into the 1950s but have slowly depopulated. Today only Haswell, Eads, and Sheridan Lake are incorporated towns. About half of the county's population resides in Eads.

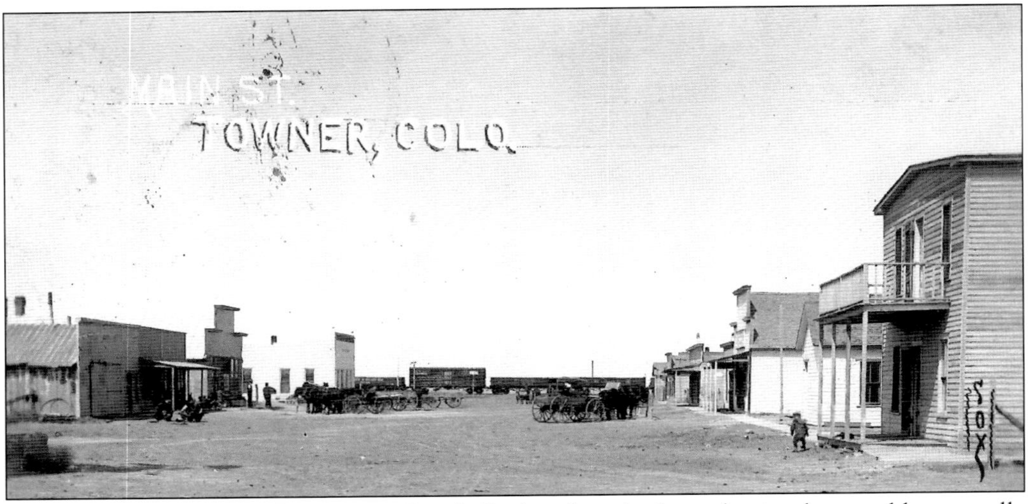

Towner Main Street. The Missouri Pacific Railroad was built on the site that would eventually become Towner in 1884, establishing a supply and work station. However, growth was slow. In 1889, only three families lived in Towner. At that period of time, a railroad official named Towner lived in the area. Many speculate that this is where the town got its name. By 1914, the population had increased to a little over 100 people.

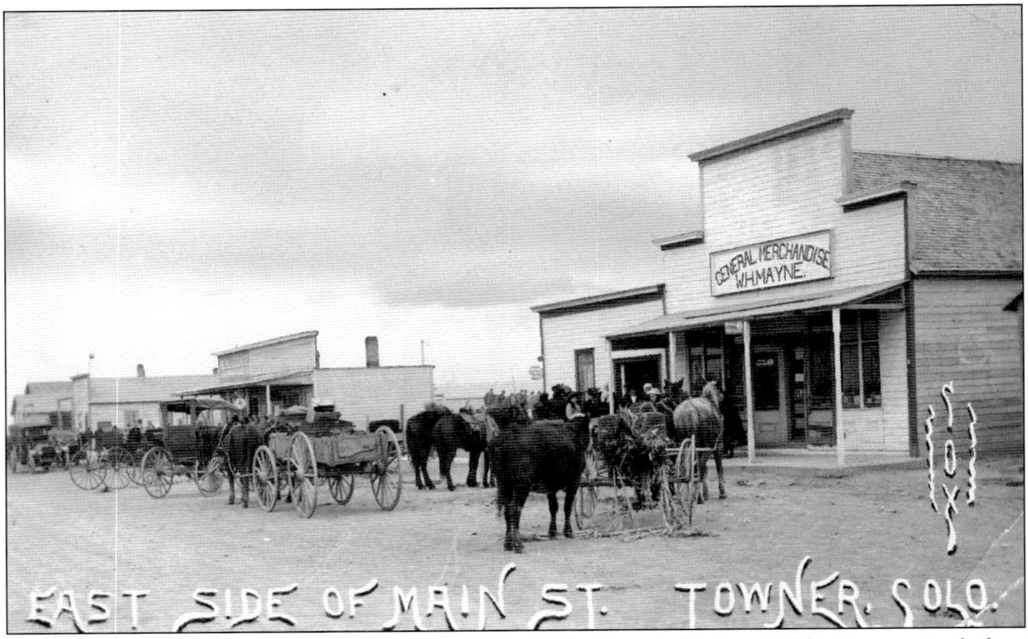

East Side of Towner Main Street. In the early 1900s, Towner had several businesses, including a general store, real estate office, bank, blacksmith shop, livery barn, and post office. A common well was drilled and a windmill erected in the middle of Main Street in 1907. Businesses got their water supply from this well, and it became a meeting place for community members.

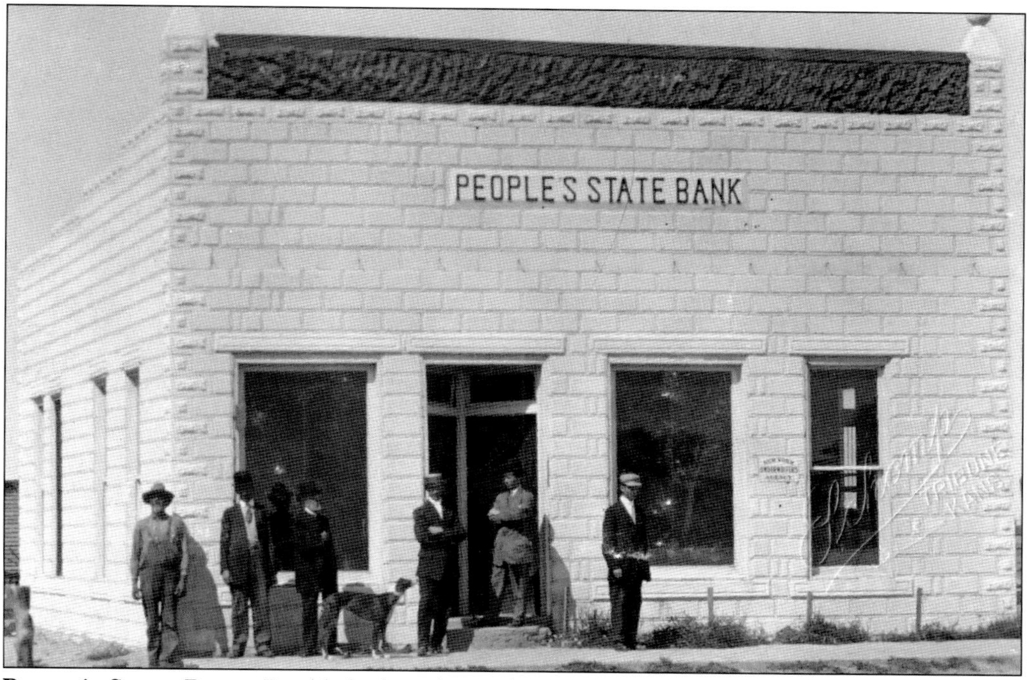

People's State Bank. Established in the early 1900s, People's State Bank was a fixture on Towner's Main Street. Charles Heaney worked at the bank as a cashier for many years. Following the federally mandated bank holiday on March 4, 1933, People's State Bank was the only bank in the county that was permitted to reopen without meeting additional federal requirements.

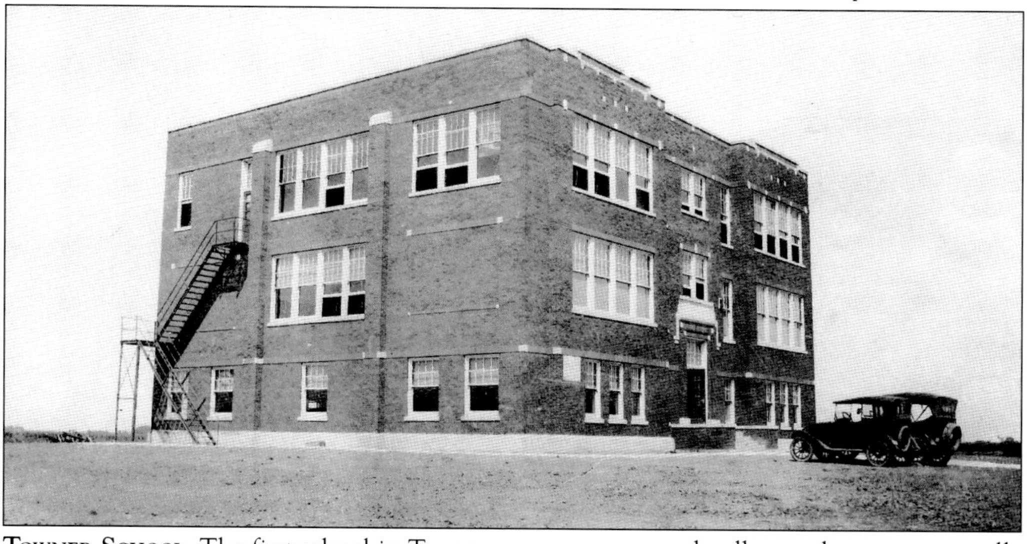

Towner School. The first school in Towner was a one-room schoolhouse that was eventually moved south of Towner in 1907. It was replaced by a two-story framed building that caught fire in the fall of 1923. The damages were extensive, and a new schoolhouse was built. The new school was constructed of brick and had a gymnasium, which also served as a community center. This building was torn down in 1963 when the school districts of Towner, Sheridan Lake, and Brandon were consolidated, and a new $400,000 schoolhouse was built in between Towner and Sheridan Lake. The children were allowed the opportunity to name the school and decided upon Plainview.

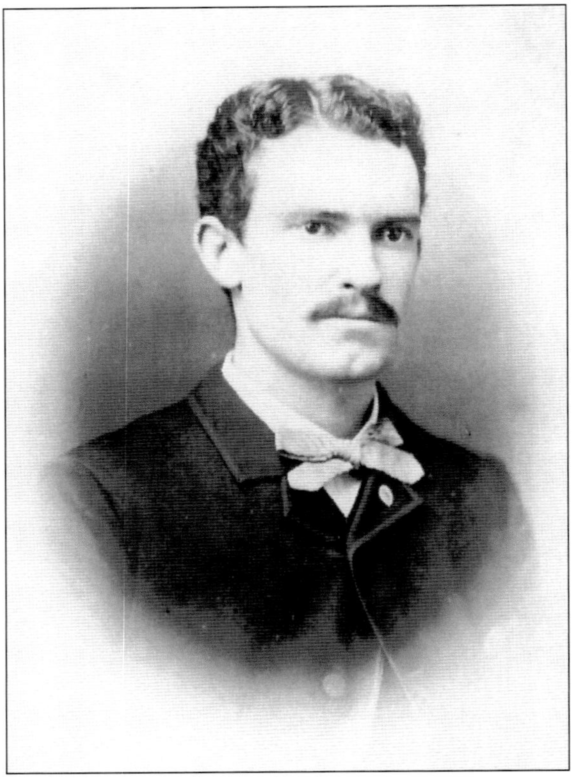

JOHN. S. BOOHER. Born in Illinois in 1861, John S. Booher moved to Arlington, Colorado, in 1887. When Kiowa County was organized in 1889, he was elected county assessor and relocated to the county seat in Sheridan Lake. Booher had many occupations, including newspaper editor, realtor, and farmer. He married Edith Reed in 1890; they had three children. The Boohers left Kiowa County in 1900.

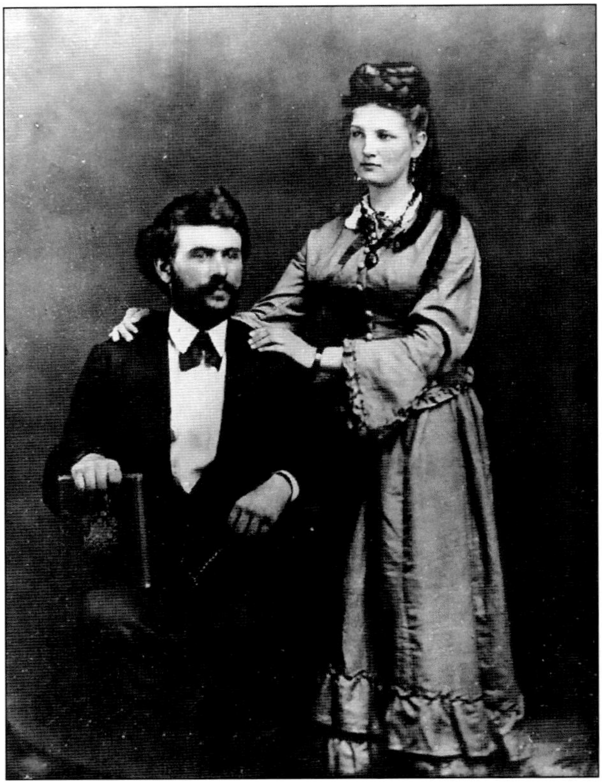

WILLIAM AND MARY ALBRIGHT. William and Mary Albright came to Sheridan Lake from Kentucky in 1887. They were attracted to Colorado's beauty and charm. Unfortunately, William died about two years after moving to Sheridan Lake, leaving Mary to raise a family of five and work and manage the Albright family homestead.

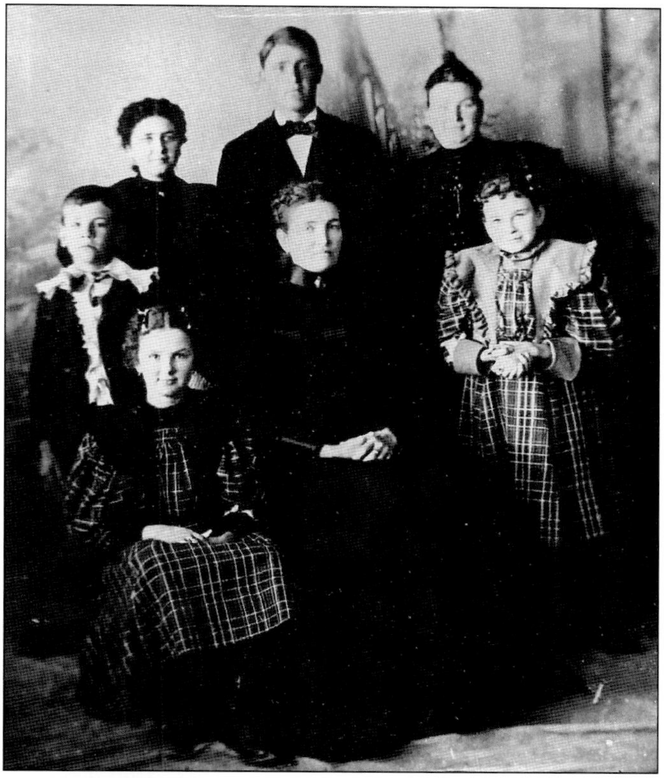

Mary Susan Albright Family. After the death of her husband, Mary Susan "Mammie" Albright successfully proved their homestead with the help of her oldest son, Willie. Willie was 14 at the time of his father's death. Mammie is pictured here with her children—Willie, Luetta, Anna, Allia, and Hughie Kiowa.

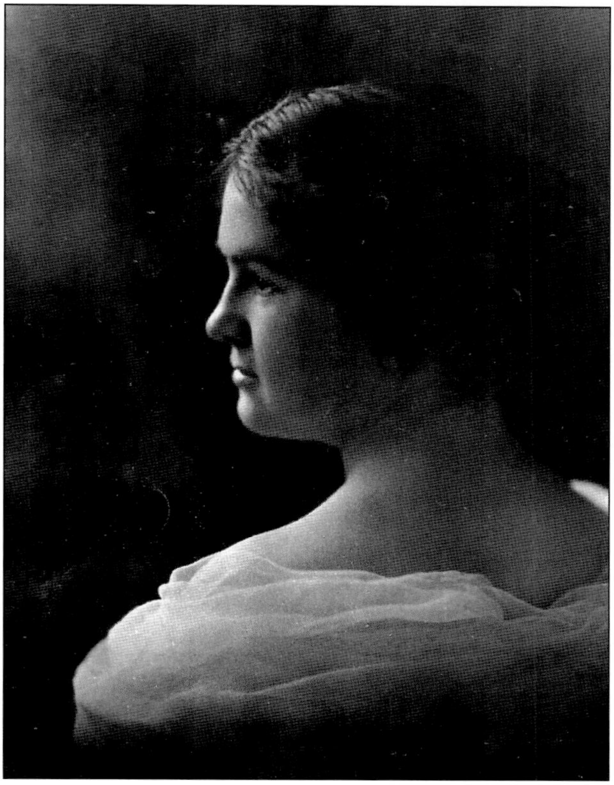

Allia Albright Severance. Allia Albright was educated in Sheridan Lake, Lamar, and Colorado Springs schools. In 1911, she married Martin H. Severance of Hutchinson, Kansas. Her only daughter, Virginia, was born in 1915. After Martin died unexpectedly in the late 1920s, Allia and Virginia moved to El Paso, Texas. Allia returned to Sheridan Lake following her mother's death in 1931. She was an active member of the Sheridan Lake community.

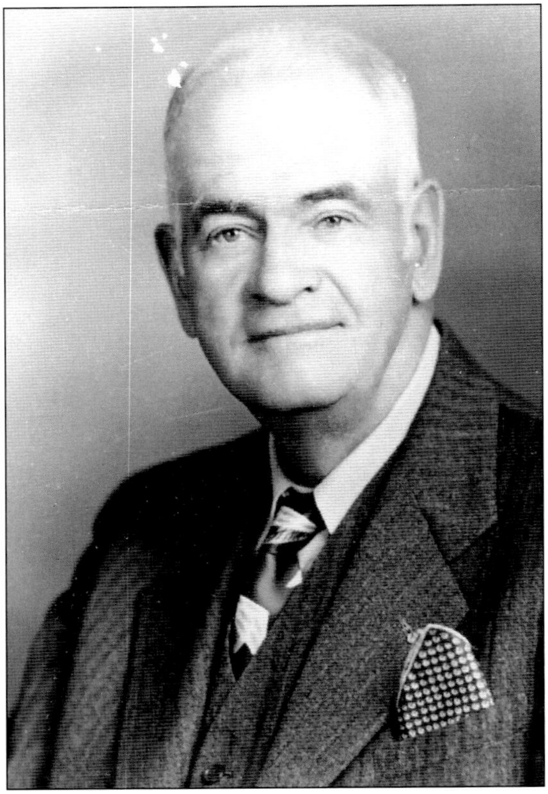

Kiowa Albright. Born on August 4, 1889, "Ki" Albright was "the first white child born in Kiowa County." He attended Sheridan Lake schools and helped his mother and brother with daily chores on the ranch. He later attended the Tonkawa Military Academy at Tonkawa, Oklahoma. Eventually, he established a homestead north of Sheridan Lake and ran his own cattle operation. Albright died in 1959, and in the 1970s, the old schoolhouse in Sheridan Lake was rededicated as the Kiowa Albright Memorial Center.

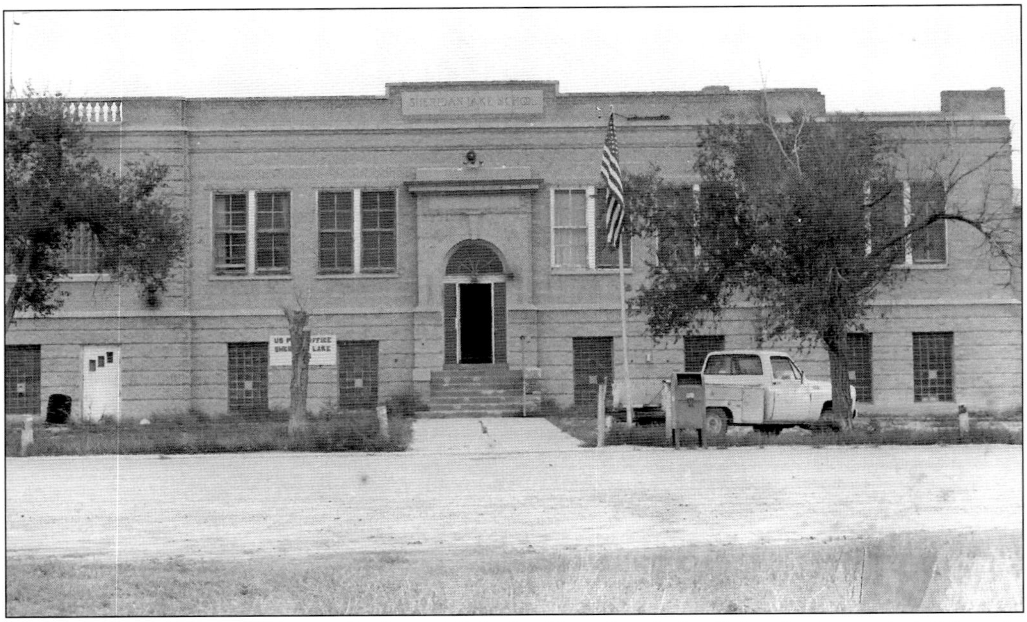

The Sheridan Lake School. Built in 1929, the Sheridan Lake School educated children in grades one through 12 from its opening until 1963, when the Towner, Brandon, and Sheridan Lake schools consolidated into the new Plainview School. The school was then restored and rededicated as the Kiowa Albright Memorial Center. The building has served as a community center since that time; it also houses the Sheridan Lake Post Office.

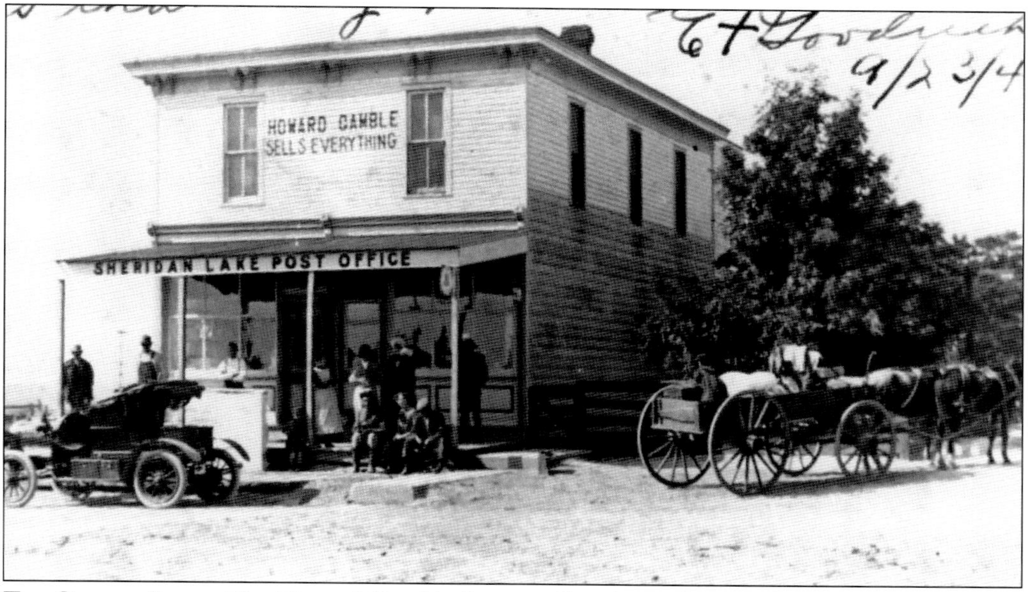

The Gamble Store. The Howard Gamble Store in Sheridan Lake served as both a general store and a post office. For 24 years, the well-known company aided in the development of eastern Kiowa County. The Gamble Store burned down on August 19, 1925. In February 1927, Gamble and his wife moved to Pueblo to pursue other job opportunities.

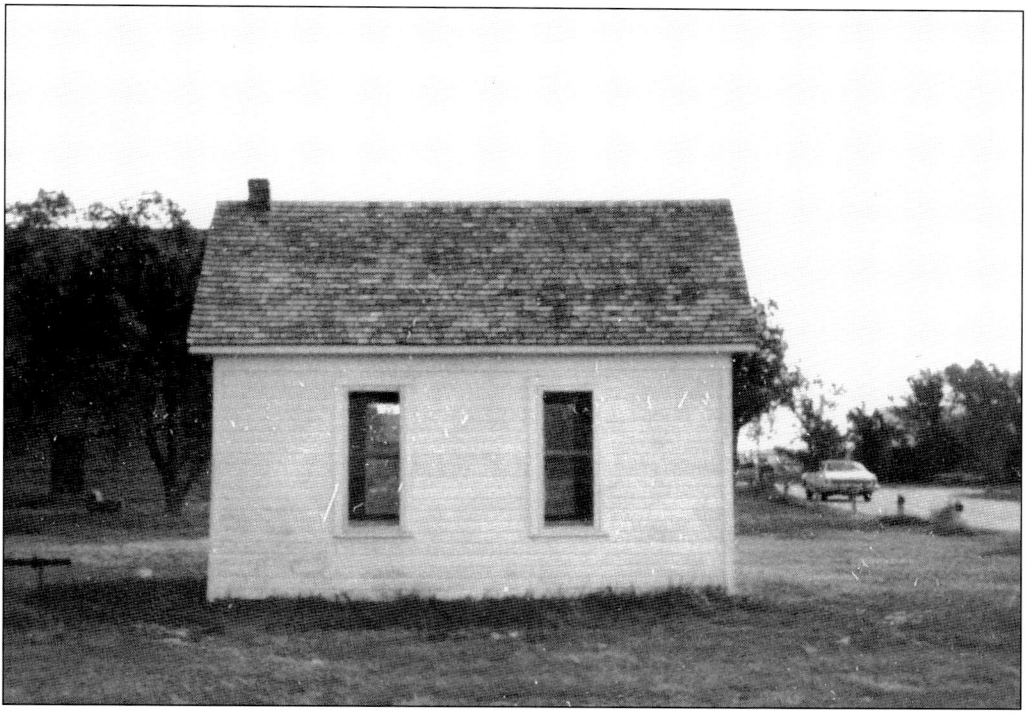

Sunny Ridge School. The Sunny Ridge School was constructed in 1910 and was part of District 11. Located north of Brandon, the community also held Sunday services and other events at the school. In 1976, the school was moved into Sheridan Lake and restored.

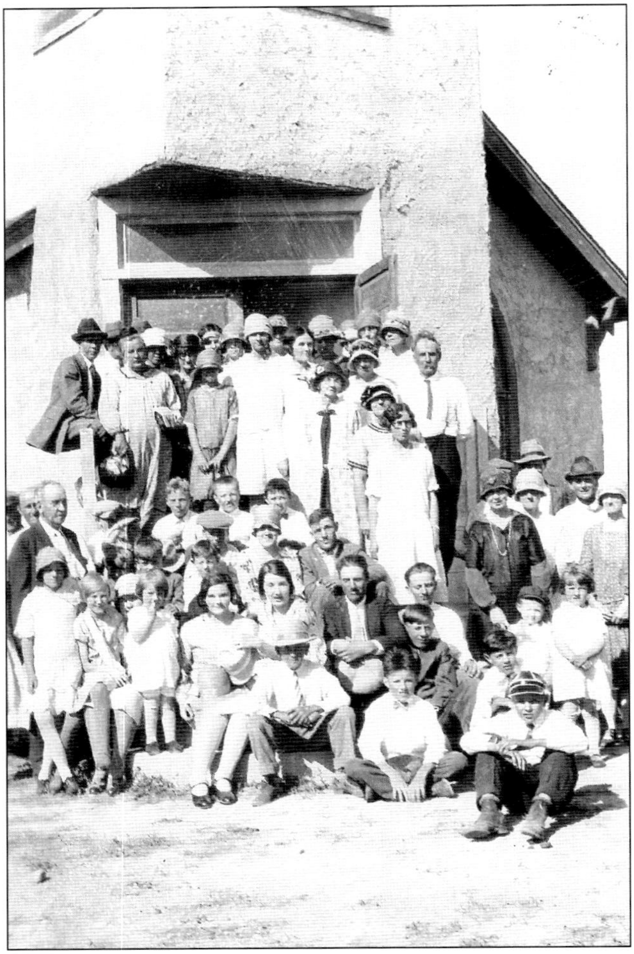

CHURCH GROUP (BEFORE REMODEL). In the late 1940s, the Methodist and Presbyterian Churches in Sheridan Lake were combined to form the Sheridan Lake Bible Church. The Methodist Church building was moved and combined with the Presbyterian building in 1949. The church is still active today.

STUART SCHOOL, 1930S. Located between the communities of Towner and Sheridan Lake, the Stuart School was a part of District 18 in the early 1900s. The school also often served as a community center with events, including basket socials and thanksgiving services.

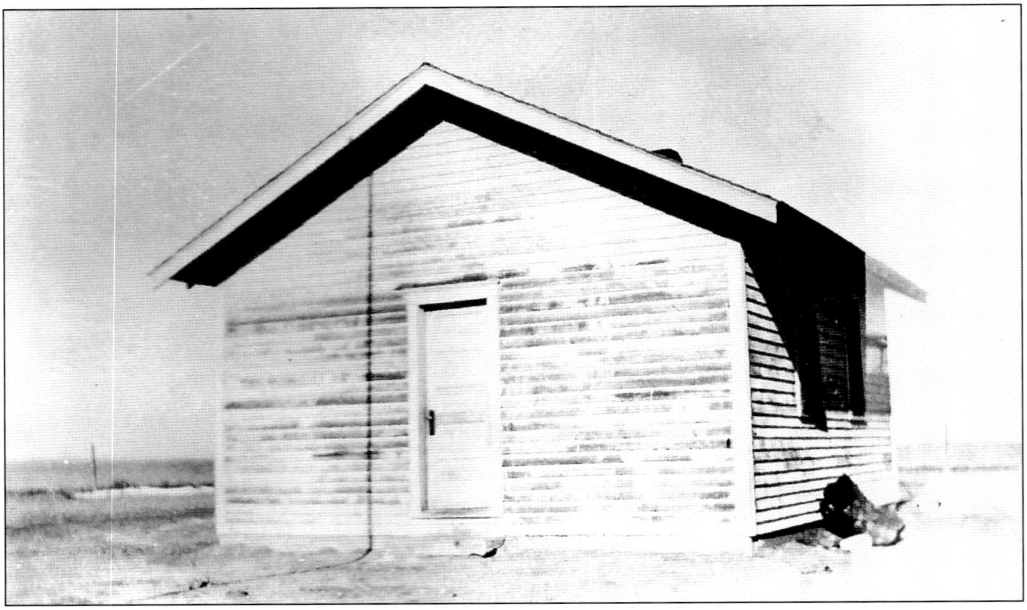

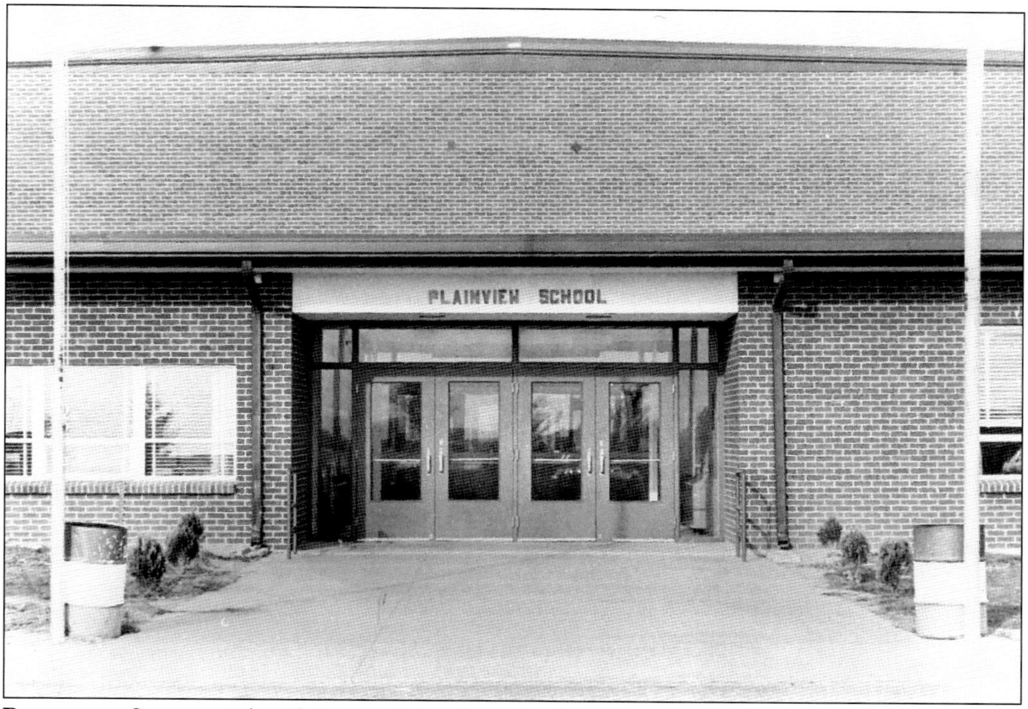

Plainview School. The Plainview School was built as a result of district consolidation in the early 1960s. Students from Towner, Sheridan Lake, Brandon, and surrounding areas attended the kindergarten through 12th grade school. Students from the east end of Kiowa County still attend this school, built near the old Stuart town site.

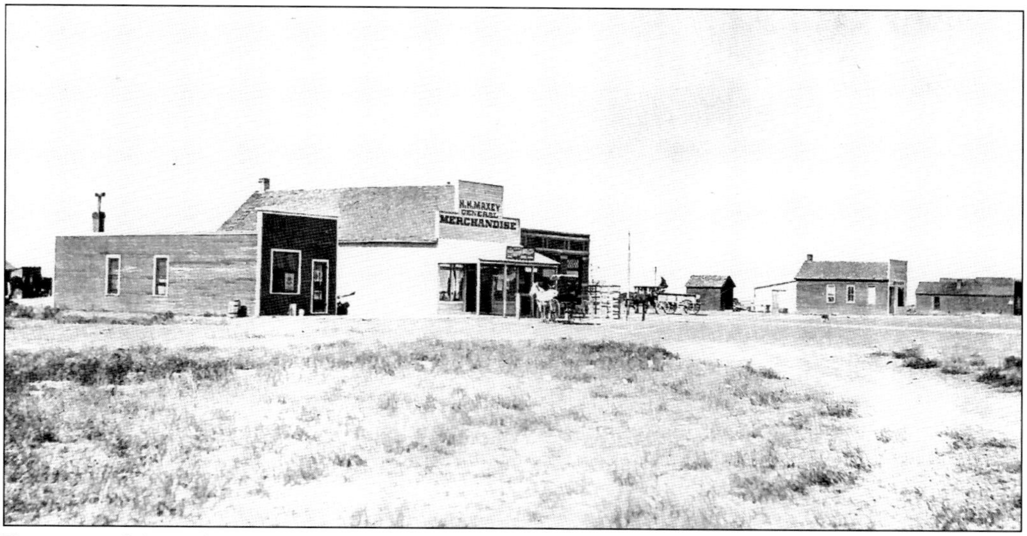

Brandon Main Street. Pictured on Brandon's Main Street is the H. H. Maxey General Merchandise Outlet. The Maxey family opened the doors in 1910 to the town of Brandon with the help of their two daughters, Imogene and Geraldine. The store was always busy, especially on Saturdays when everyone from town and surrounding farms and ranches came to purchase their goods for the next week. At one time, Brandon had two grocery stores, a hardware store, pool hall, barbershop, two cafés, a filling station, garage, lumberyard, depot, railroad section house, stockyards, cream station, and a section house.

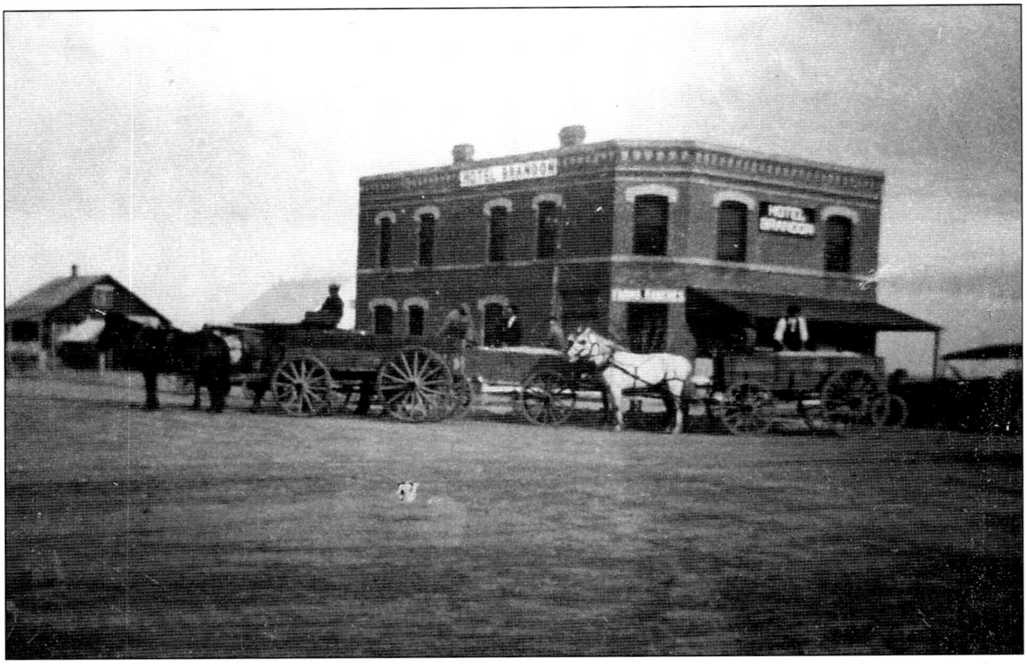

Brandon Hotel. The Brandon Hotel was an outlet for many things during the town's glory days. Dr. O. B. Hugg was a physician and surgeon, and his office was in the hotel. The local post office was also located in the Brandon Hotel. On December 10, 1915, Lena Ingrams became the owner and operator of the hotel.

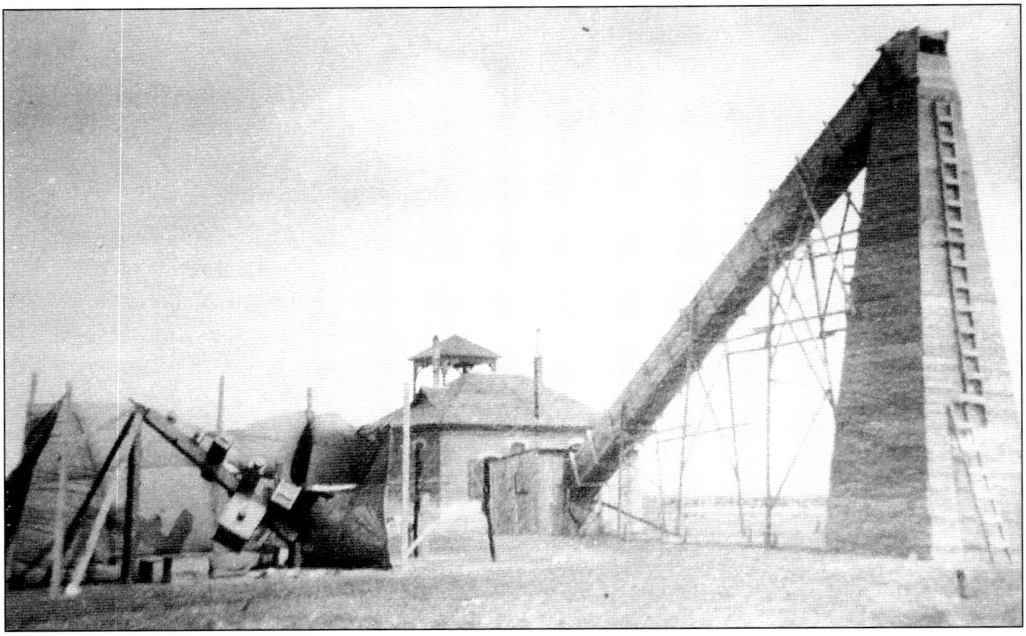

Brandon Observatory. On June 8, 1919, at 5:37 p.m., a total eclipse of the sun was to be seen in Brandon, only one of two places in the world. Estimated to last only 88 seconds, astronomers Dr. John A. Miller and E. C. Slipher came in early May with equipment to record the phenomenon. The observatory was built in May. While in Brandon, the astronomers gave many lectures to the students and townspeople. The eclipse brought much publicity and people to Brandon.

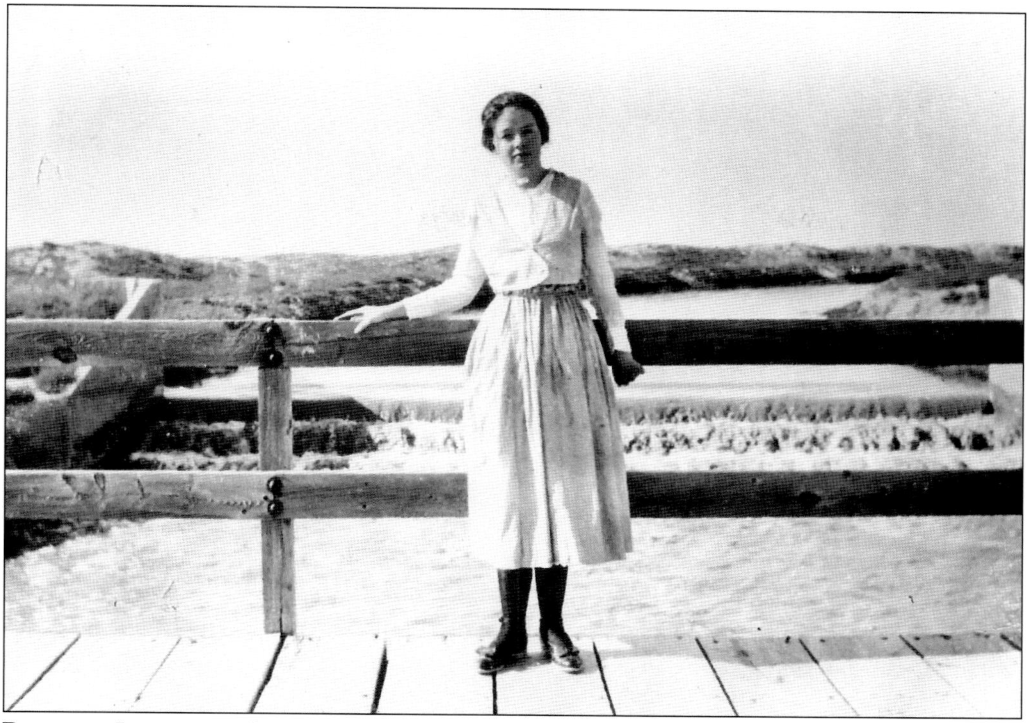

Brandon Irrigation Canal. Built by local townspeople using horses and crude equipment, the Brandon Irrigation Canal (also known as the Chivington Canal) was the highlight of the town for many years. Imogene (Maxey) Seamans is standing on the bridge that overlooks the canal. The drops were located east of Brandon, a quarter of a mile on the north side of present Highway 96. The canal ran from Sand Creek southeast for 20 miles to Brandon Lake.

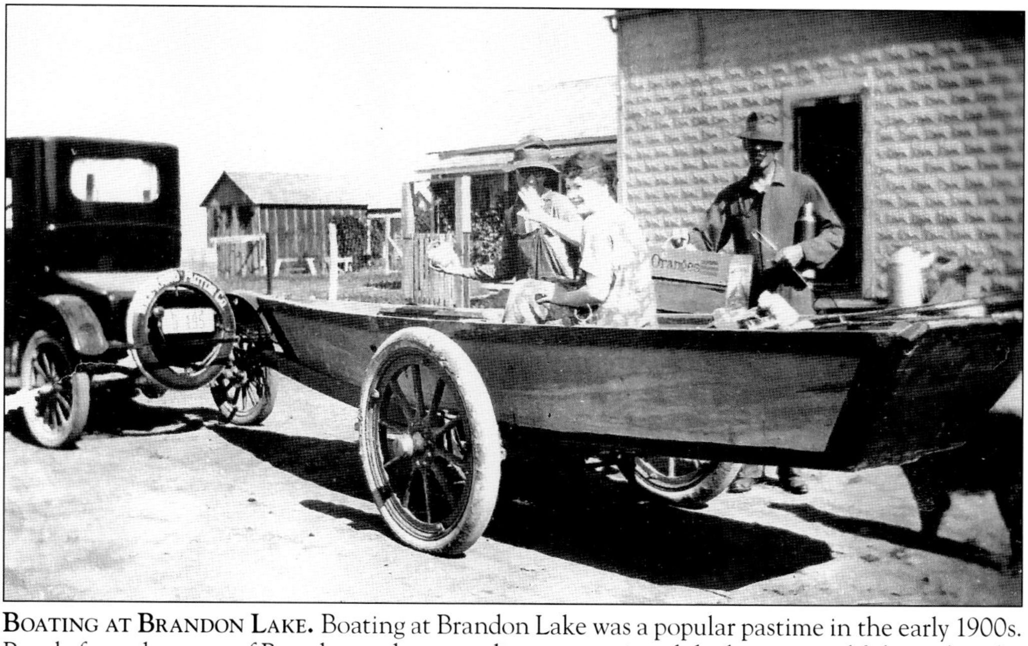

Boating at Brandon Lake. Boating at Brandon Lake was a popular pastime in the early 1900s. People from the town of Brandon and surrounding areas enjoyed the boating and fishing that the lake had to offer. The Brandon community also hosted events at the lake.

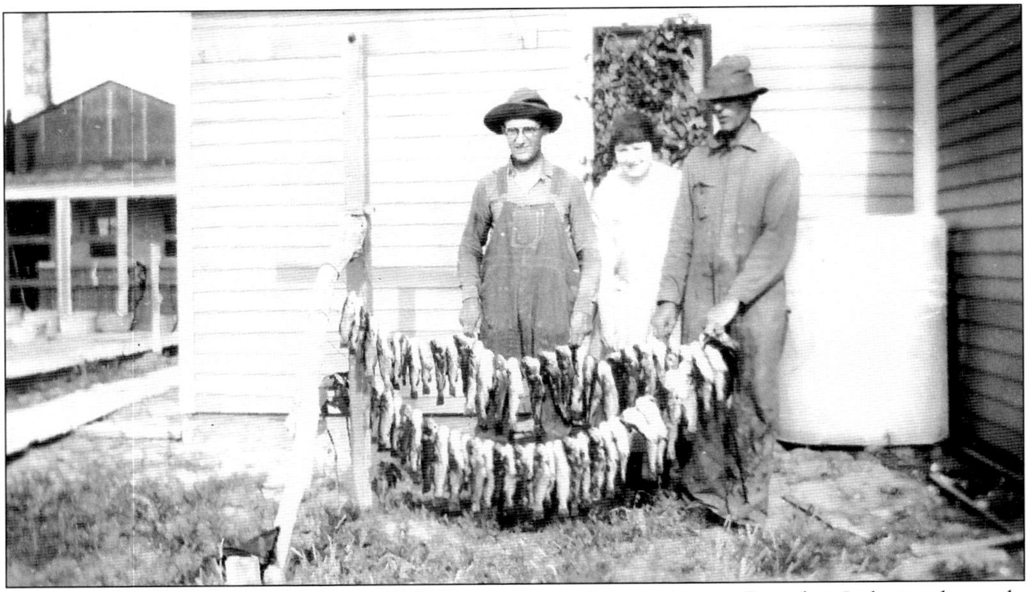

After Catch at Brandon Lake. Fishing was a popular pastime at Brandon Lake in the early 1900s. The Brandon Canal was used from 1908 to 1920 and then abandoned. Although it was no longer used as a reservoir, Brandon Lake continued to be a popular place to hunt, fish, boat, and picnic.

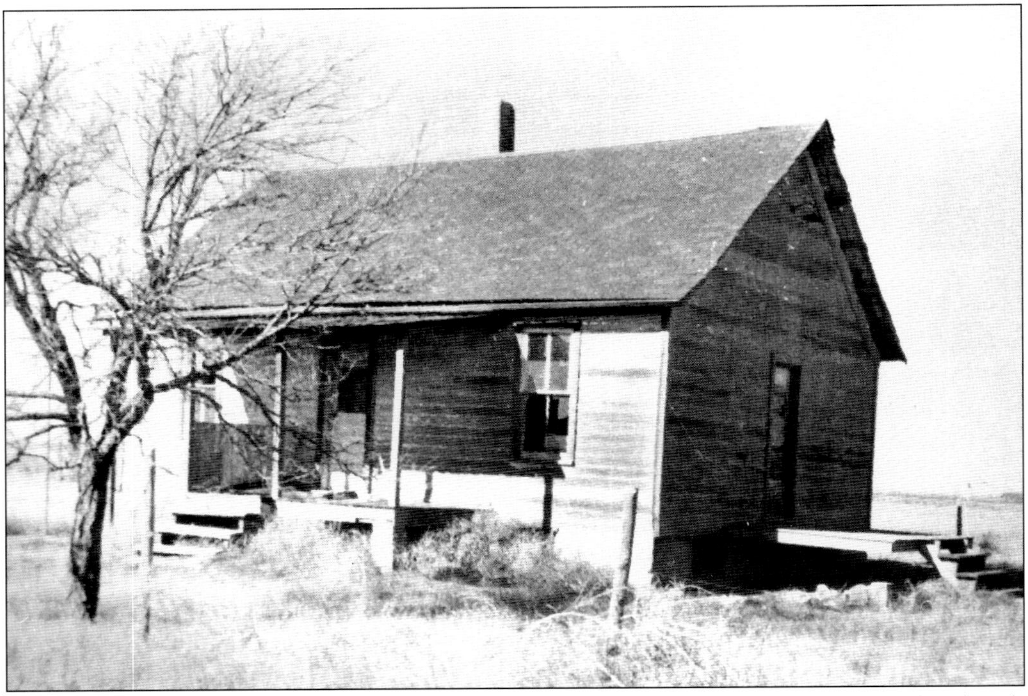

Water Valley School. The Water Valley School served as both a schoolhouse and a church building for the United Brethren in Christ Church during the settlement of Water Valley. The church was organized in 1909, and people worshipped there until 1921. The structure was later moved west of Eads and used as a residence. Water Valley was also called Kansas Valley due to the number of homesteaders from Kansas in the area.

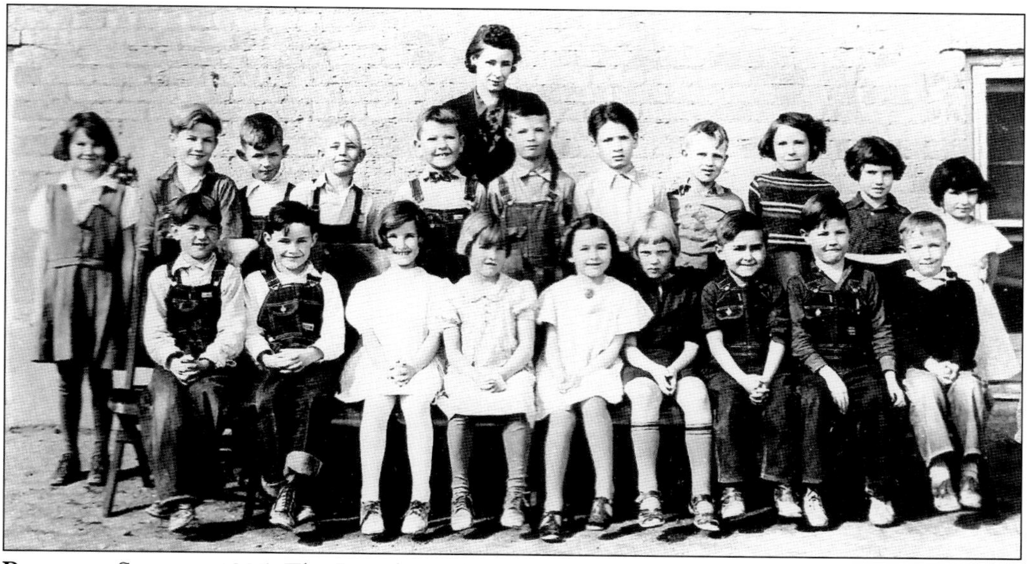

Brandon School, 1935. The Brandon School was located on Main Street on the south end of town. In the 1930s, the population of Brandon was about 150 people. Ruth France Dawson was the teacher of first through third grades at the Brandon School at that time. She was the daughter of Kent and Mary Rittgers France, both the children of Kiowa County pioneers.

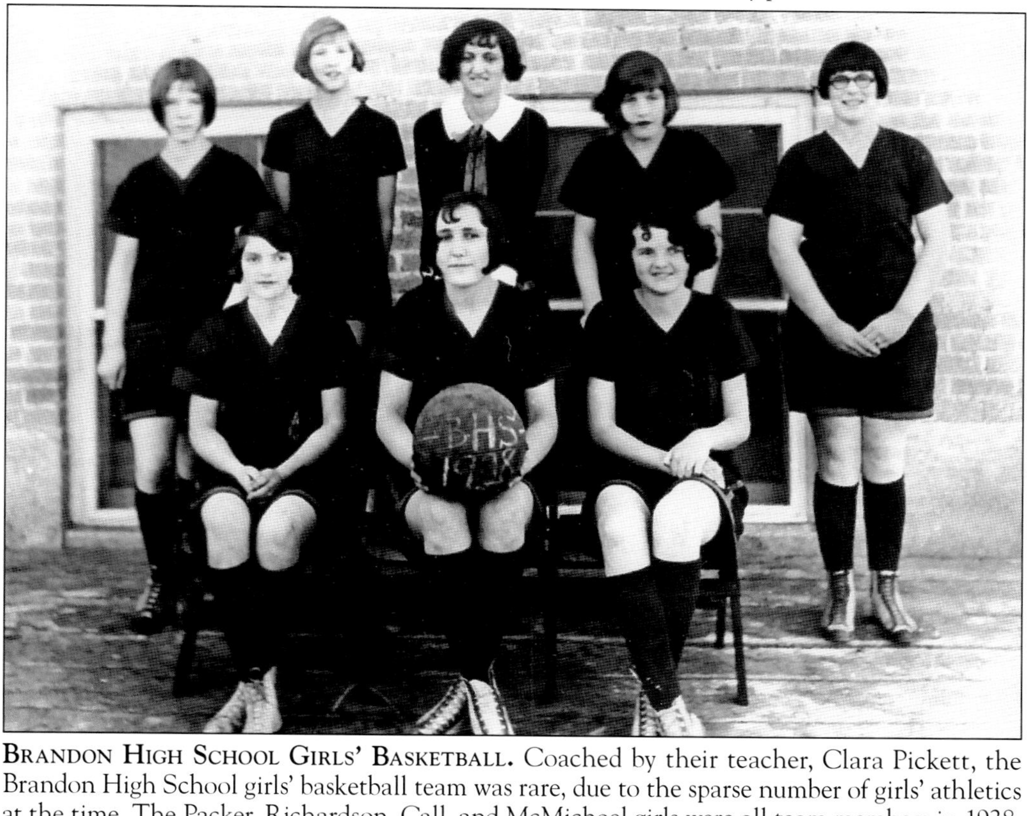

Brandon High School Girls' Basketball. Coached by their teacher, Clara Pickett, the Brandon High School girls' basketball team was rare, due to the sparse number of girls' athletics at the time. The Packer, Richardson, Call, and McMichael girls were all team members in 1928. Clara Pickett and her sister, Alvah, who taught first through third grades, were born and raised in Weld County and graduated from Colorado State Teacher's College.

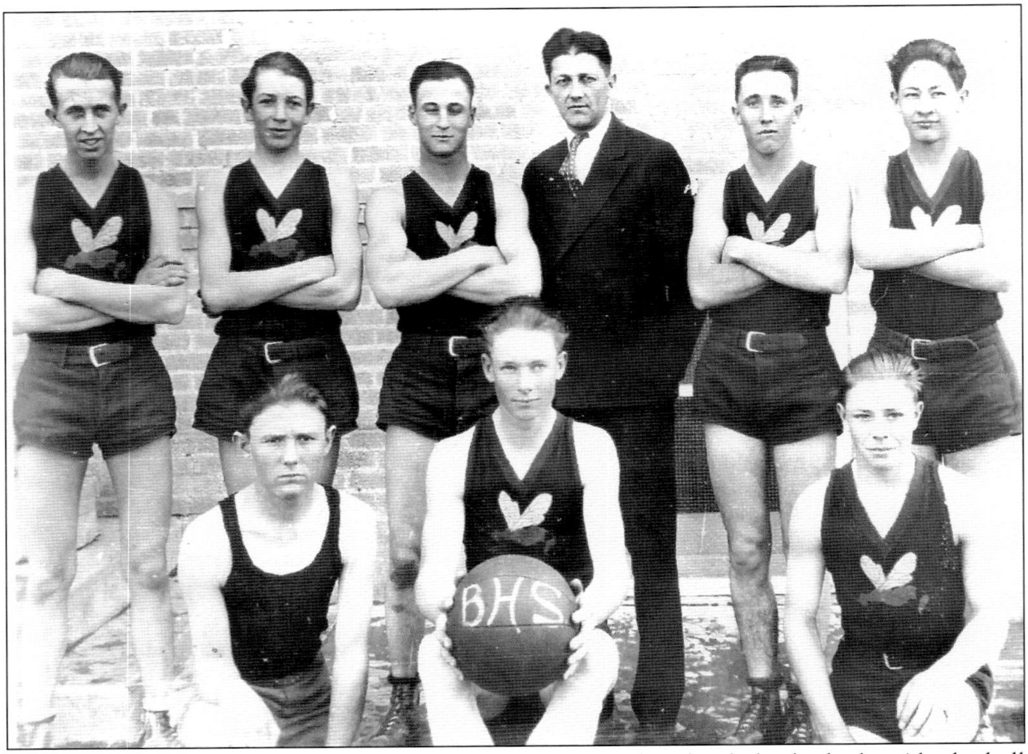

Brandon High School Boys' Basketball. Brandon High School also had a boys' basketball team. The superintendent, A. A. Hall, was the basketball coach at the time and taught the boys the fundamentals and skills needed to play the game. They played schools in the county and in some surrounding counties and were said to be very competitive.

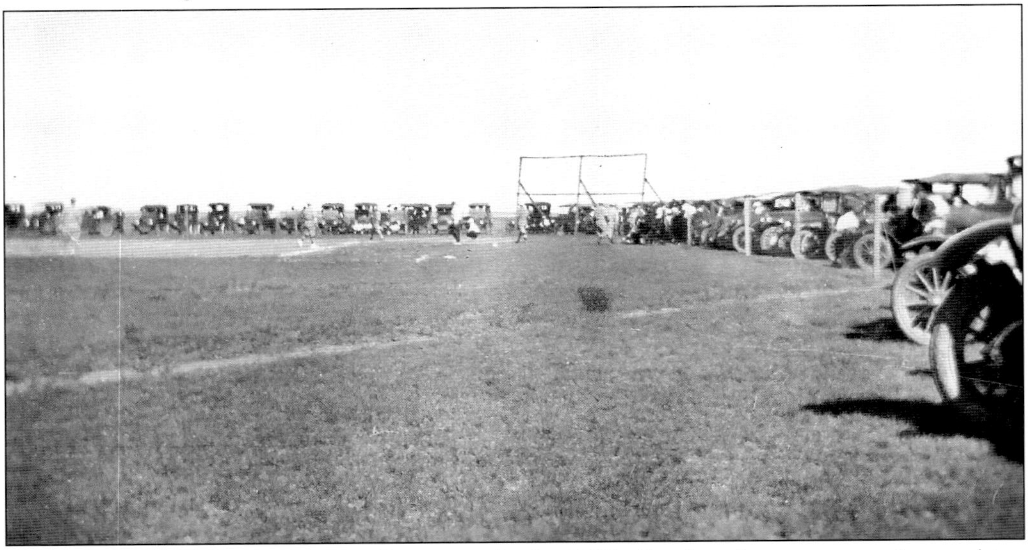

Baseball Game, Haswell Versus Brandon. In the 1930s, Sunday afternoons were for watching baseball. There were many teams in Kiowa County: Eads, Haswell, Galatea, Sheridan Lake, and Black Lake. Many of the teams were invited to play for area celebrations, fairs, and tournaments. The teams were very competitive, and playing allowed farmers and ranchers to get away from the fields and enjoy the summer months with a good game of baseball.

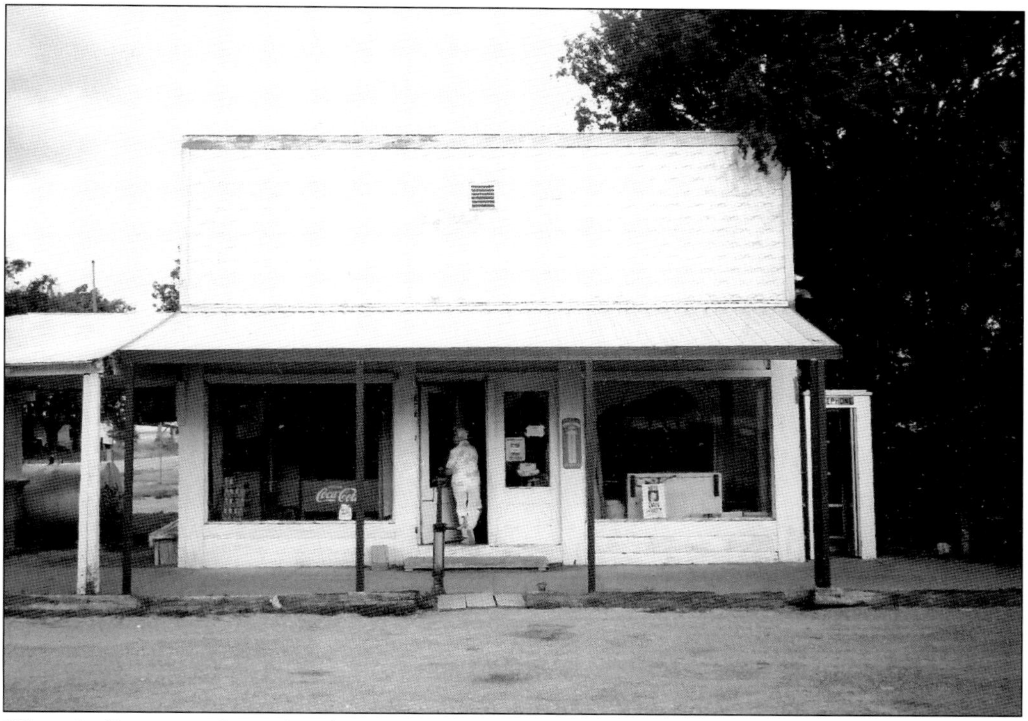

White's Grocery. Owned and operated by Thurman "Clink" and Alvah White, the country store was the social hub for many of the local farmers, ranchers, drilling contractors, and roughnecks. Clink became the owner of the store in 1937, when he bought it from his brother, H. L. White. The Whites were never spoiled with an overabundance of modern conveniences in the early days of their store. Until 1946, the propane was not refrigerated and not until 1951 did the store, or town, have electricity.

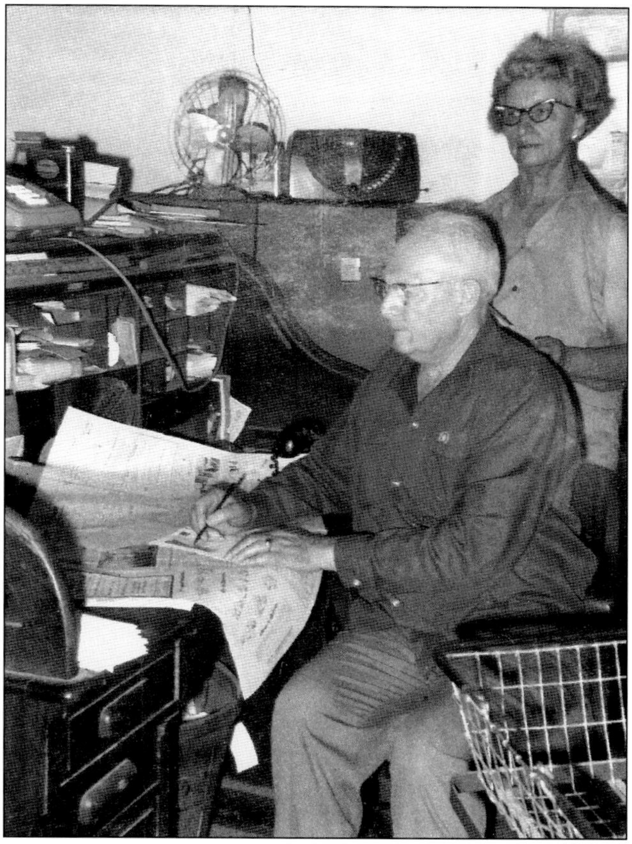

Clink and Al White. Thurman "Clink" White was born in Missouri in October 1898; his family filed a homestead claim near Brandon in 1898. Alvah Pickett came to Brandon to teach school in the early 1930s. The couple married in 1937. Alvah taught school in Kiowa County for 43 years.

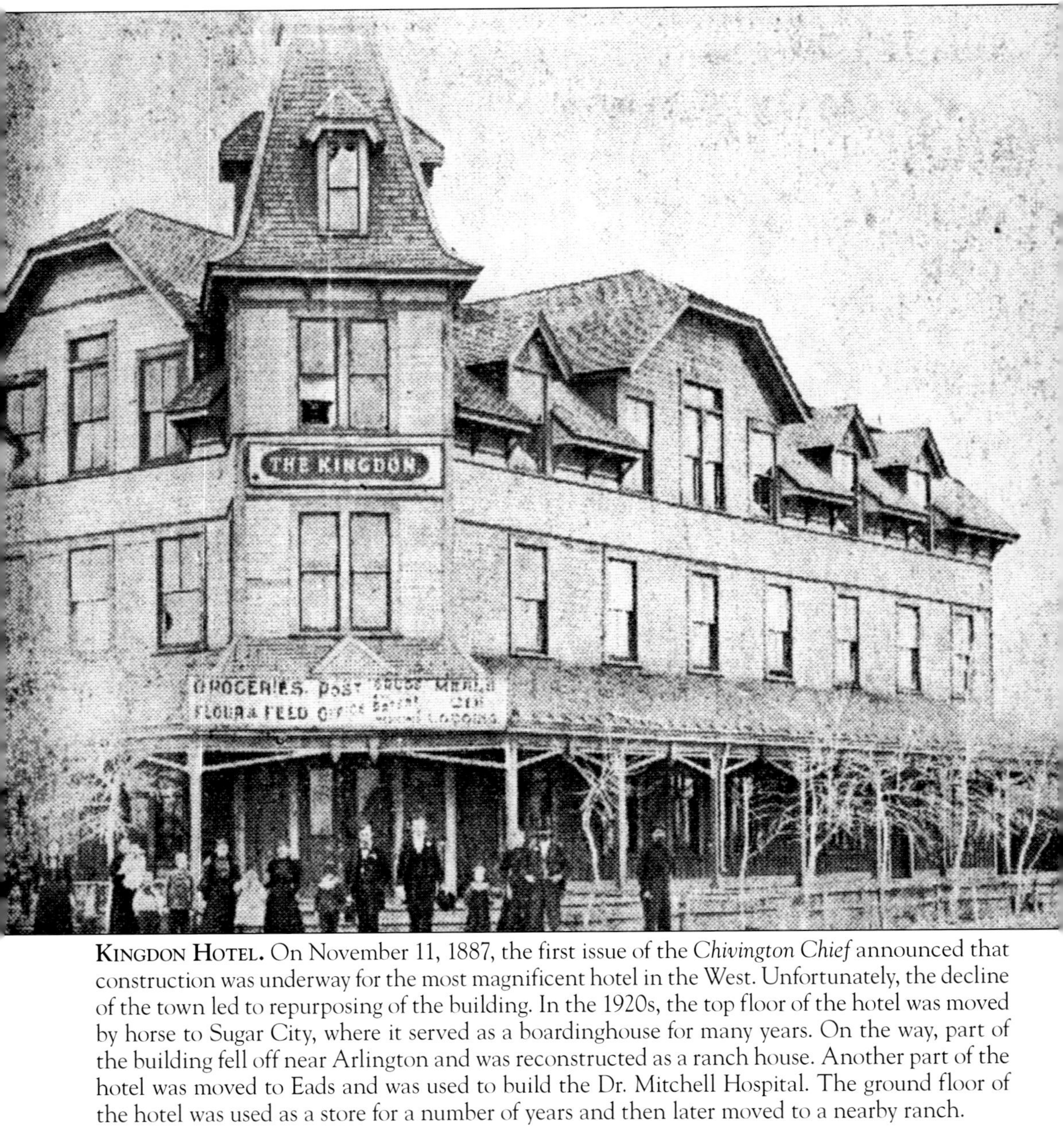

Kingdon Hotel. On November 11, 1887, the first issue of the *Chivington Chief* announced that construction was underway for the most magnificent hotel in the West. Unfortunately, the decline of the town led to repurposing of the building. In the 1920s, the top floor of the hotel was moved by horse to Sugar City, where it served as a boardinghouse for many years. On the way, part of the building fell off near Arlington and was reconstructed as a ranch house. Another part of the hotel was moved to Eads and was used to build the Dr. Mitchell Hospital. The ground floor of the hotel was used as a store for a number of years and then later moved to a nearby ranch.

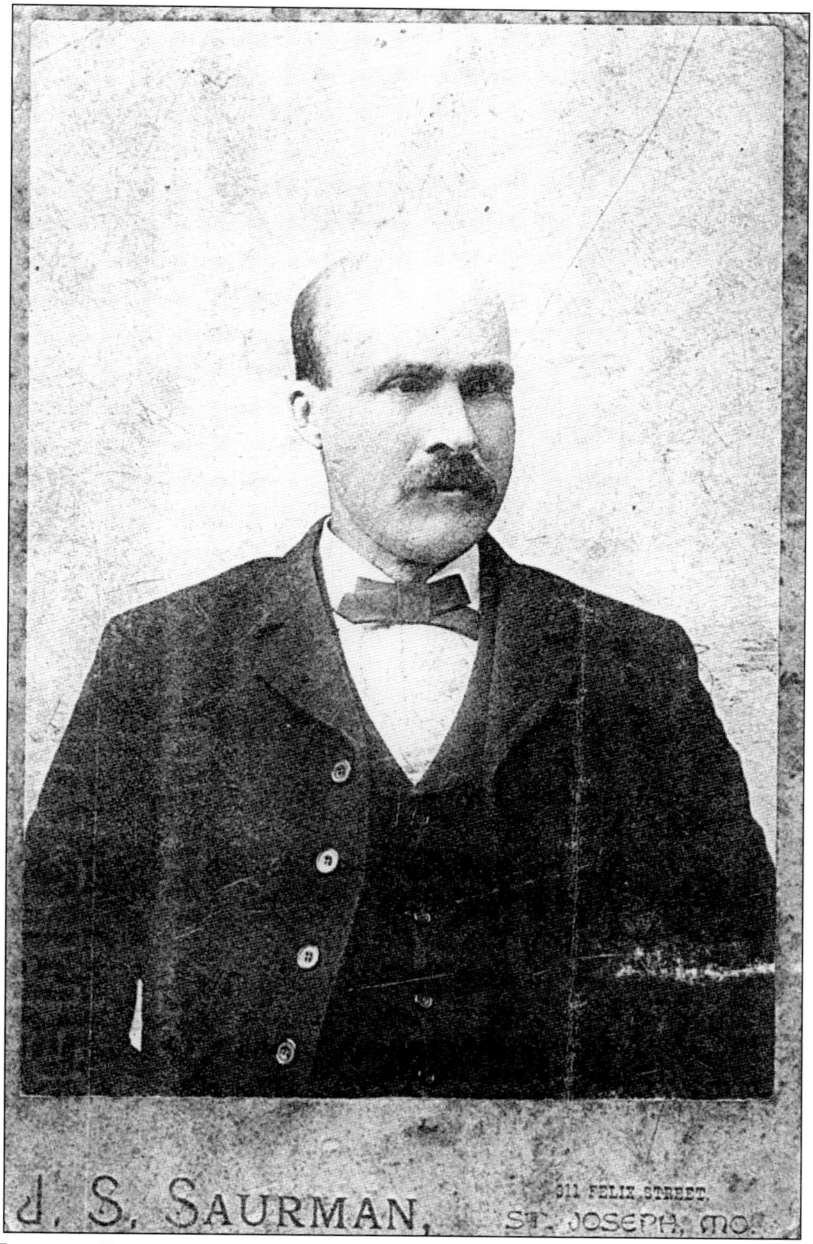

C. FROST LIGGETT. Pioneer C. Frost Liggett purchased a 2,000-acre ranch near Big Sandy Creek in 1879; a few years later, the Missouri Pacific Railroad crossed through his ranch and established the town of Chivington nearby. Liggett operated the first mercantile store in Chivington. He purchased the *Chivington Chief* in 1888. Liggett moved the *Chief* to Sheridan Lake and renamed it the *Kiowa County Press* in 1895. When the county seat changed in 1902, Liggett moved the *Press* to Eads. Liggett also served as a county commissioner and deputy county treasurer for several years. He married his wife, Emily, in 1888; she taught school in Sheridan Lake and became the superintendent of schools in 1896. The Liggetts moved to Lamar in 1897, following his appointment as receiver of the United States Land Affairs. They moved to California in the late 1930s; from there, Liggett wrote many articles under the title "Pioneers I Remember" for the *Kiowa County Press*.

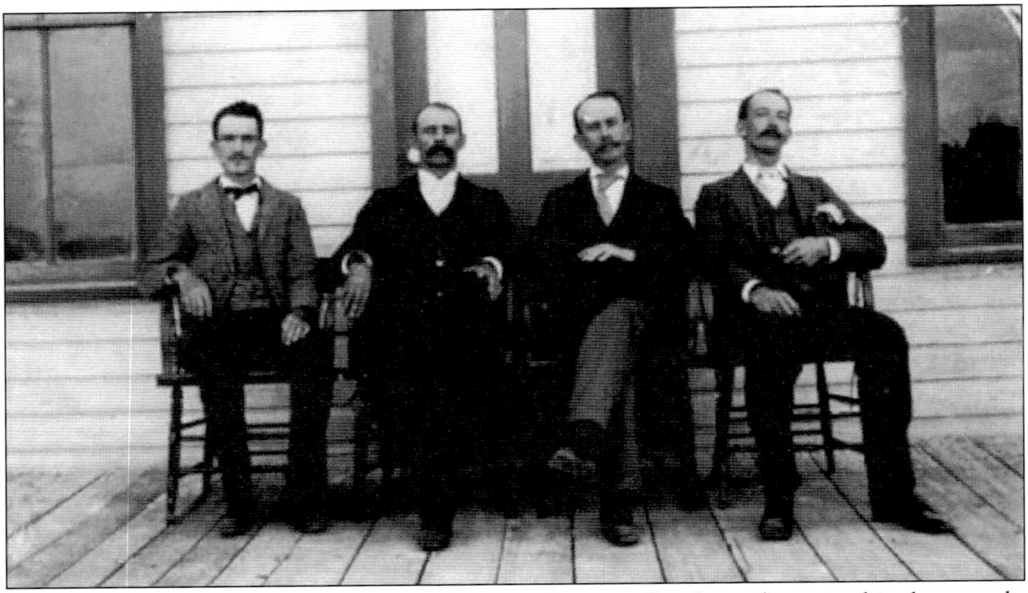

EARLY KIOWA COUNTY OFFICIALS. Four early Kiowa County officials are shown in this photograph. In 1890–1891, county officials included W. A. Lafferty, clerk; Raymond Miller, treasurer; R. W. Hutchcraft, county judge; John S. Booher, assessor; W. S. Harvey, sheriff; J. A. Venable, coroner; F. E. Torbit, superintendent of schools; D. E. Jones, surveyor; W. K. Dudley, clerk of the district court; and O. A. Rush, H. J. Beal, and J. Sherman, commissioners.

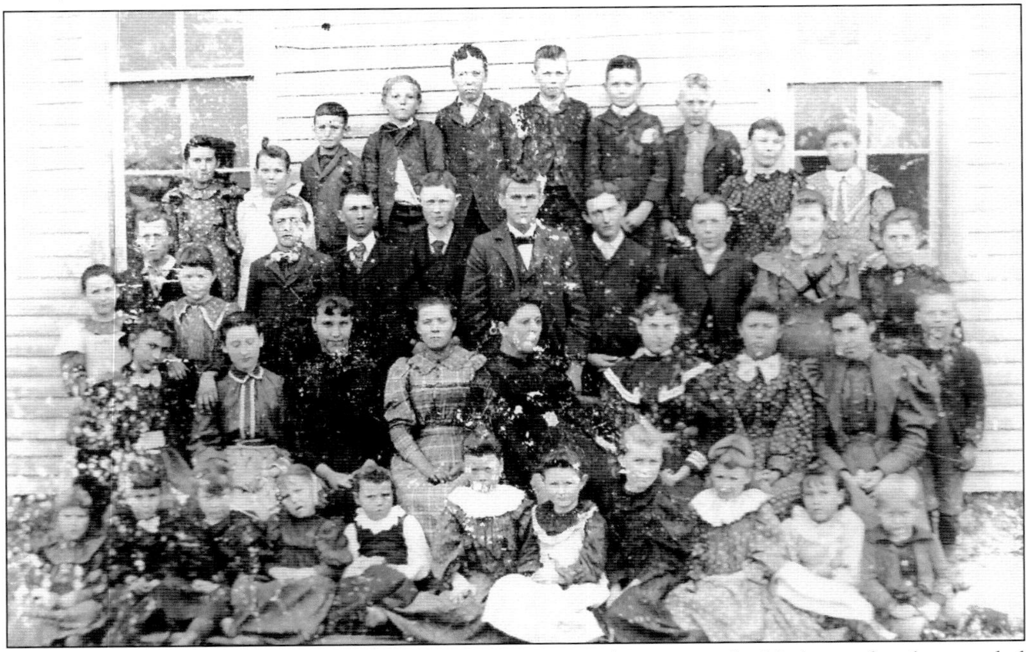

CHIVINGTON SCHOOL, EARLY 1900S. Homesteading near Chivington, the Hickman family attended school there. Coral (third row, fifth from left)) and Ziza (third row, second from right) Hickman are identified in the picture above with a cross on their chests. There were several families at this time that set the stage for a county that would soon be known to all as Kiowa County. Martha Adamson, whose family also homesteaded nearby, was a teacher at the Chivington School for a considerable amount of time.

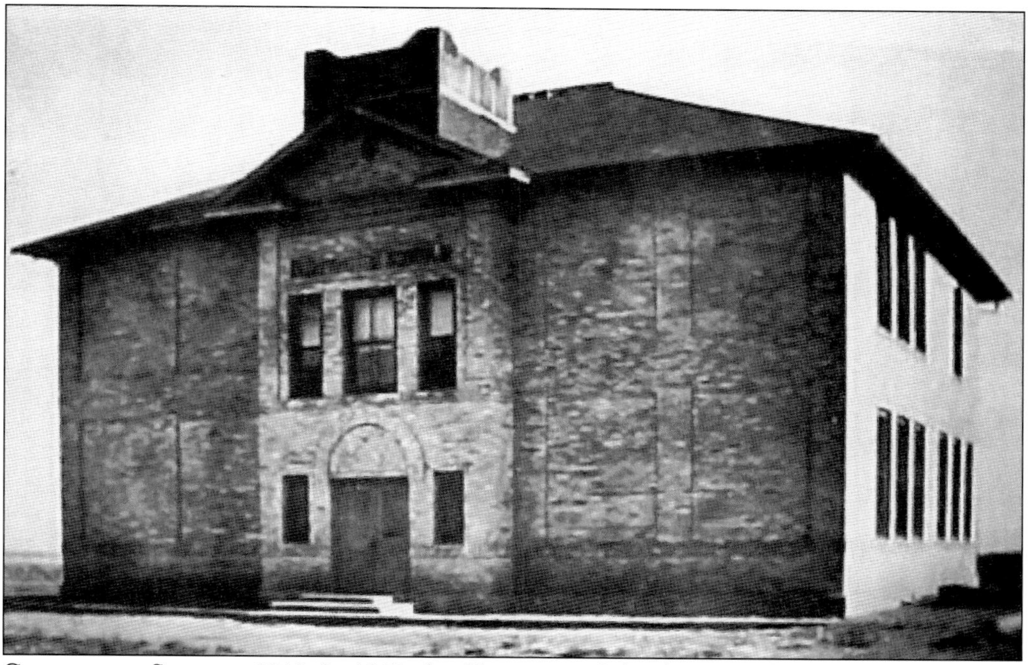

Chivington School, 1919. In 1918, the Chivington School District held a bond election to fund the construction of a new school, as the current building was overcrowded. It passed, and the new school was complete by 1919. The school operated until the early 1960s, when the district was consolidated with Eads to form Kiowa County School District RE-1.

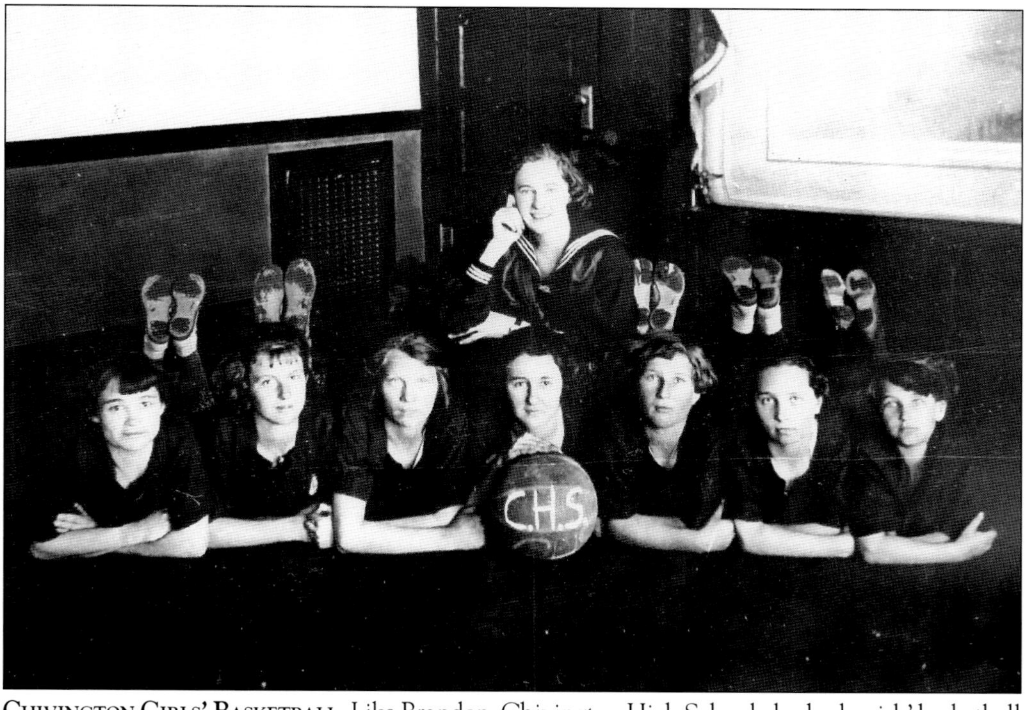

Chivington Girls' Basketball. Like Brandon, Chivington High School also had a girls' basketball team in the 1920s. Pictured here from left to right are Fern Woodmansee, Cleta France, Esther Sarah, unidentified, Gladys Meyers, Beulah Roth, Wilma Wise, and Catherine Meyer.

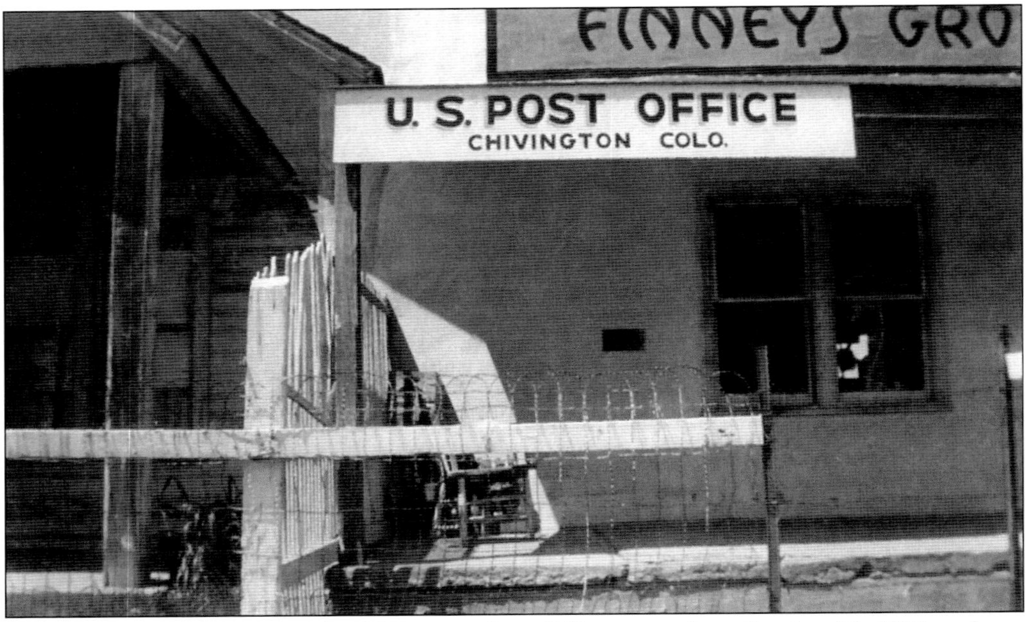

CHIVINGTON POST OFFICE. The Chivington Post Office opened on October 24, 1887, and was first located in the Kingdon Hotel. Since its establishment, 10 postmasters have had the honor of serving the community. For many years, the post office was the only business located in Chivington. The post office closed in 1992.

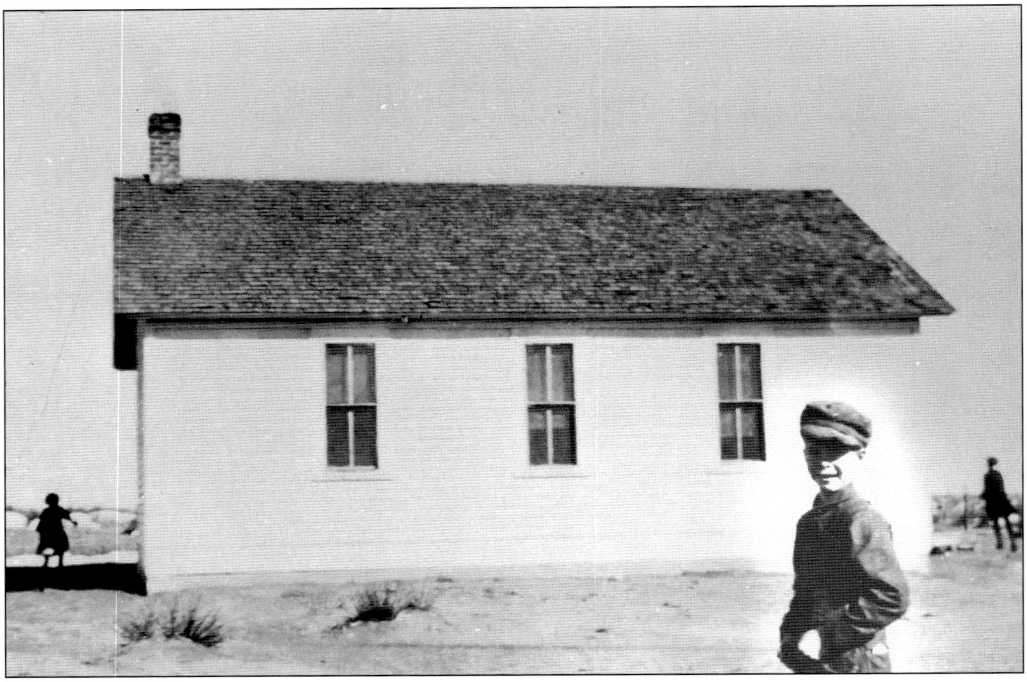

DISTON SCHOOL. District 12, located in Diston, bonded itself for $800 to build and furnish the schoolhouse. Furnishings included a library and organ, which broke the district. However, the school was opened. Both Martha Adamson Sherman and Grace Gilbert taught at this school.

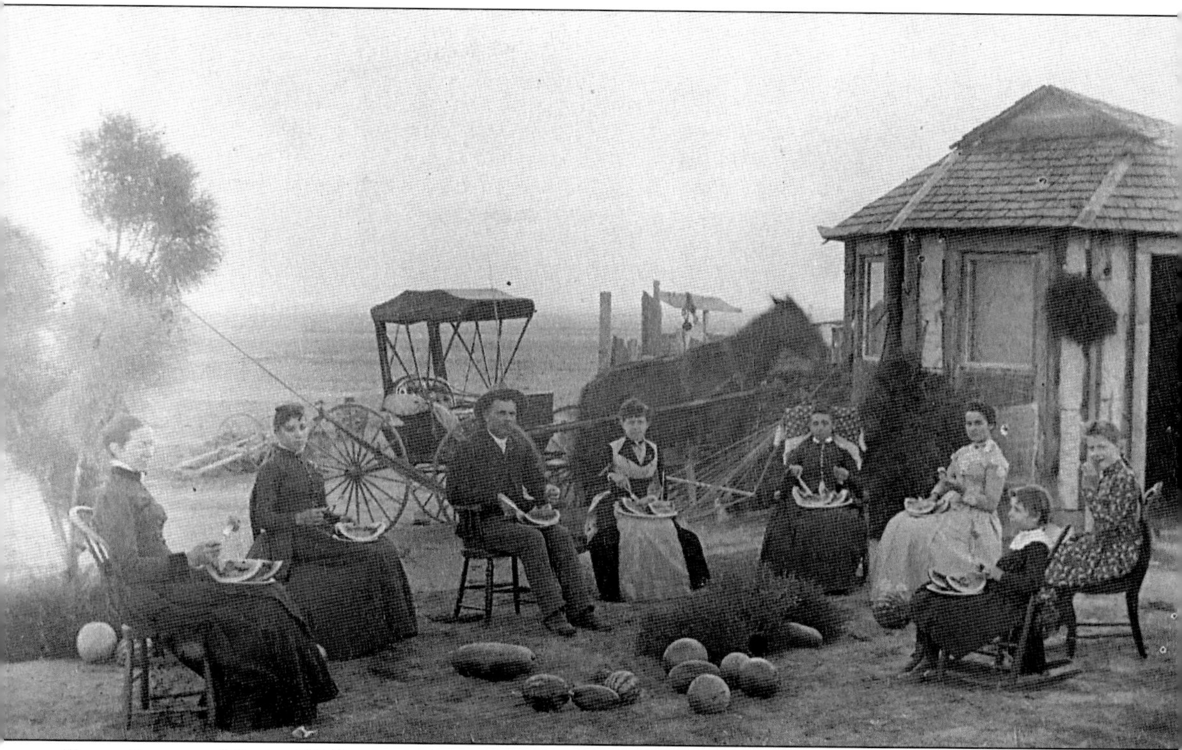

KERR FAMILY, 1890S. William and Mattie Kerr and their children, William Victor (Vic), Alida Alice (Lida), and Josephine Elizabeth (Bessie), arrived in Kiowa County on January 10, 1889. They homesteaded about 4.5 miles southeast of Eads. After William's passing on December 10, 1890, the family moved to Eads; they had successfully proved their homestead. This photograph shows a family picnic, and the location would become the south end of Maine Street in Eads.

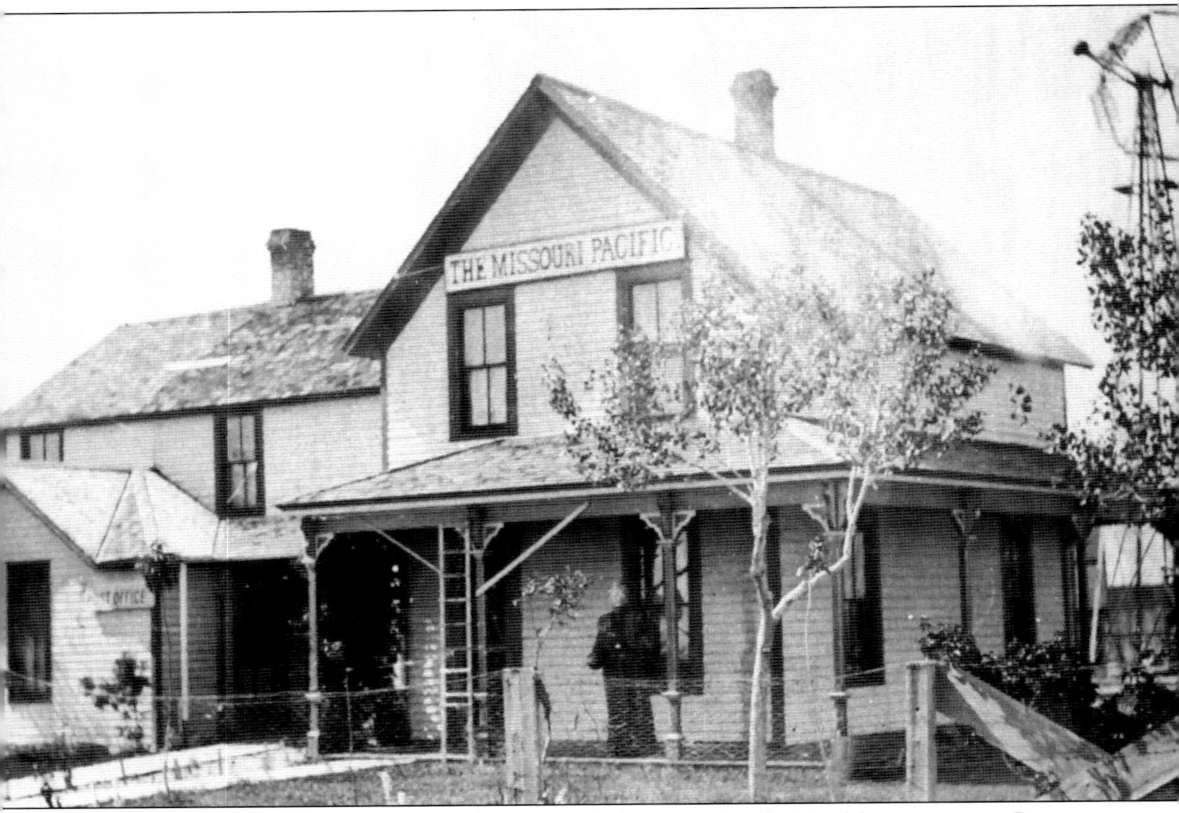

Missouri Pacific Hotel. The Kerr family ran the Missouri Pacific Hotel for many years. Passengers on overnight train journeys often stayed at the hotel; many passengers also dined at the hotel, as trains did not have dining cars in the early 1900s. The first post office in Eads was located in the Missouri Pacific Hotel, and Mattie, Vic, and Lida Kerr each served as the town postmaster at various times.

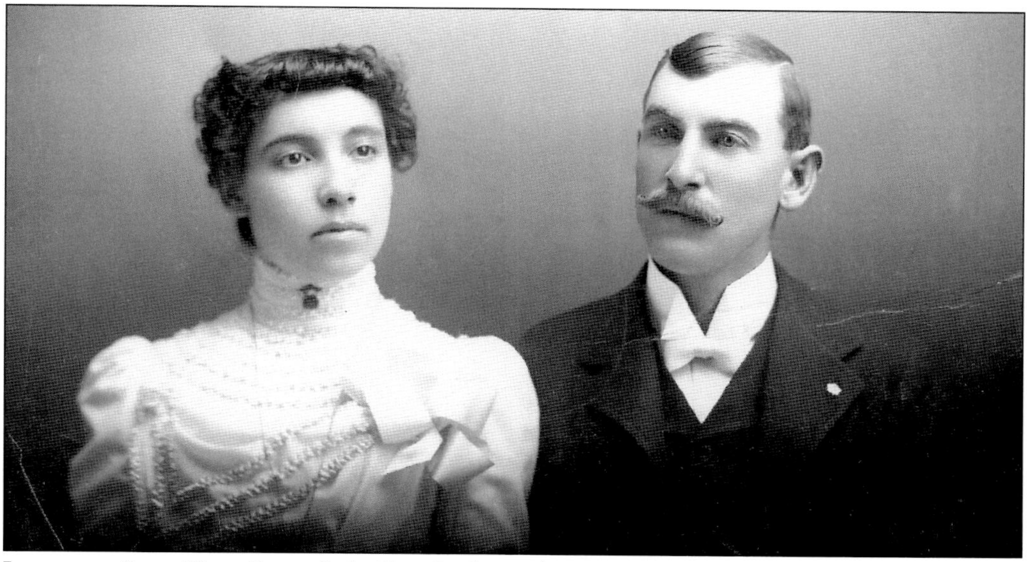

JOHN AND LIDA KERR LINK. Lida Kerr Link was born on December 13, 1874, on her parents' homestead in Nebraska. When the Kerr family moved to Kiowa County, Lida was 15. She married John Henry Link, a rancher from Pueblo, Colorado, in 1898. The couple bought a 1,400-acre ranch near Eads in 1902, and Lida accompanied John on horseback every day to check cattle. After John's sudden death on October 16, 1916, Lida continued to run their ranch for over 25 years. She was an active member of the Eads community and shared some of her pioneer memories in the *Kiowa County Press*.

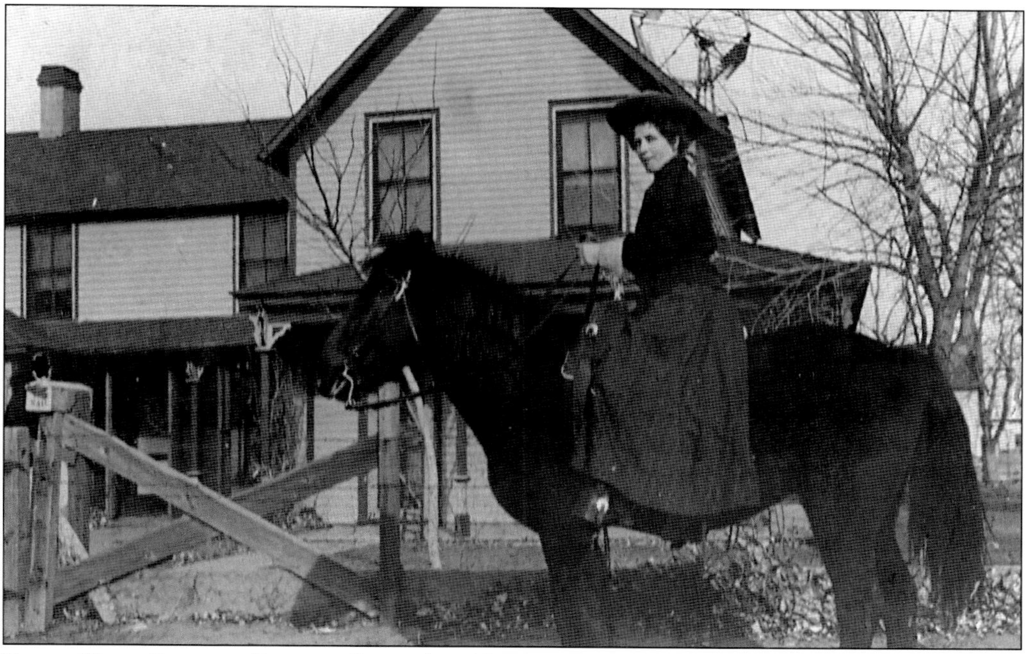

BESSIE KERR SUNDAY. Born on December 10, 1880, Bessie Kerr was eight years old when the Kerr family moved from Nebraska to Kiowa County. She married Howard Sunday on October 8, 1919. She was the bookkeeper at Sunday's garage until they sold the business in 1929. Howard and Bessie then farmed near Rush Creek until 1963. Howard died October 31, 1967, and Bessie passed away January 2, 1971.

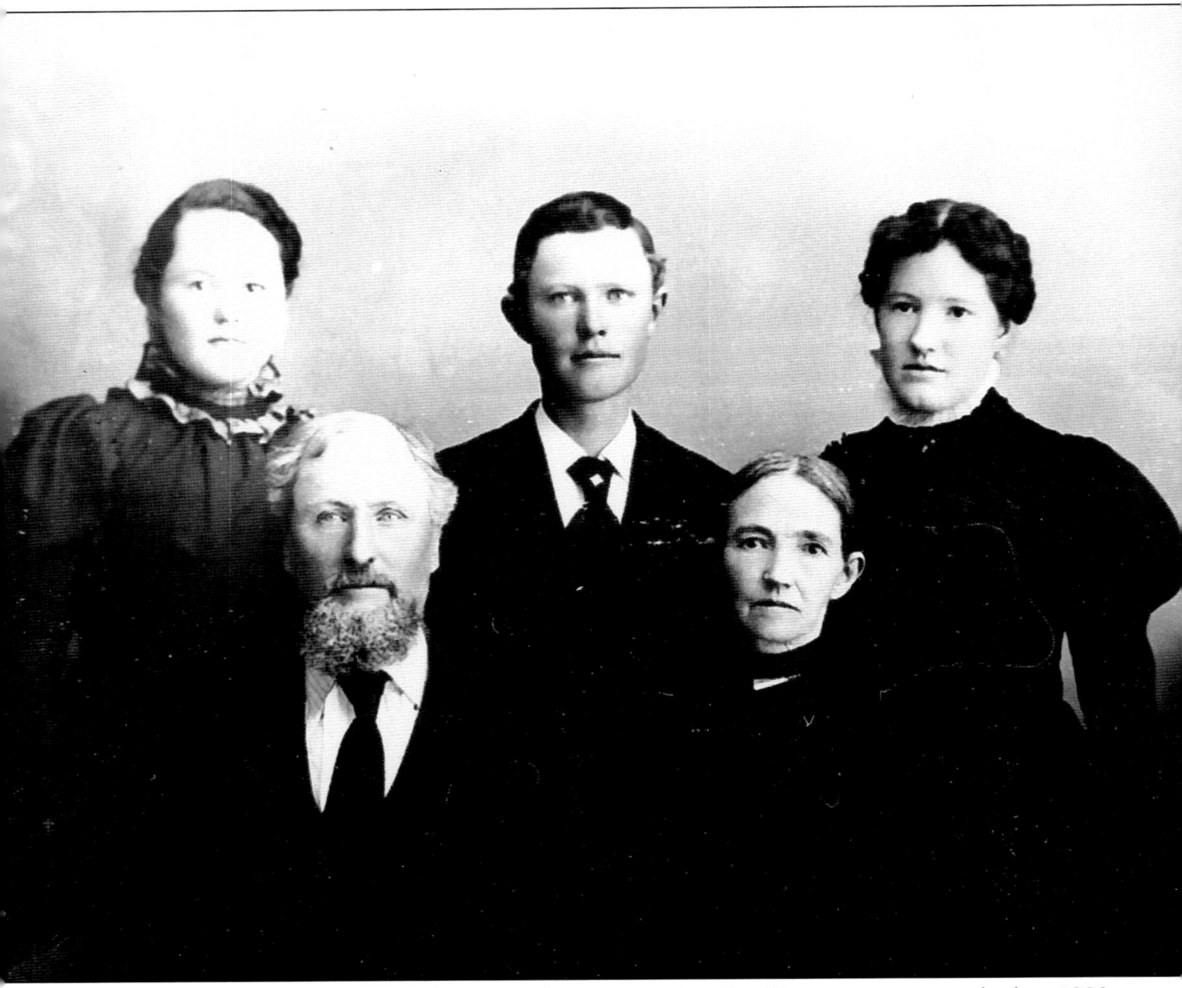

Hickman Family. Byard and Eleanor Hickman moved to the Chivington area in the late 1880s, before the railroad was constructed, and established a homestead there. The Hickmans had nine children: Anderson, William, Coral, Thomas (Ed), Nellie, Ziza, Maggie, Susan, and Nettie, who died young. Most of their children ended up in Kiowa County. Byard helped relocate the county records from Sheridan Lake to Eads in 1902; he was elected Kiowa County commissioner in 1903 and 1907. The Hickmans later moved from the Chivington area to Eads. Pictured, from left to right, are Nellie Hickman McKeever, Byard Hickman, Coral Hickman, Eleanor Zane Hickman, and Ziza Hickman Low.

WALTER FRANCE FAMILY. In 1912, Walter France (right), son of Eads pioneers George and Carrie France, married Irene Gish (left), the daughter of John and Maggie Hickman Gish. The couple lived at the C. D. Thompson ranch headquarters from 1912 to 1919; they moved household and home to the France homestead, south of Eads at that time. The couple raised their two daughters, Betty (pictured) and Margret, in Eads, and they were active members of the community. Irene passed away in 1938; Walter then married Madge Mason Murphy of Rocky Ford, and he lived in Eads until his death in November 1973.

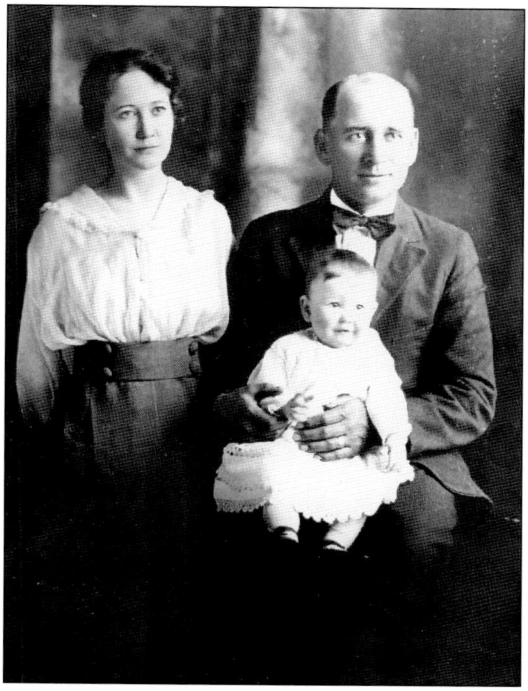

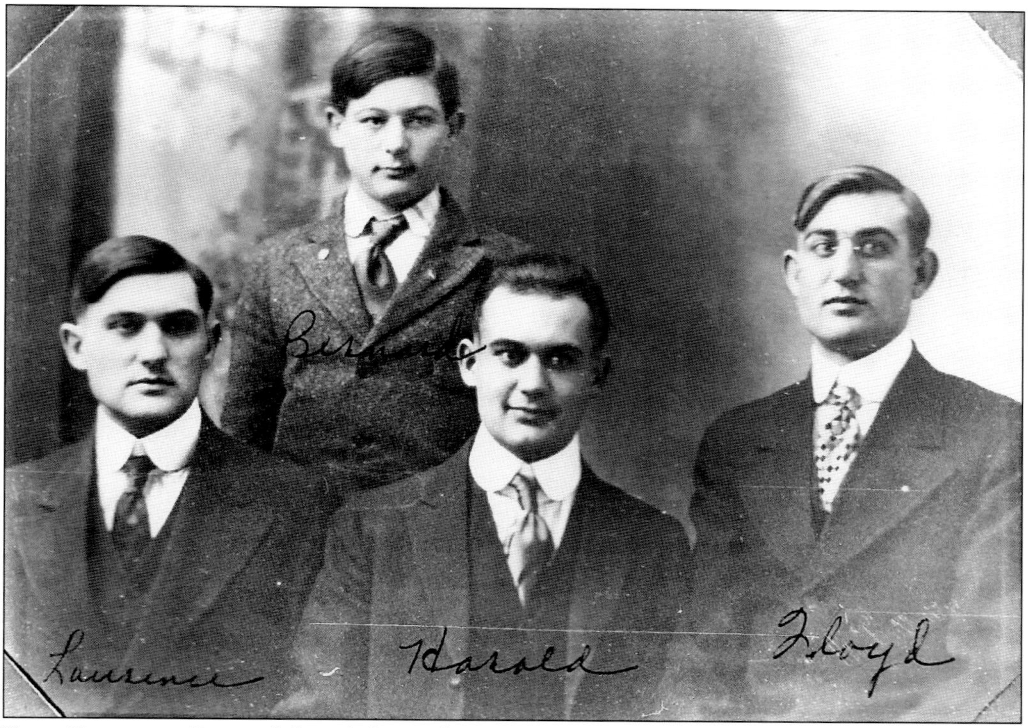

PYLES BROTHERS. Pictured, from left to right, are Lawrence, Bernard, Harold, and Floyd Pyles, the sons of John L. and Emma Pyles, who came to Eads in June 1903, increasing the town population to 65. John bought the *Kiowa County Press* from C. Frost Liggett and published the weekly paper until 1915, when he bought the *Greeley County Republican* in Tribune, Kansas, and moved the remainder of the family there. F. Lawrence married Bertha Lee Whitelaw in 1915 and remained in Eads.

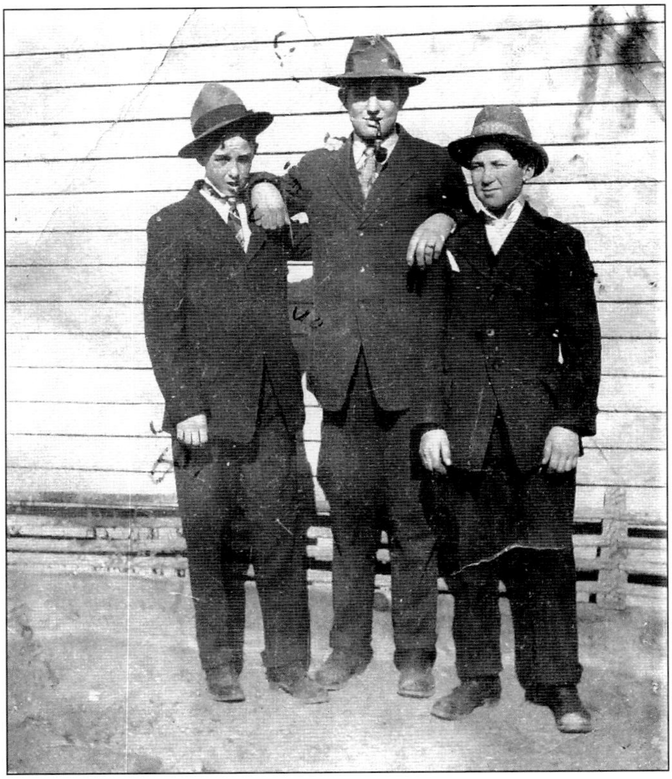

Fay Hines, Floyd Pyles, and Leland Whitelaw. The sons of early Eads citizens, these gentlemen grew up in Eads together. Fay Hines (left), son of Mr. and Mrs. George A. Hines, helped his father construct the Commercial Hotel and later owned and operated several businesses in the area. Floyd Pyles (center) helped his father publish the *Kiowa County Press* until 1915, when he married Bess Belshe and moved shortly thereafter. Leland Whitelaw (right) married Ruby Blair in 1916 and was involved in many business affairs until the couple moved to California in 1926.

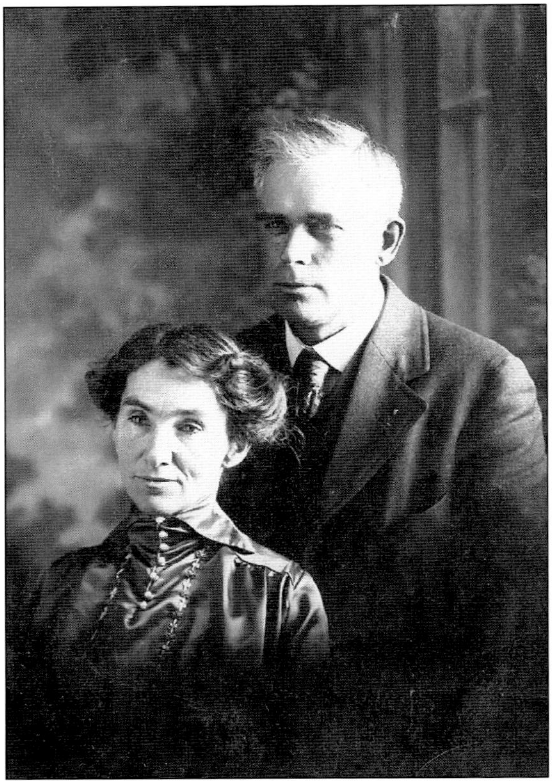

William and Rose Nipps. Dr. William H. Nipps, a dentist, and his wife, Rose Hartley Nipps, came to Kiowa County in 1908. In 1912, Dr. Nipps began the construction of a new building on Maine Street. John Paul Musselman and George W. France, among others, helped construct the building. Dr. Nipps's dental office was located on the second floor of the building; Wilmot and Son's Grocery Store was on the ground level.

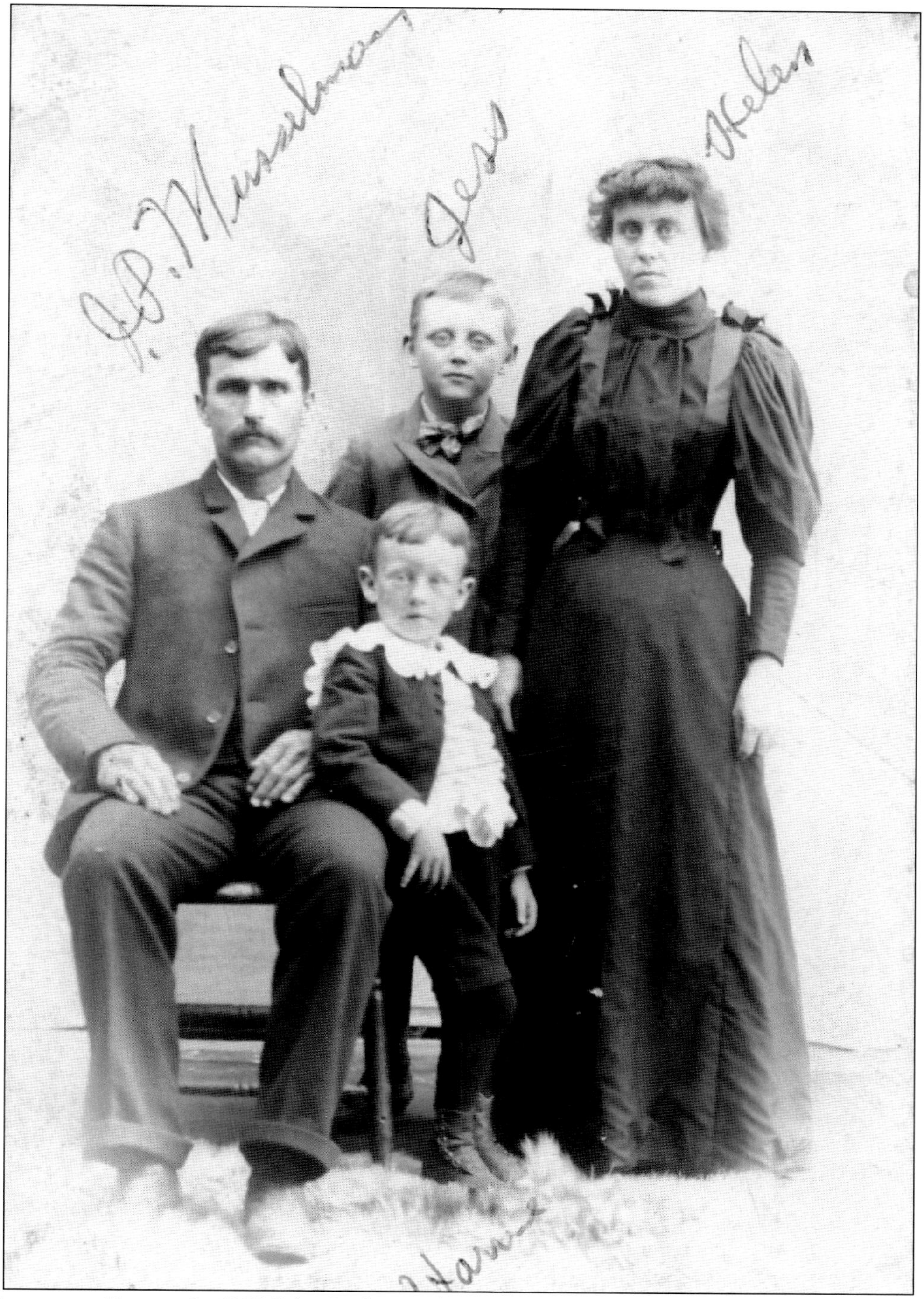

Musselman Family. In 1907, John Paul Musselman came to Kiowa County with his wife, Helen, and claimed a homestead south of Eads. John worked in construction locally and farmed and ranched; he and Helen lived in Eads until they moved to Pueblo in 1933. Their son, Harve, married Elizabeth Kirby and homesteaded northwest of Eads; they raised their five children in Eads. Harve was the superintendent of Kiowa County Road and Bridge for many years; he was also the foreman for many WPA projects in the area.

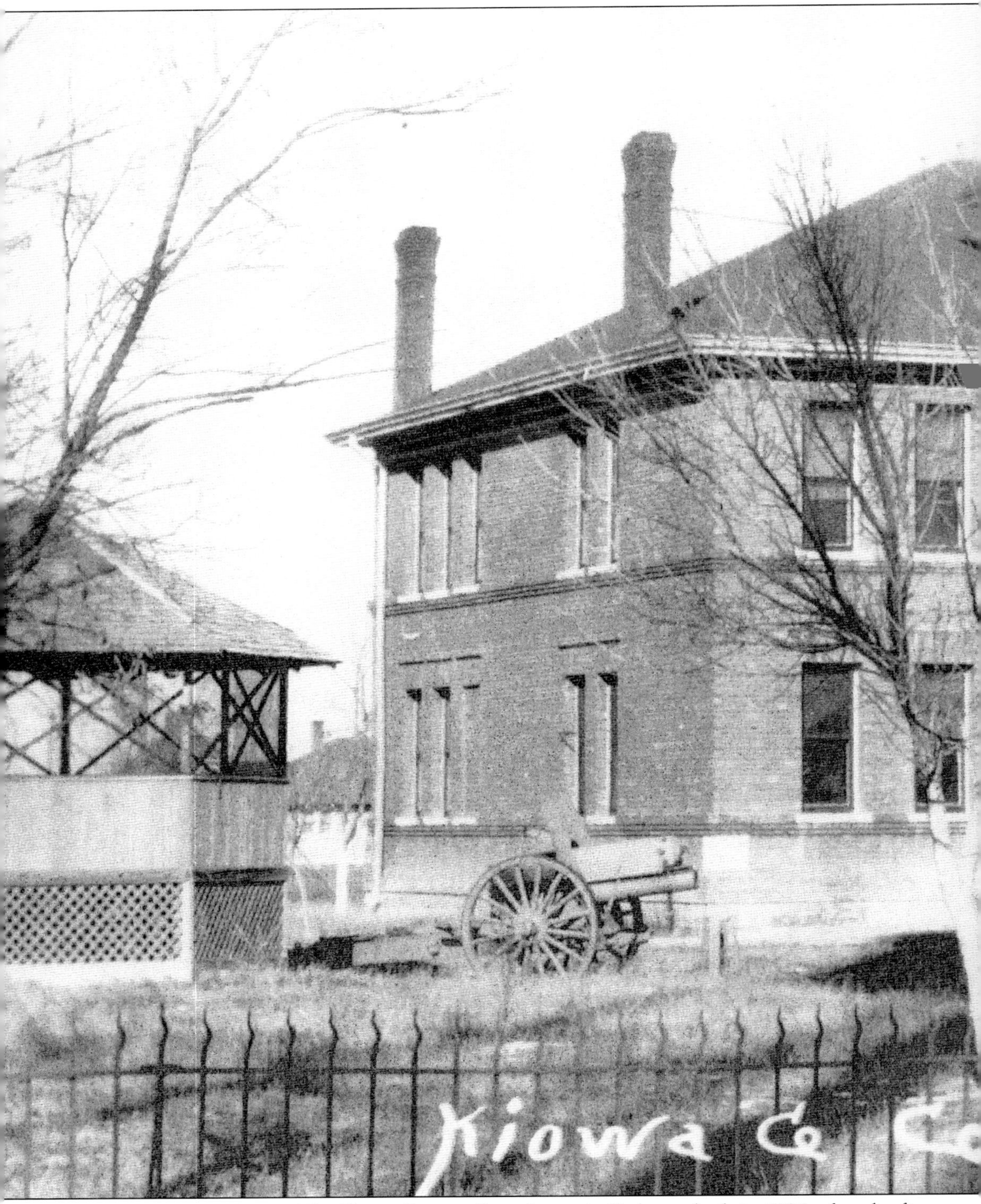

Courthouse in Eads. The Kiowa County Courthouse in Eads was built in 1904, after the first courthouse burned to the ground on December 3, 1900. When Kiowa County was established in 1889, the county seat was in Sheridan Lake; however, as the years passed, there was a growing demand to move the county seat to Eads. In December 1901, a fire destroyed the courthouse in

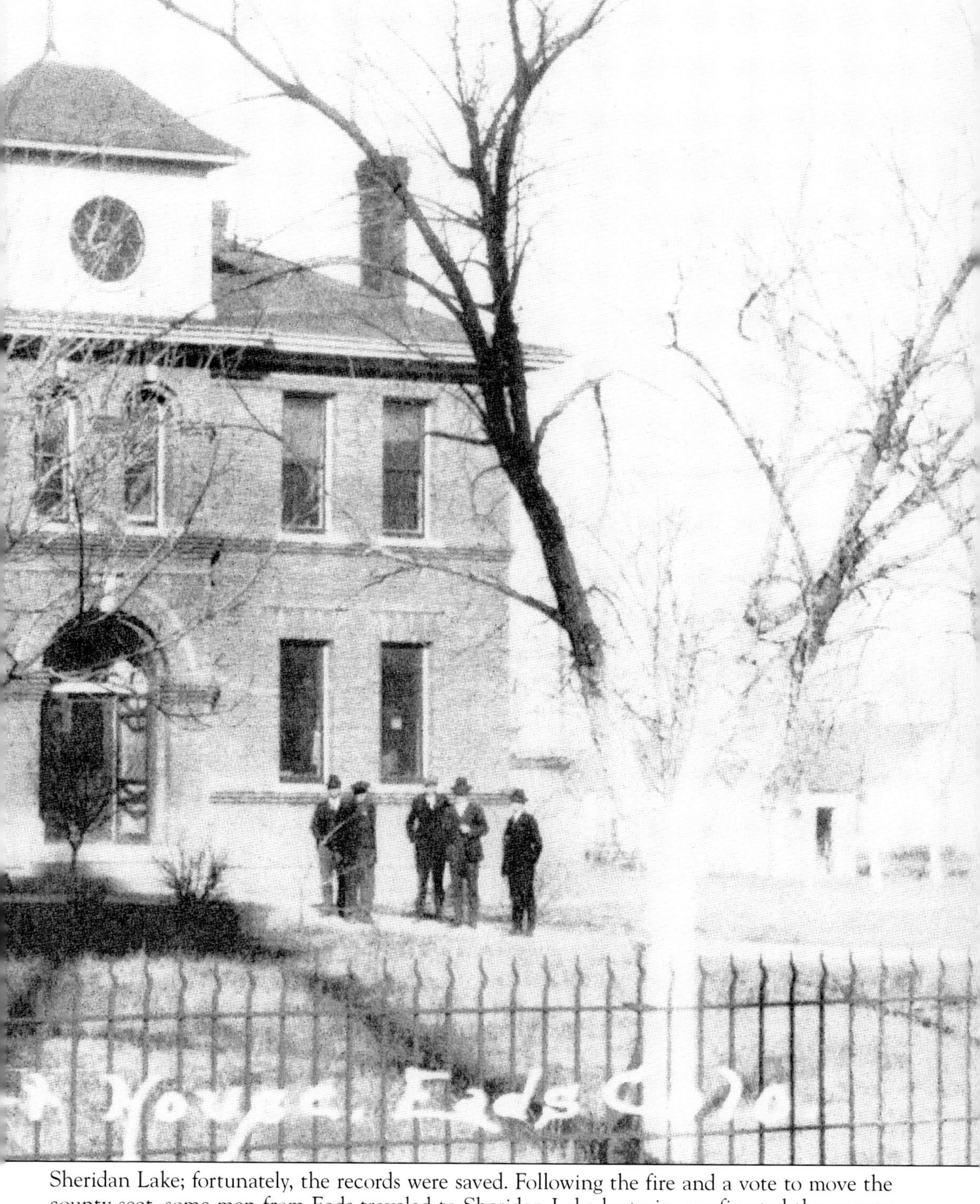

Sheridan Lake; fortunately, the records were saved. Following the fire and a vote to move the county seat, some men from Eads traveled to Sheridan Lake by train, confiscated the county documents and records, and took them to Eads on a railcar. Thus, Eads became the county seat of Kiowa County and still remains so to this day.

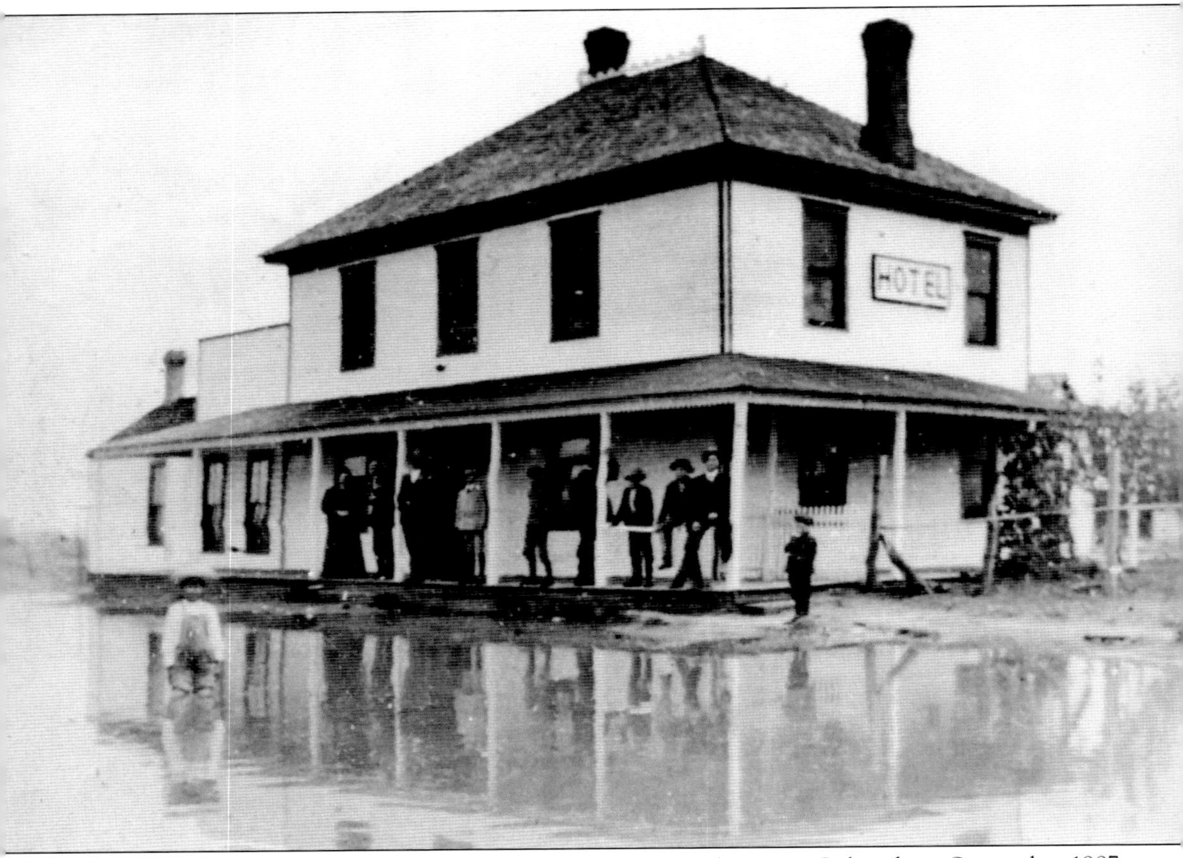

Goff Hotel. The Goff family came from Indiana to southeastern Colorado in September 1887. They first lived in Lamar, then the settlement of Dayton, and finally in Eads. They homesteaded at Kiowa Springs, thus the area was also known as Goff Springs. Constructed in 1889, the Goff Hotel was the first hotel in Eads. Lizzie Goff Wolever ran the hotel for many years. The building still stands today.

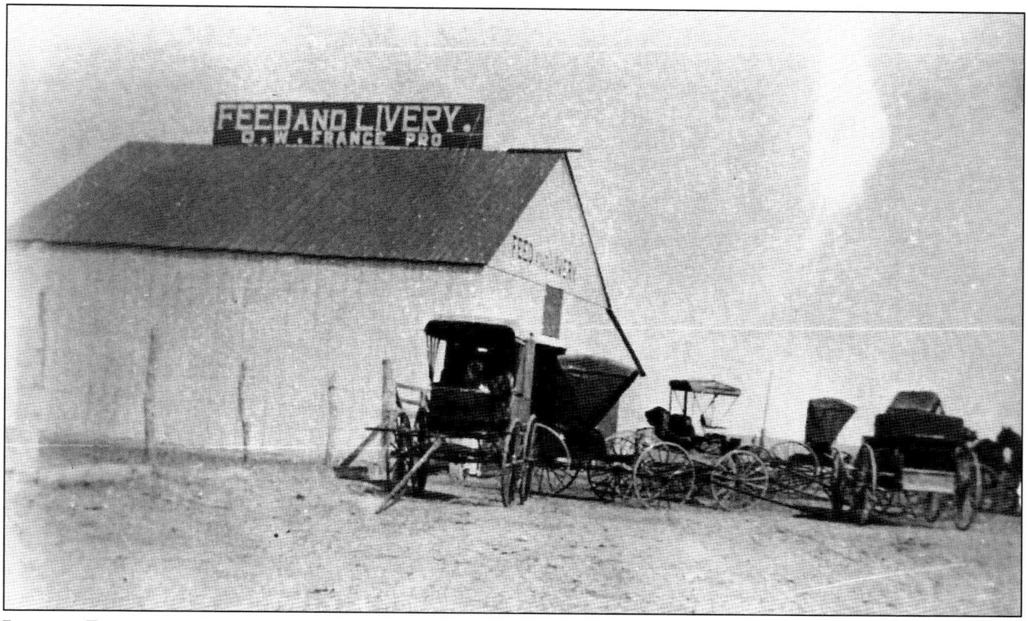

Livery Barn, 1906. At age 18, Walter France borrowed money to start a livery business with Clyde Corbett. On June 15, 1906, they advertised in the *Kiowa County Press*: "Feed and Livery Barn. D.W. France, Prop. For Sale—fine lot of horses. Either work horses of saddlers, broken or unbroken. We also repair wagons and do carpenter work. We respectfully solicit your patronage. D.W. France, Eads, Colorado." By 1912, France had sold the business to Fred E. Colvin; it later burned down.

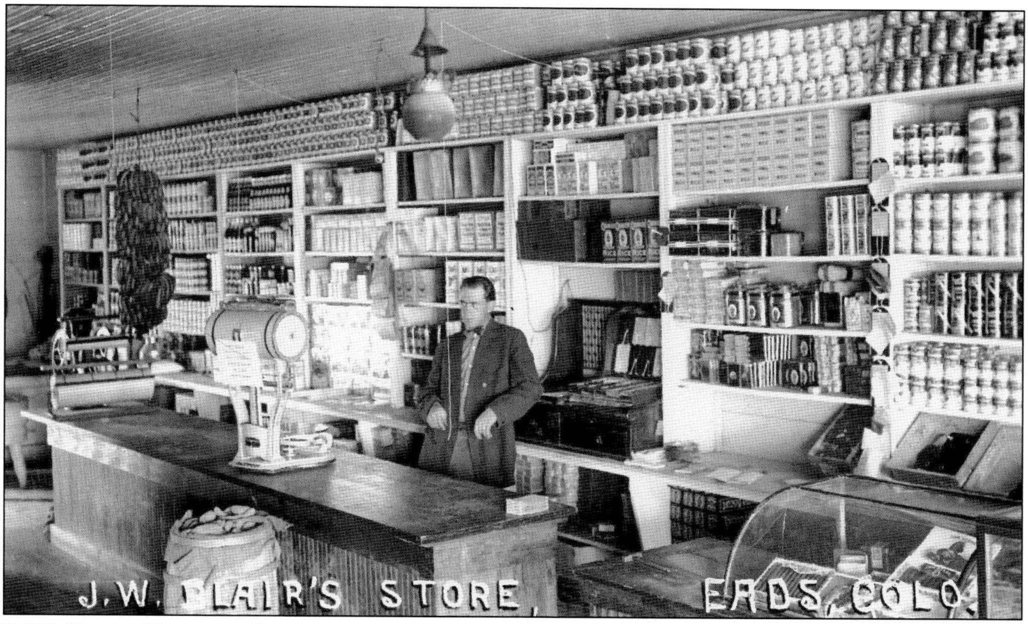

J. W. Blair General Store, 1908. In 1908, John Blair started the J. W. Blair General Store in Eads. This business became successful and met the needs of many happy customers. John Blair sold his business in 1916 to C. C. Wolever and his business partner, John Sanborn, when he and his family moved out of Eads. Wolever was a resident of Towner, so he was well known throughout the town of Eads.

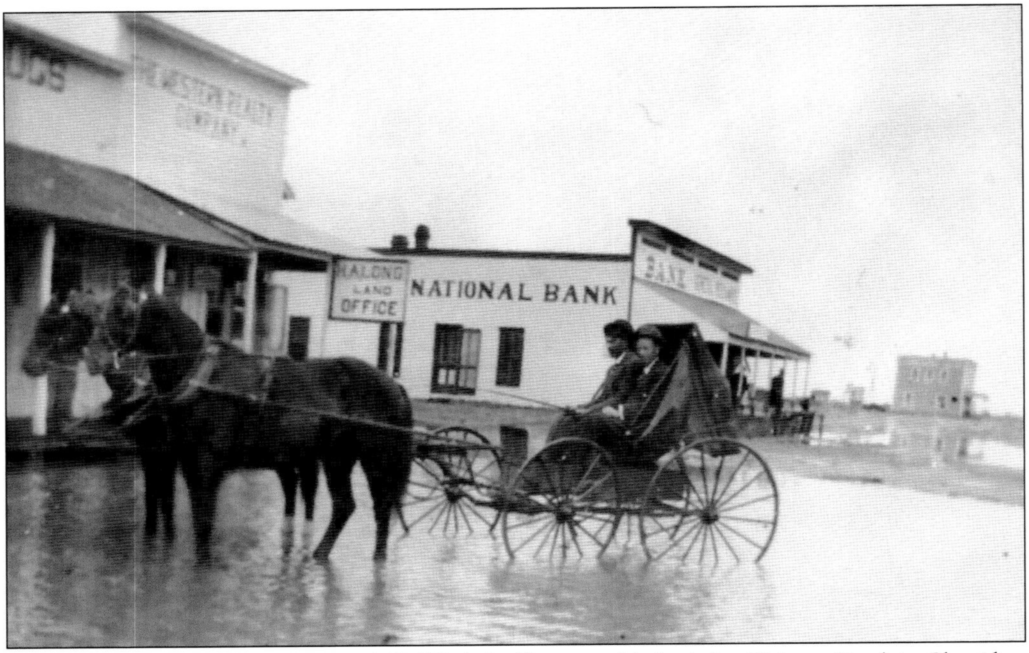

EADS FIRST NATIONAL BANK. In 1887, W. A. Lafferty established the Citizens Bank in Sheridan Lake. After the county seat moved to Eads, J. H. Slater relocated the business to Eads and renamed it; the bank was a private institution. In 1906, the bank was granted a charter and became the First National Bank of Eads.

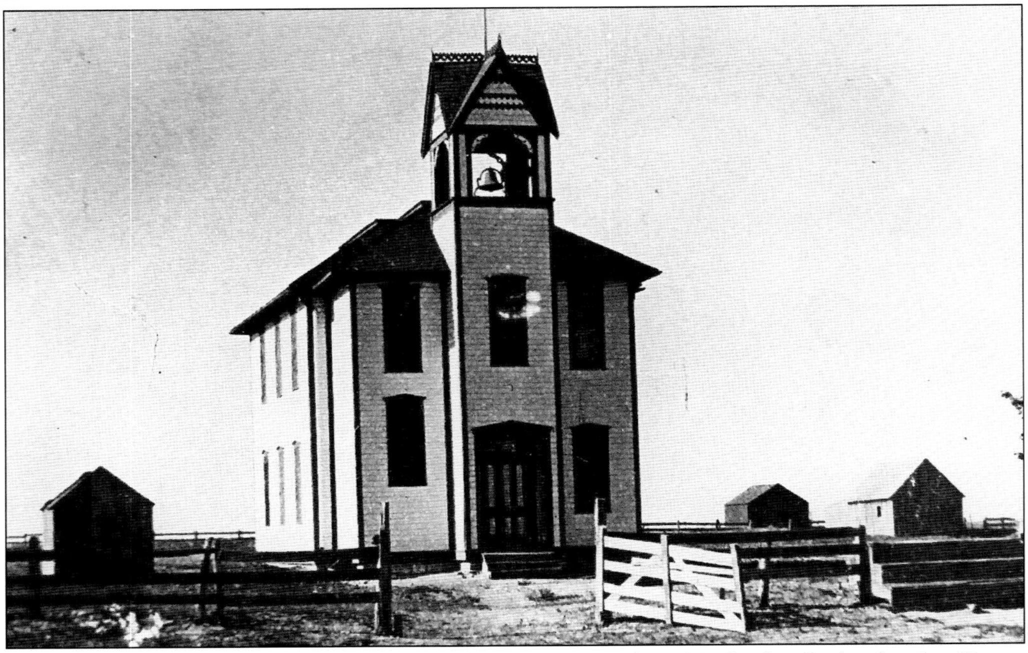

THE FIRST EADS HIGH SCHOOL. Constructed in approximately 1908, the first high school in Kiowa County was a two-story frame building in Eads. It was also the social center of town; citizens had literary meetings and spelling bees, hosted box suppers and dances, and attended Sunday school. In 1916, the community built a new brick school, so the old school was moved near the railroad tracks and converted to a grain elevator. The school/elevator was torn down in the 1970s.

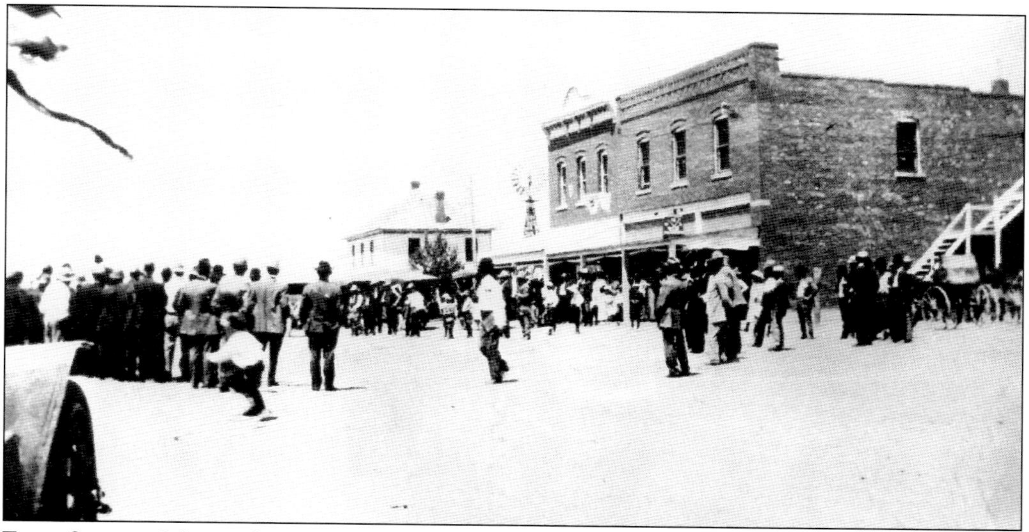

EAST SIDE OF MAINE STREET, EARLY 1900S. The Goff Hotel and Whitelaw and Company mercantile store are shown in this photograph of Maine Street in Eads in the early 1900s. Previously employed at a general store in Missouri, Walter Paul Whitelaw and his family moved west to start their own general store. Another employee of the same Missouri general store, Mary Etta O'Brien, also moved to Kiowa County and became their business partner, owning half interest; she lived in the apartments on the second floor.

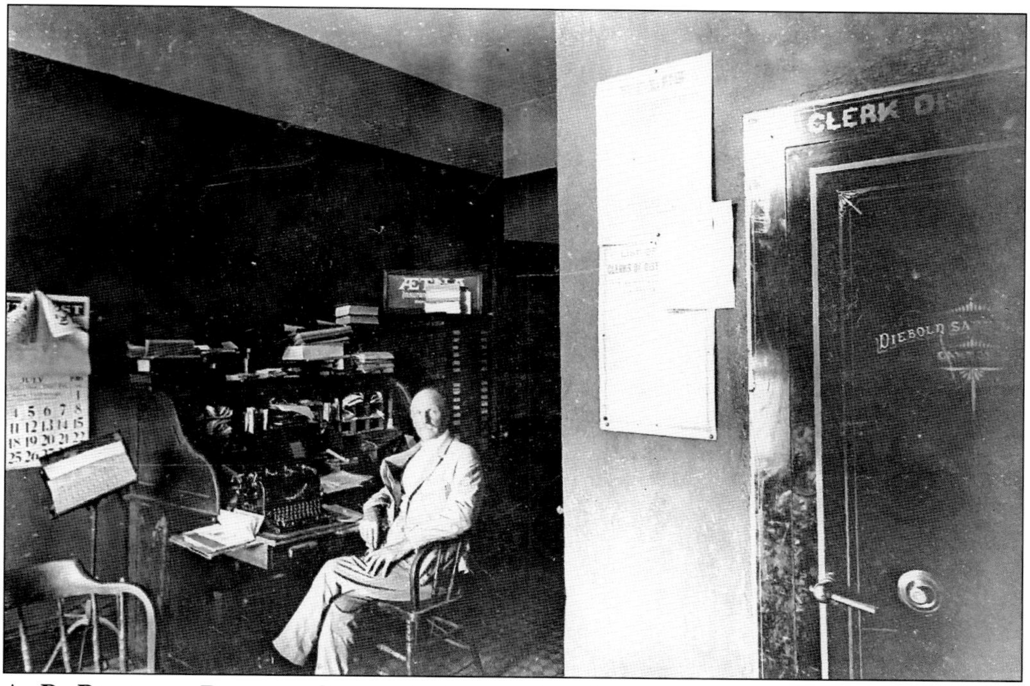

A. R. RITTGERS, DISTRICT CLERK. Ambrose Robert Rittgers came to Kiowa County in the late 1880s and taught at the North Towner school in 1889. He married Verta Alice Snyder in Iowa in 1891, and the couple returned Kiowa County. They had 12 children. Ambrose worked with C. Frost Liggett as a printer for the *Kiowa County Press*; he also served in various county government positions, including district court clerk (as pictured), justice of the peace, school board clerk, and mayor of Eads.

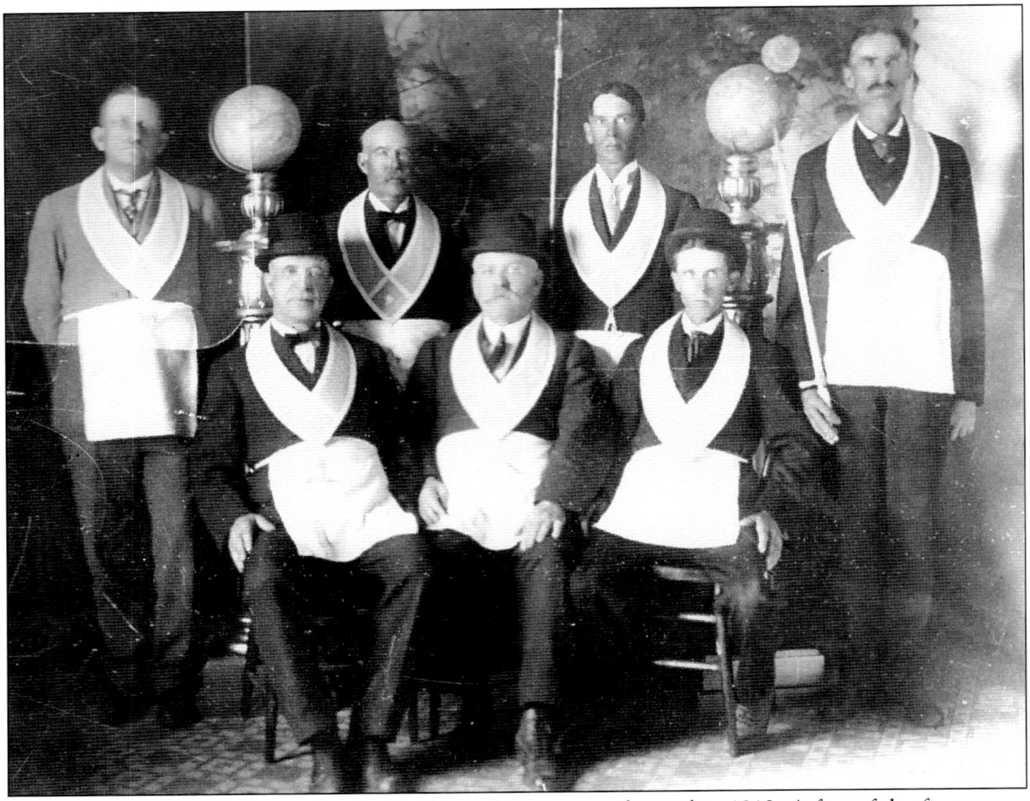

MASONS, 1912. The Masonic Lodge in Kiowa County was formed in 1912. A few of the first group of Masons are pictured here, from left to right, (first row) W. P. Whitelaw, senior warden; John T. Gough, worshipful master; and Gerald Spurgeon Jr., warden; (second row) Boon Best, secretary; A. S. Baldwin, treasurer; Dick Moldenhauer, senior deacon; and Charles Tracey, tyler.

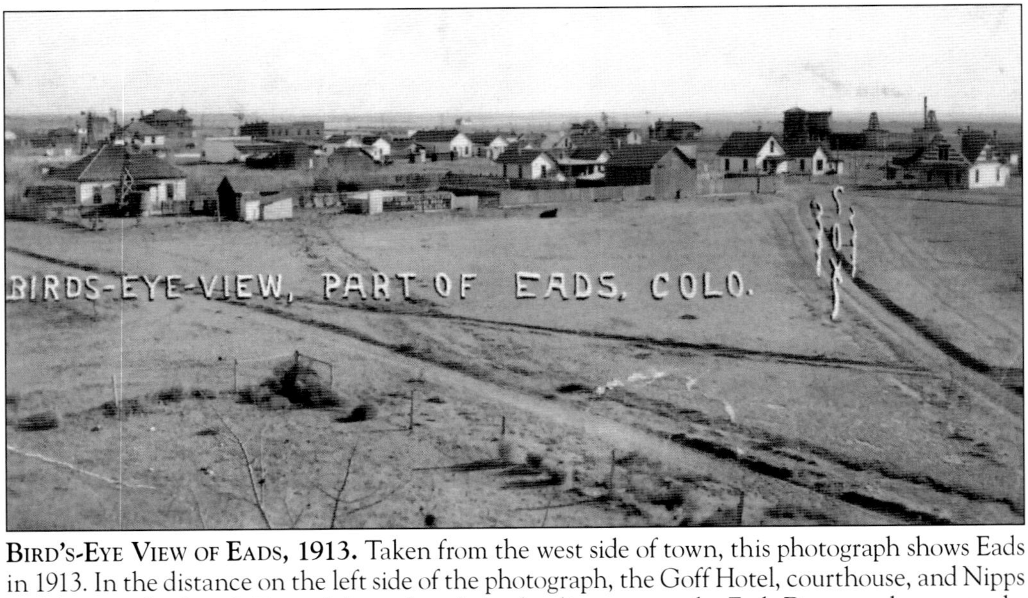

BIRD'S-EYE VIEW OF EADS, 1913. Taken from the west side of town, this photograph shows Eads in 1913. In the distance on the left side of the photograph, the Goff Hotel, courthouse, and Nipps building can be found. Toward the right side in the distance are the Eads Depot and water tanks for the railroad.

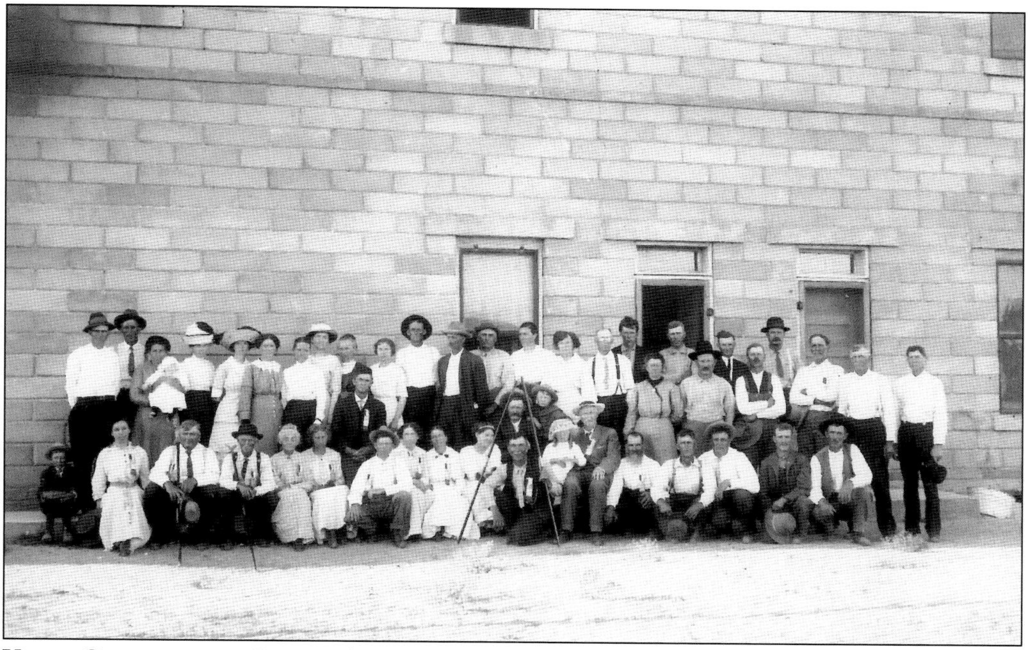

KIOWA GRANGE, 1914. During the 1910s, Kiowa County had several local units of the National Grange, an agricultural organization that emphasized community service. Lida Kerr Link was the grange secretary for the Kiowa Grange in Eads; the National Grange was one of the first organizations to admit women with membership equality of men. Other granges in Kiowa County were located in Arlington, Chivington, Haswell, and Towner.

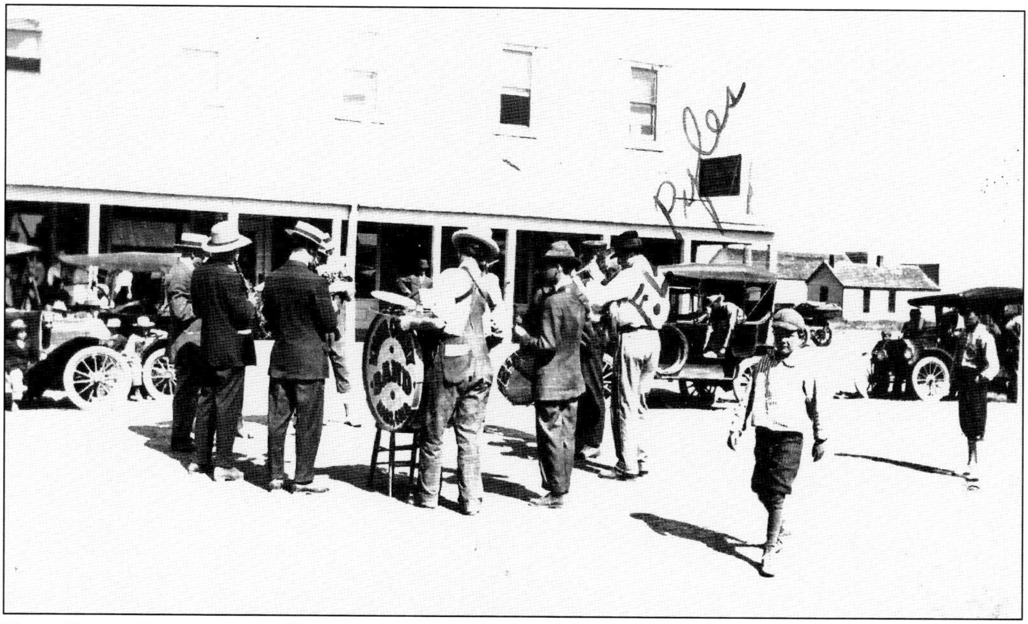

EADS BAND, JUNE 1915. The Kiowa County Band was a popular group that entertained citizens at many county events. The band is shown here playing on Maine Street in front of the Nipps Building in June 1915. Members included brothers Farrel and Fay Hines and F. Lawrence Pyles. Into the 1920s, several articles in the *Kiowa County Press* praised the Eads Band and encouraged more concerts.

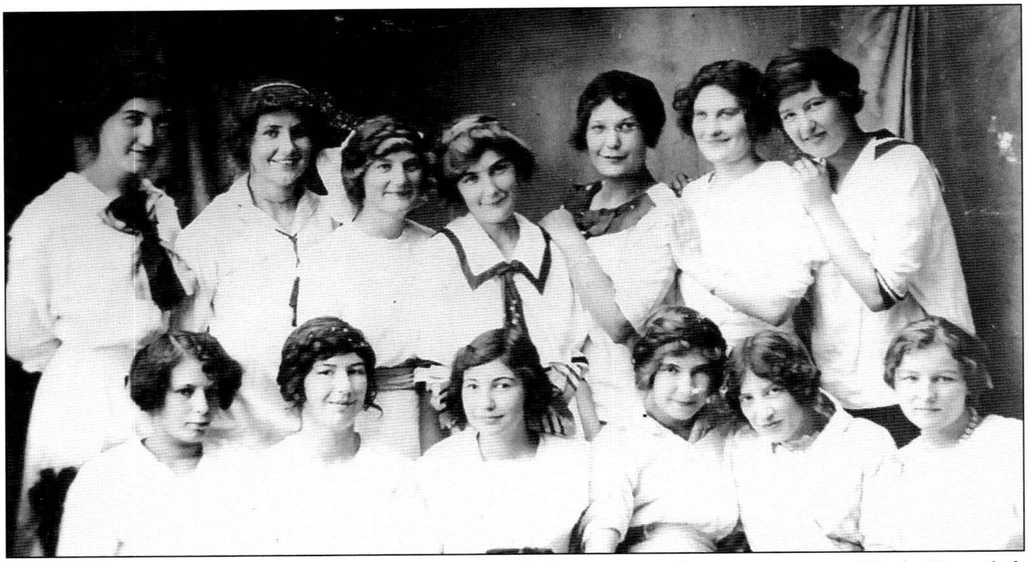

Eads Girls, 1915. Taken in 1915, this photograph shows several young women of Eads. From left to right are (first row) Zelma Snapp, Helen Barlow, Ruby Blair, Gladys Denney, Lee Whitelaw, and Blanche Rittgers; (second row) Reba Wilson, Bess Belshe, Lucile Pyles, Mary Thompson, Catherine Witmar, Nela Campbell, and Ida Wiley.

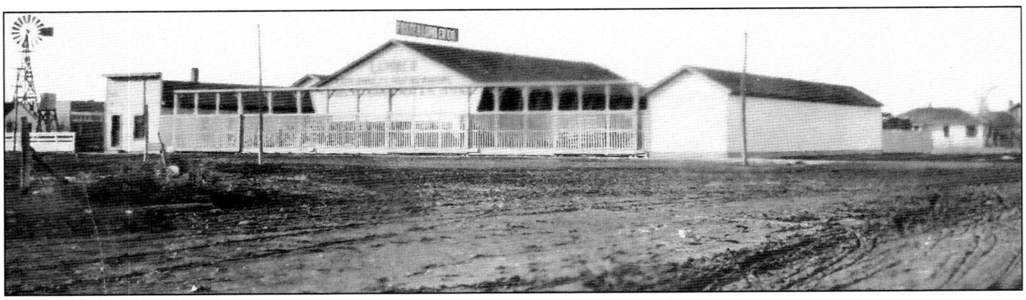

Foster Lumber Company. Foster Lumber Company constructed a new, three-building lumberyard in 1915. They brought in lumber from railroad cars and also sold coal, paint, roofing supplies, and other miscellaneous repair supplies. Foster Lumber ran the business until 1966, when George Crow purchased it and began Eads Building Supply, Inc. P. L. and Mary Reed and John and Doris Forsyth of Haswell Lumber Company bought it in 1973.

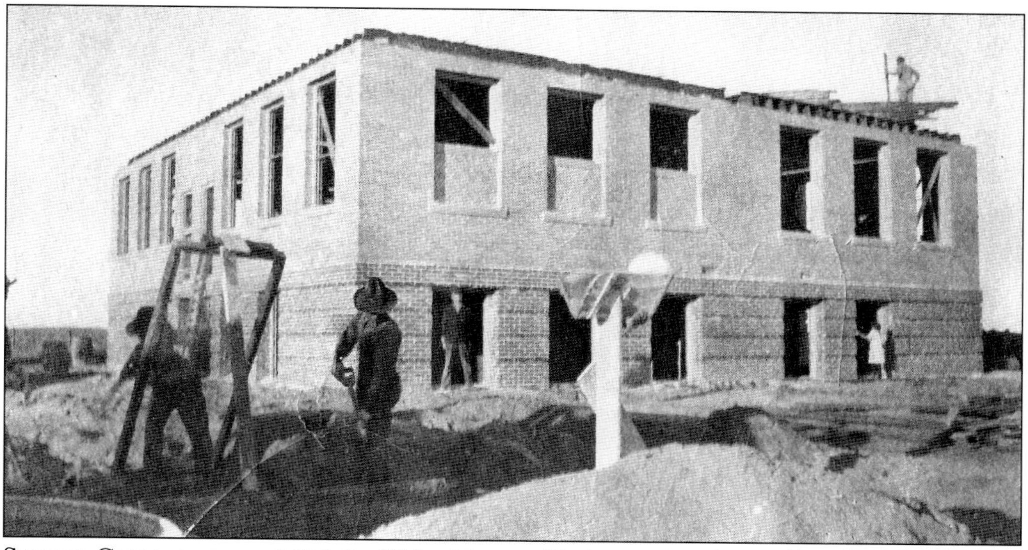

School Construction, 1916. In 1915, citizens of Eads voted in favor of bonds to build a new and larger school in Eads. The school, a two-story brick building, was constructed at a cost of approximately $15,000. The school was dedicated on April 7, 1916.

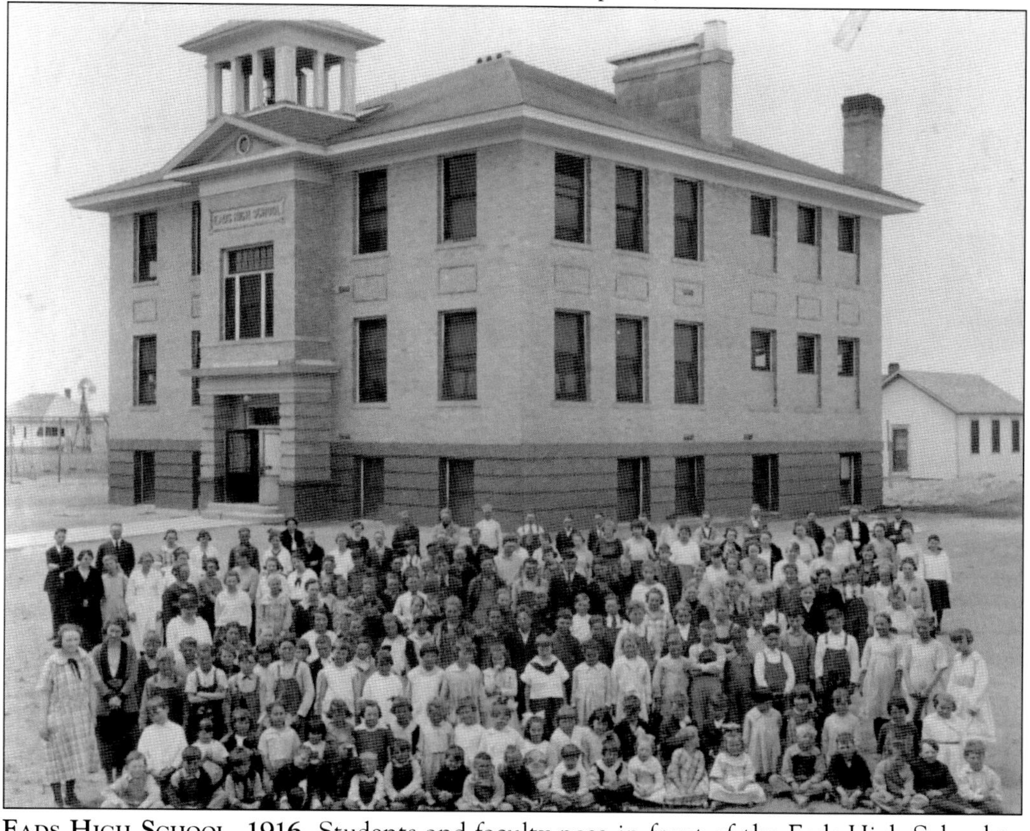

Eads High School, 1916. Students and faculty pose in front of the Eads High School to commemorate the new school. Built in 1916, the school had the first accredited high school and was also the first consolidated school in Kiowa County. First through 12th grades attended school there. The school burned to the ground in 1937.

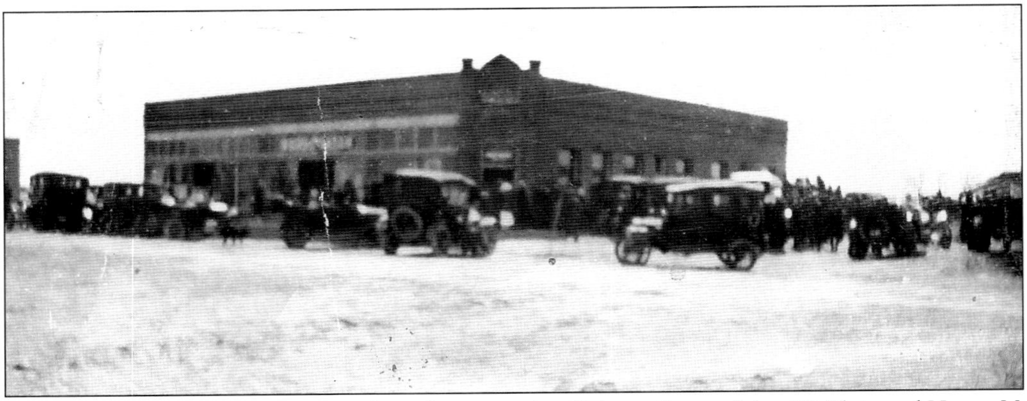

Post Office Block, 1917. Located on the west side of Maine Street, John W. Blair and Henry V. Fluke organized the construction of a $10,000 three-storefront brick building in 1917. J. H. Peck was the contractor. Blair Hardware opened for business in August 1917; he sold the business to James M. Kelley in 1925. T. F. Prajer operated a drugstore from the middle portion of the building, and Fluke located the new post office in the northern section on the corner.

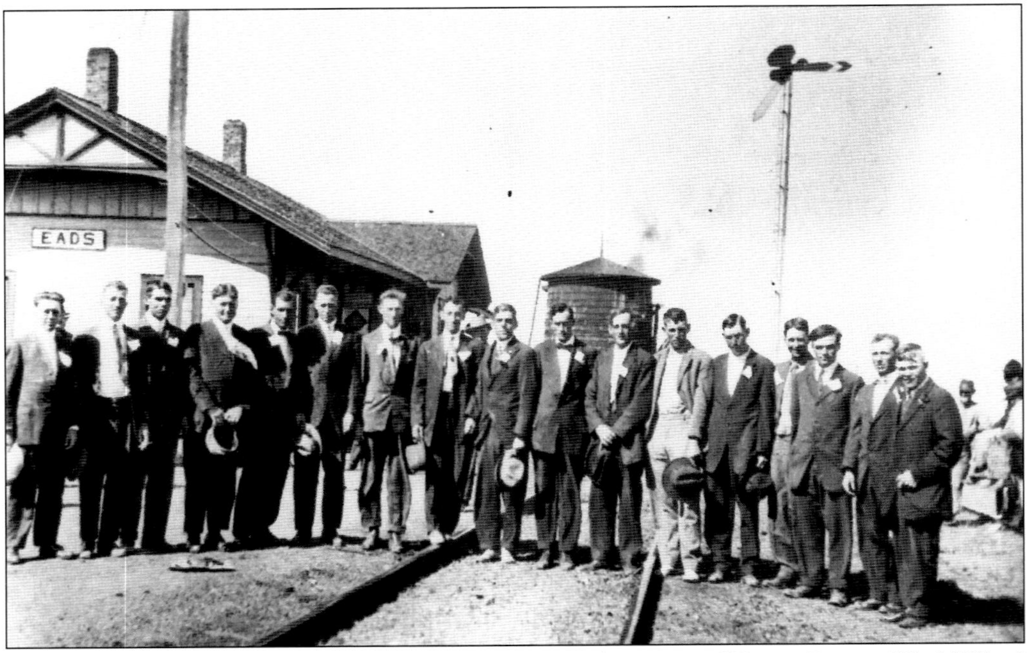

World War I Draftees, Eads, 1918. Taken in 1918, this group of Kiowa County World War I draftees waits at the Eads Depot for the train to take them to boot camp. Pictured here are Ernest Center, Paul Moore, Wilbur White, Paul Zygmunt, Otho Ferris, James Hensley, Hardy Boyd, Vinton Brown, James Griswould, Robert Marlof, Robert Benner, Oscar Hainer, James O'Connor, Roy Crum, Orin Matthews, and John Allen.

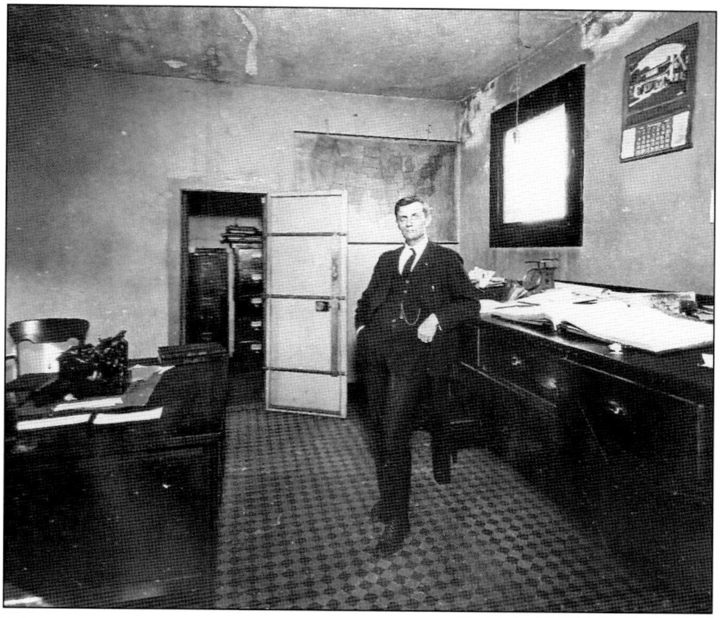

Hal King, Abstract Office, 1918. Henry V. and Fara K. Fluke organized the Kiowa County Abstract Office in 1906. From 1921 to 1943, Harold H. (Hal) King, Fara's brother, operated the business. His parents, John and Emma King, moved from Ohio and received a homestead on April 18, 1887. King also acquired a 160-acre homestead in 1910 where he ranched; he moved to town in 1946. King's nephew, Theron Fluke, operated the abstract office from 1943 to 1975.

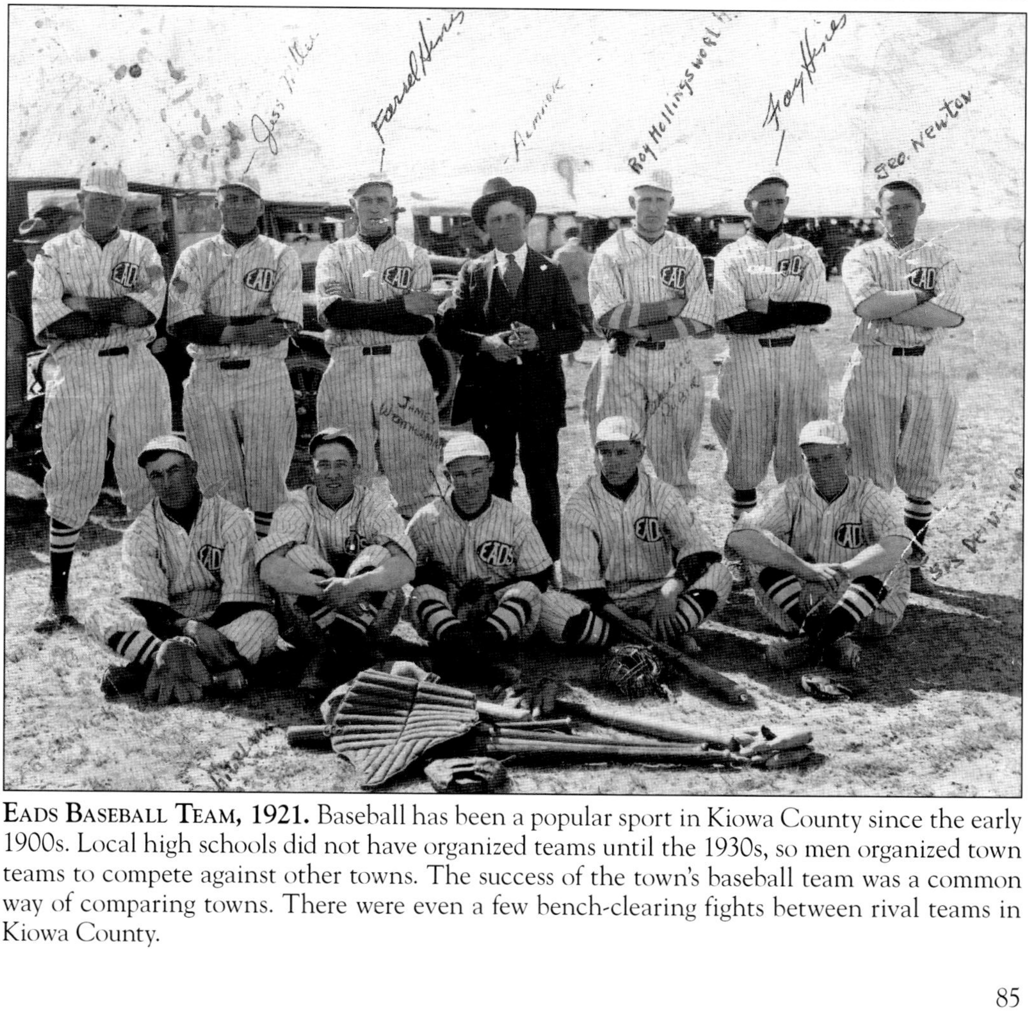

Eads Baseball Team, 1921. Baseball has been a popular sport in Kiowa County since the early 1900s. Local high schools did not have organized teams until the 1930s, so men organized town teams to compete against other towns. The success of the town's baseball team was a common way of comparing towns. There were even a few bench-clearing fights between rival teams in Kiowa County.

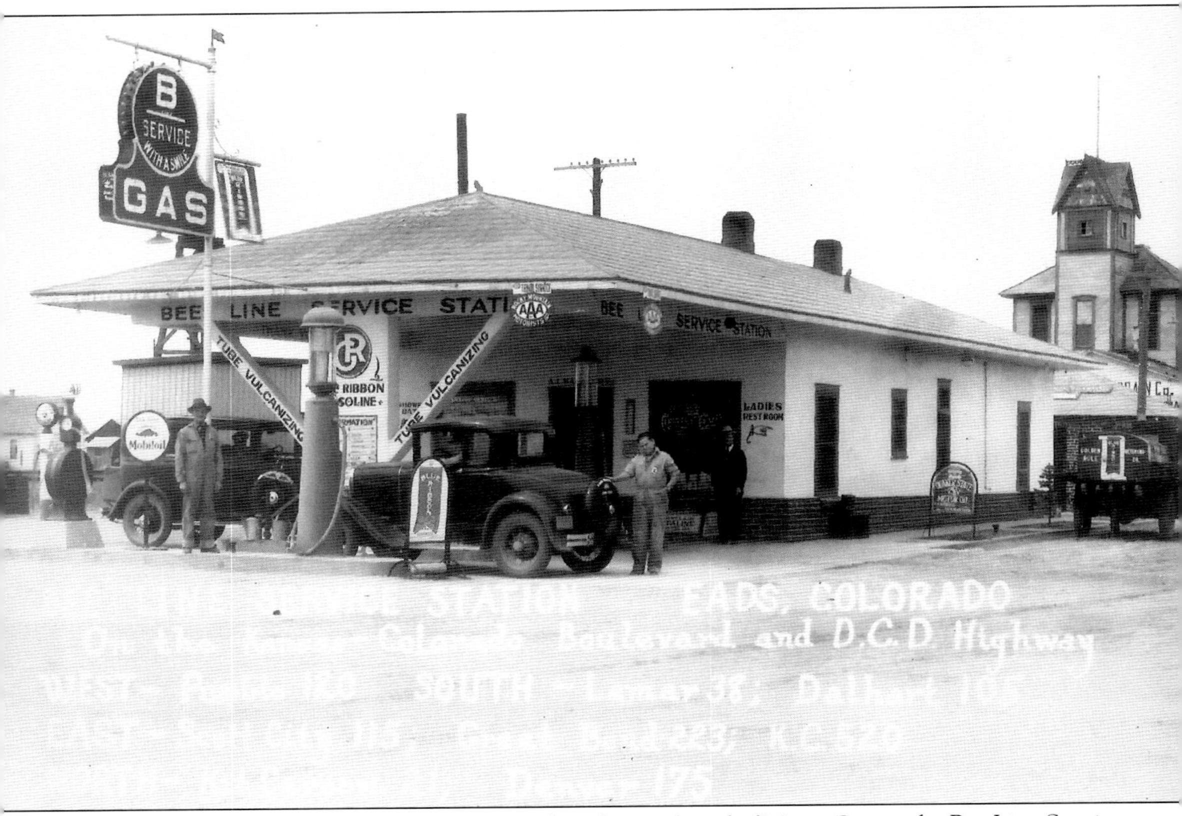

Bee Line Service Station, 1920s. Located on the south end of Maine Street, the Bee Line Service Station was owned by A. L. Mansker in the 1920s. A modern store, Mansker sold gasoline, tires, and other automobile needs. John Osolin purchased the store in 1937 and added a small stock of groceries, making the Bee Line Service Station a predecessor to modern convenience stores.

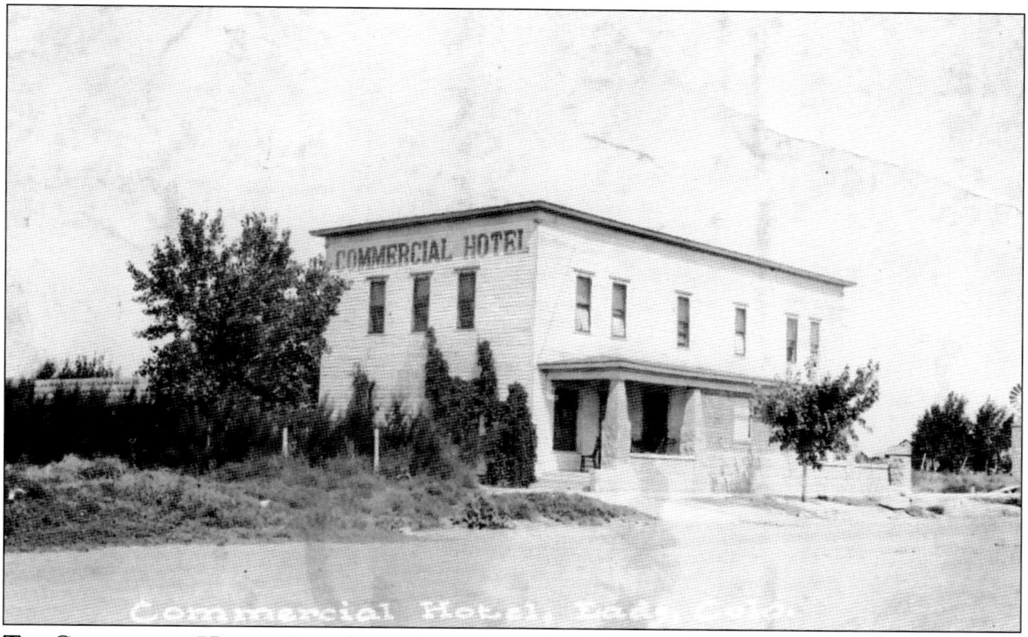

The Commercial Hotel. Once located on Maine Street, across the street from Sunday's Garage, the Commercial Hotel was a fixture in town until it was torn down in the 1960s. In 1922, there was a smallpox outbreak in Eads, and the sick were quarantined in the Commercial Hotel. Following the quarantine, the hotel was thoroughly cleaned to ensure "absolutely no danger of any germs being alive in the building," reported the *Kiowa County Press*.

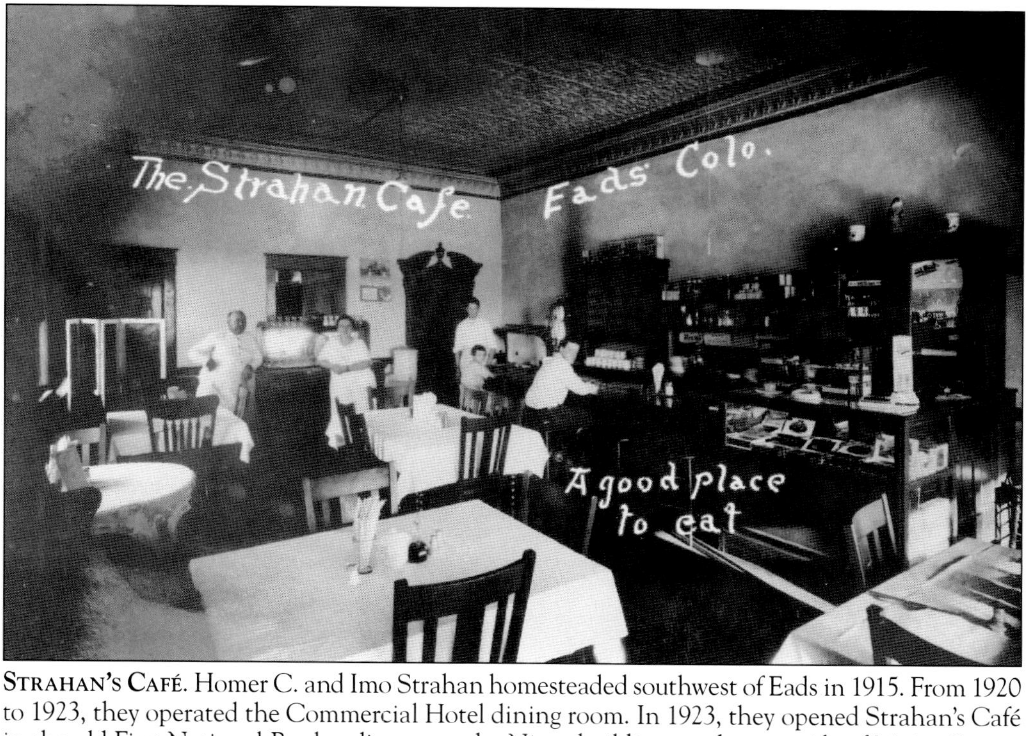

Strahan's Café. Homer C. and Imo Strahan homesteaded southwest of Eads in 1915. From 1920 to 1923, they operated the Commercial Hotel dining room. In 1923, they opened Strahan's Café in the old First National Bank, adjacent to the Nipps building on the east side of Maine Street. They later added a hotel on to the building. The Strahans retired from business in 1945.

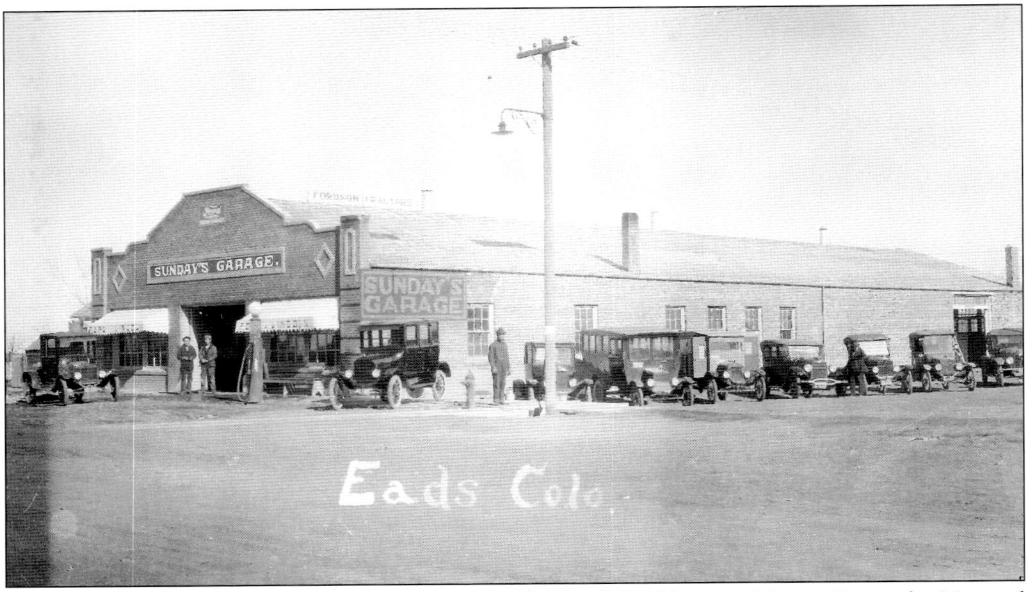

SUNDAY'S GARAGE. In 1917, J. H. Peck completed a brick building on Maine Street for Howard Sunday. Open for business in 1917, Sunday's Garage repaired cars and sold gas, tires, and Ford Model Ts. In the 1920s, the *Kiowa County Press* reported that Howard exchanged cars for cows. He was also an amateur inventor. Howard and his wife, Bessie Kerr Sunday, owned and operated Sunday's Garage from 1917 to 1929. In 1956, Clyde Crow purchased the building and remodeled it; Crow's Stop 'N' Shop moved to its current location in 1960.

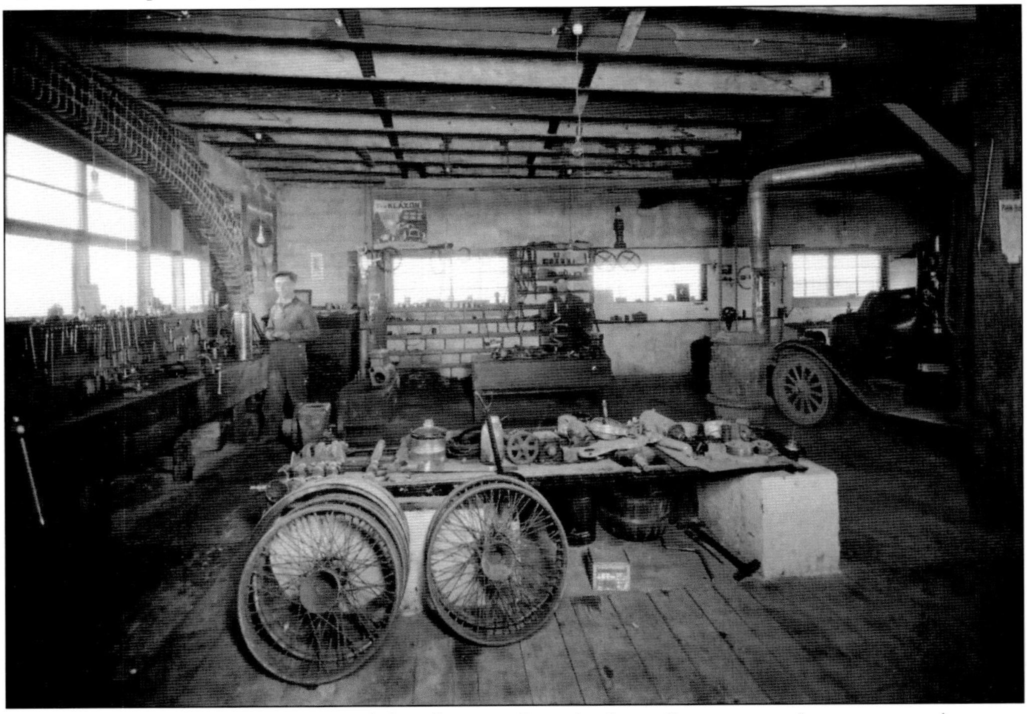

INSIDE SUNDAY'S GARAGE. Howard Sunday was described as a "pioneer in the garage and tractor business." Sunday invented and patented the back-drive fluid engine as a possible solution to the pollution problem. He is pictured here inside his garage on Maine Street.

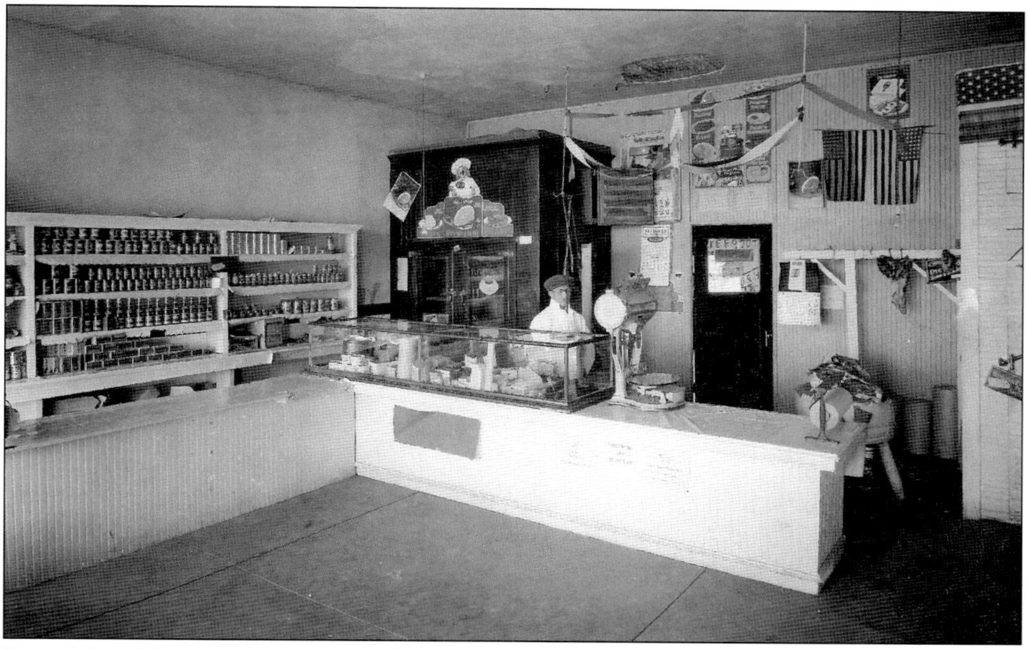

EADS MEAT MARKET, 1925. In the late 1910s, George France constructed a brick building on Maine Street next to Kelley Hardware. He opened the Eads Meat Market for business in 1920 and operated it until 1924. In February 1924, Theodore Windecker (pictured) purchased the business from George France. He remodeled the interior of the shop and served as a butcher for two years. Clyde and Bernice Crow moved their grocery store into the building in 1943.

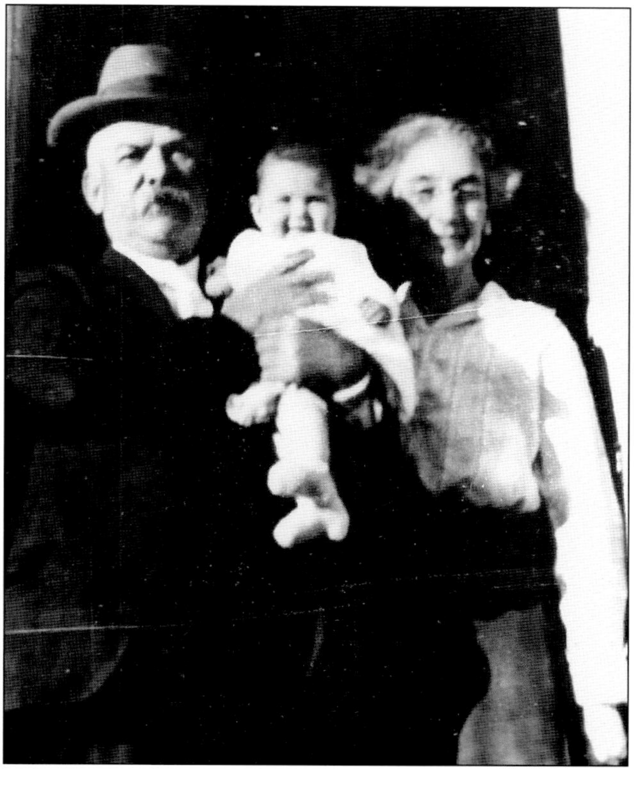

THE GOUGHS AND BARBARA ANN PYLES. John T. Gough, Porter A. Thompson, and Field Bohart purchased J. A. Slater's interest in the First National Bank in 1910. Gough was elected president and held that office until 1928. Barbara Ann Pyles was the daughter of F. Lawrence and Bertha Lee Whitelaw.

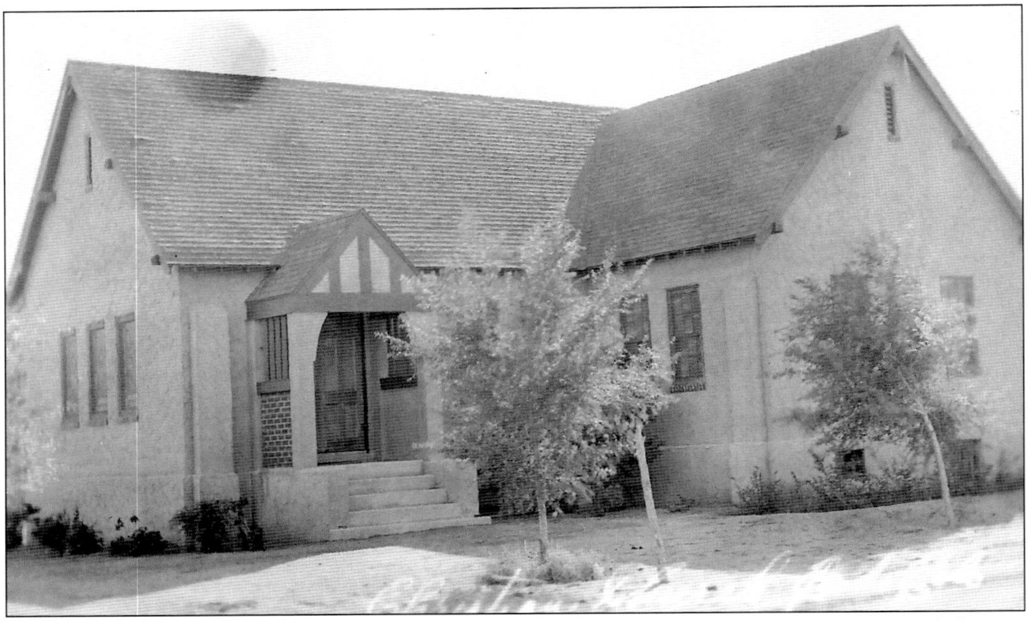

First Christian Church. Organized in 1925, the First Christian Church in Eads began construction on its first church (pictured) in 1930. The church, located on Maine Street, was dedicated on May 15, 1932, and served the congregation for many years. A new church on the north end of Maine Street was dedicated January 16, 1972; the first church building was sold and converted to a residence in 1973.

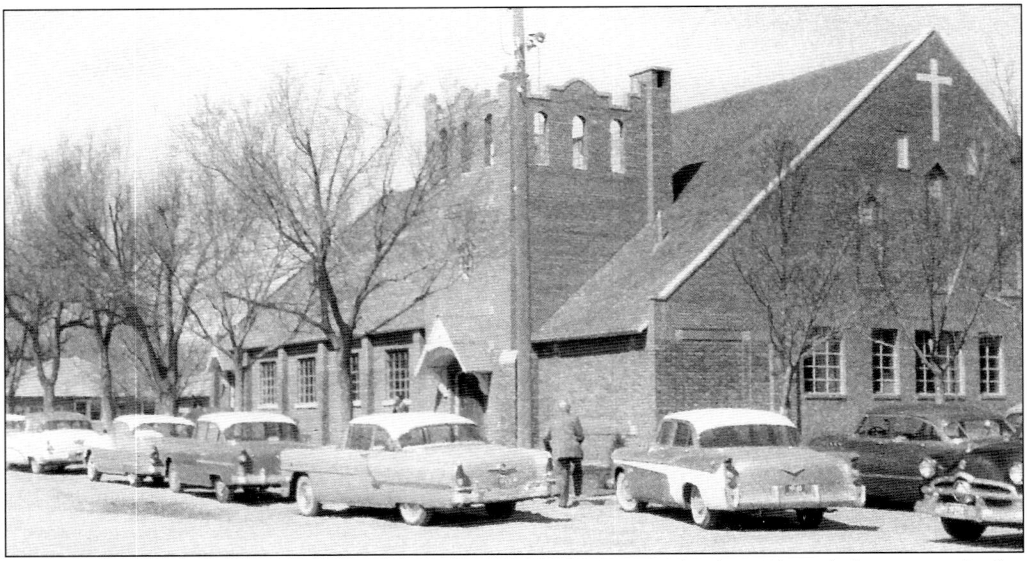

United Methodist Church. The construction of the Methodist Church began with the basement in August 1920 by volunteer labor. After cement was poured for the basement floor and walls, construction was stopped due to a decline in cattle prices and crop losses that put many community members in financial hardship. A roof was added, and the building was used as it was. Until the school gymnasium was completed in 1928, the basement hosted basketball games and graduation ceremonies. In 1951, construction resumed; the church was dedicated on November 30, 1952. In 1969, the two Methodist congregations in Eads combined as the United Methodist Church. (Photograph courtesy Cardon and Joyce Berry.)

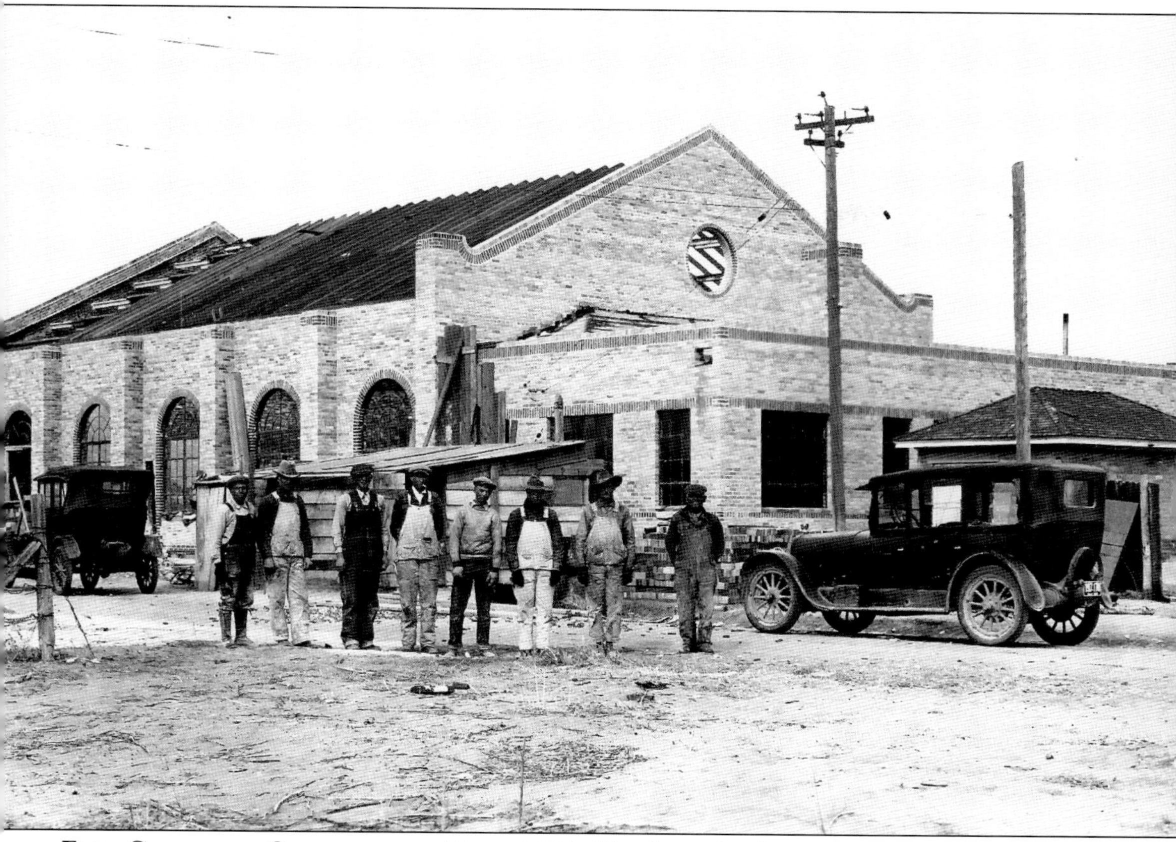

EADS GYMNASIUM CONSTRUCTION CREW, 1928. The first school gymnasium was constructed in Eads in 1928. Designed by Colorado Springs architect Elmer E. Nieman, local residents Cal Benner and son Bill helped construct the gym. The one-story portions on the east and west sides of the gym were originally used as classrooms.

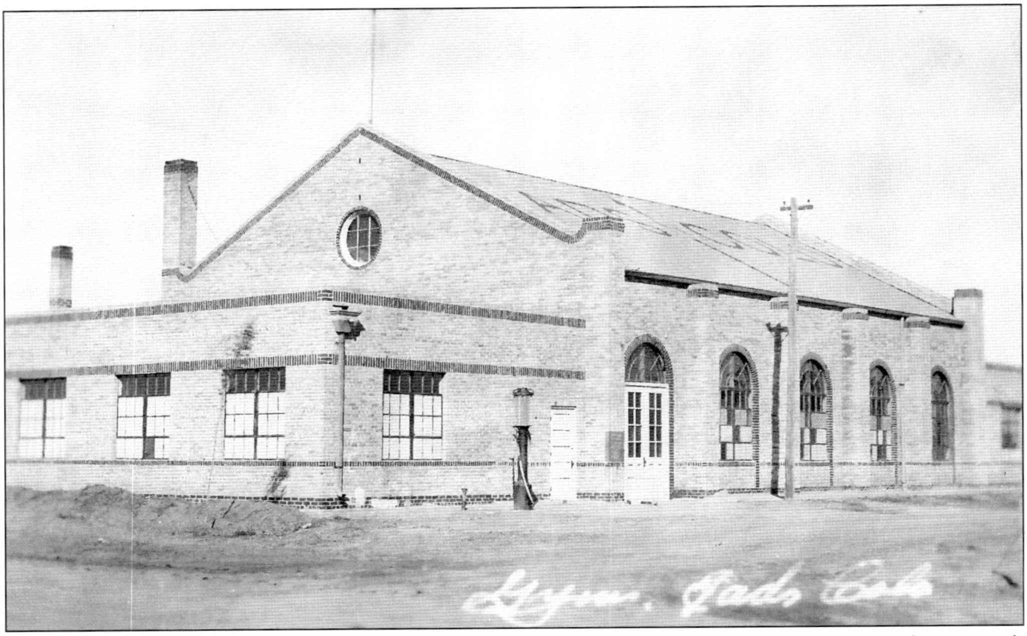

EADS GYMNASIUM. Once completed, the new gymnasium became an important educational, recreational, and cultural facility. Prior to the construction of the gym, basketball games had been held in the basement of the United Methodist Church. The building was saved in 1937 when the brick school burned down. Until the new school was completed in 1940, many classes were held in the gym as well as other locations in town.

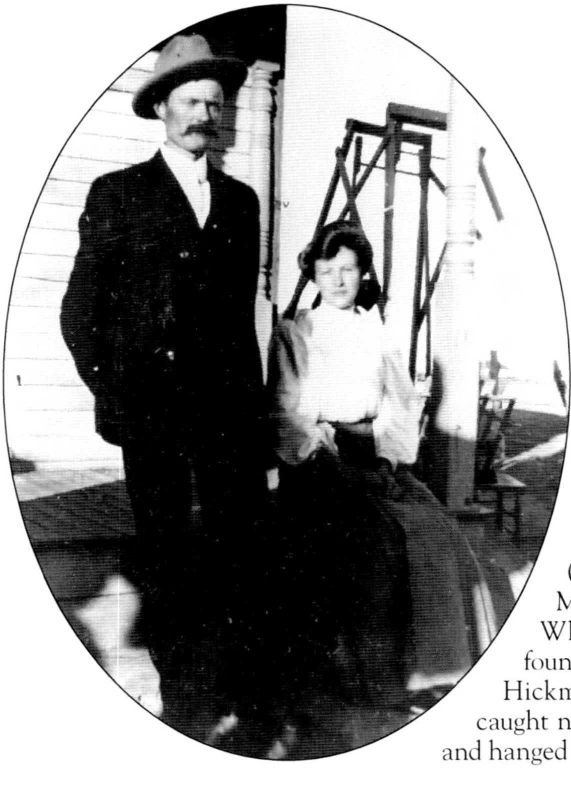

CORAL HICKMAN'S MURDER. On March 14, 1930, three bandits robbed a bank in Kansas. Alerted that they were headed toward Eads, deputy sheriffs Coral Hickman (pictured with his wife, Mamie) and William Mosher chased their Model A Ford sedan. When the bandits pulled over, the deputies found themselves in a gunfight. Shot six times, Hickman died immediately. The bandits were caught near Jetmore, Kansas, put on trial in Eads, and hanged within a year.

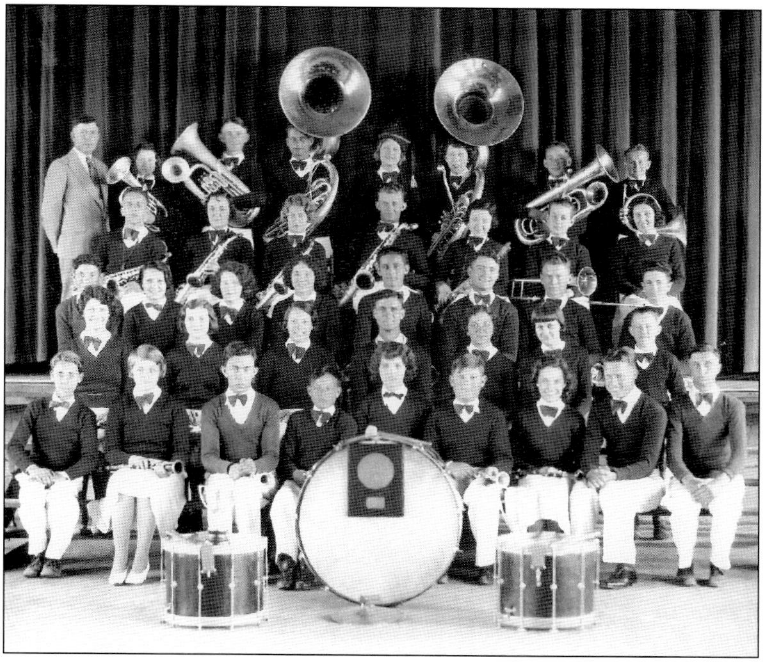

State Championship Band, 1932. Band has been a legacy of Eads High School for many years. The band won several state championship titles in the 1930s; it also received numerous awards under the direction of Philomene and Thomas Liesen in the 1950s and 1960s.

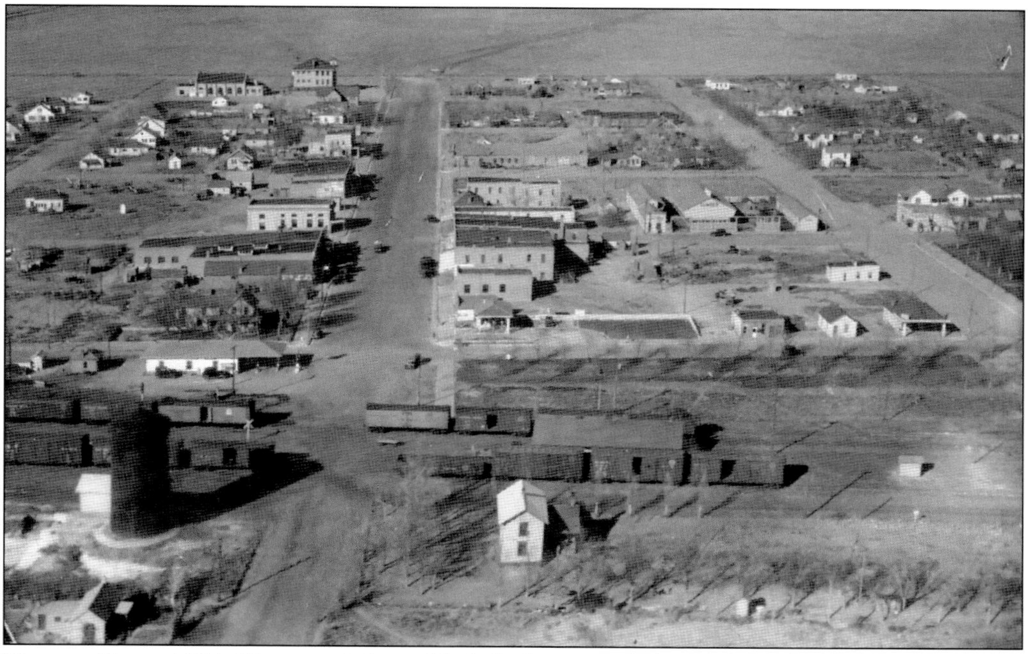

View of Eads, 1936. This aerial shot of Eads looking north shows the railroad tracks and water tank in the foreground. On the west side of Maine Street are the Bee Line Service Station, Missouri Pacific Hotel, First National Bank, France/Kelley/post office buildings, and Commercial Hotel. The Christian Church, Eads School, and Eads Gymnasium are in the distance on the left. The Nipps building, Whitelaw building, Rialto Hotel, and Sunday's Garage are visible on the east side of Maine Street.

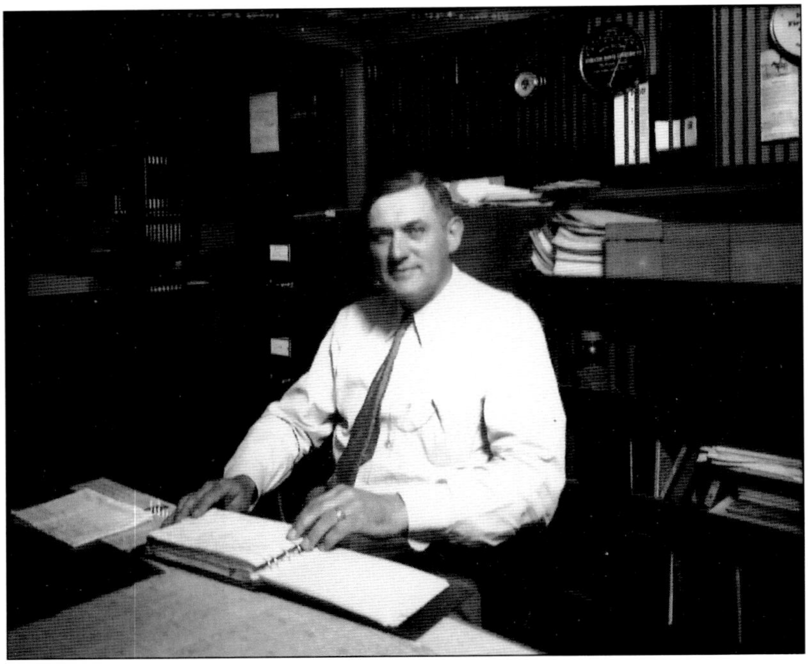

F. L. Pyles, Bank President. F. Lawrence Pyles began working at First National Bank in Eads in 1909 at age 17; his duties included teller work, bookkeeping, and janitorial tasks. He became a cashier in 1914 and vice president in 1925. On June 30, 1931, Pyles became the president, serving in that capacity for 36 years until his death in 1970.

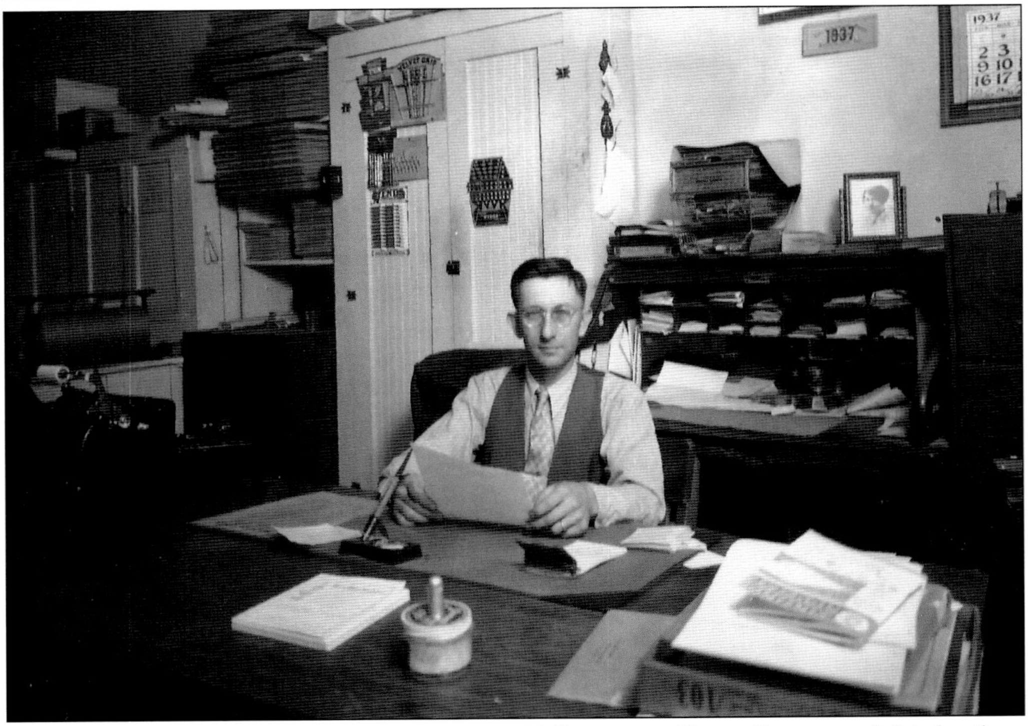

James LaVelle, *Kiowa County Press*. James LaVelle came to Kiowa County with his family at age three, when his father claimed a homestead west of Eads in 1910. He graduated from Eads High School in 1925 and learned the printing trade from J. C. Miller at the *Kiowa County Press*. LaVelle purchased the *Haswell Herald* in 1927 and merged it with the *Kiowa County Press* in 1937. LaVelle published the *Press* until 1963. He and his wife, Edith, were active members of the Eads community.

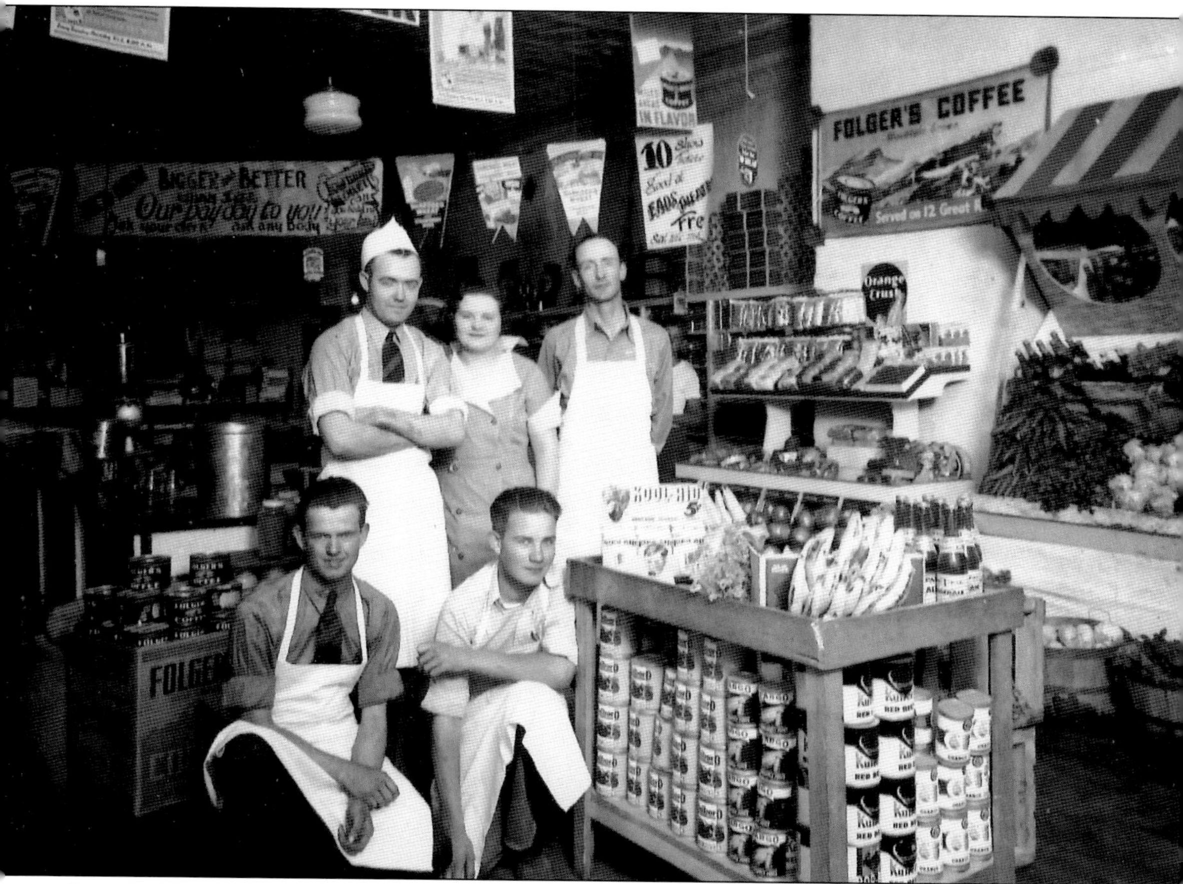

Crow's Stop 'N' Shop, 1937. Born and raised in Eads, Clyde Crow opened Crow's Stop 'N' Shop for business in 1937. Prior to opening his own store, Crow worked at Schoggen's Grocery and Higginbottom's Grocery in Eads. He married Bernice Barksdale on May 20, 1933; they later built and operated the first motel in Eads in the 1960s. The Crows sold their business to their son, Gary, and his wife, Pam, in 1975; their son, Keith, and his wife, Jennifer, bought the store in 2009, keeping the business in the Crow family for three generations.

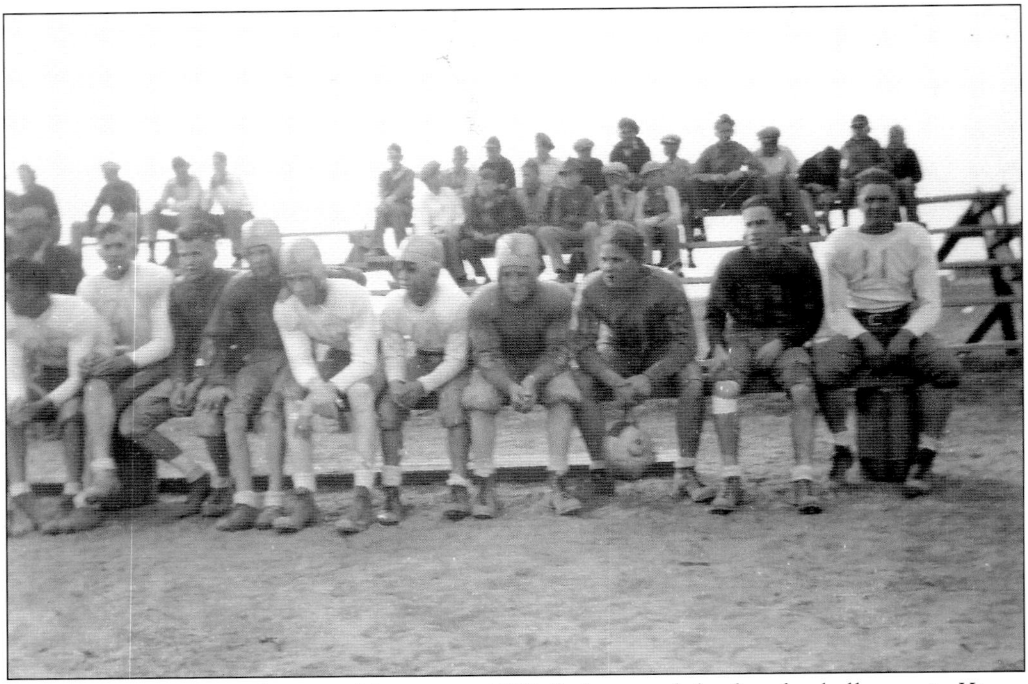

Eads Versus Sharon Springs, November 1937. Eads started the first football team in Kiowa County in 1931. In that same year, a nearby pasture was donated to the school and used as a football, baseball, softball, and track field. Today the track is located on that field. Members of the 1937 football team are pictured here.

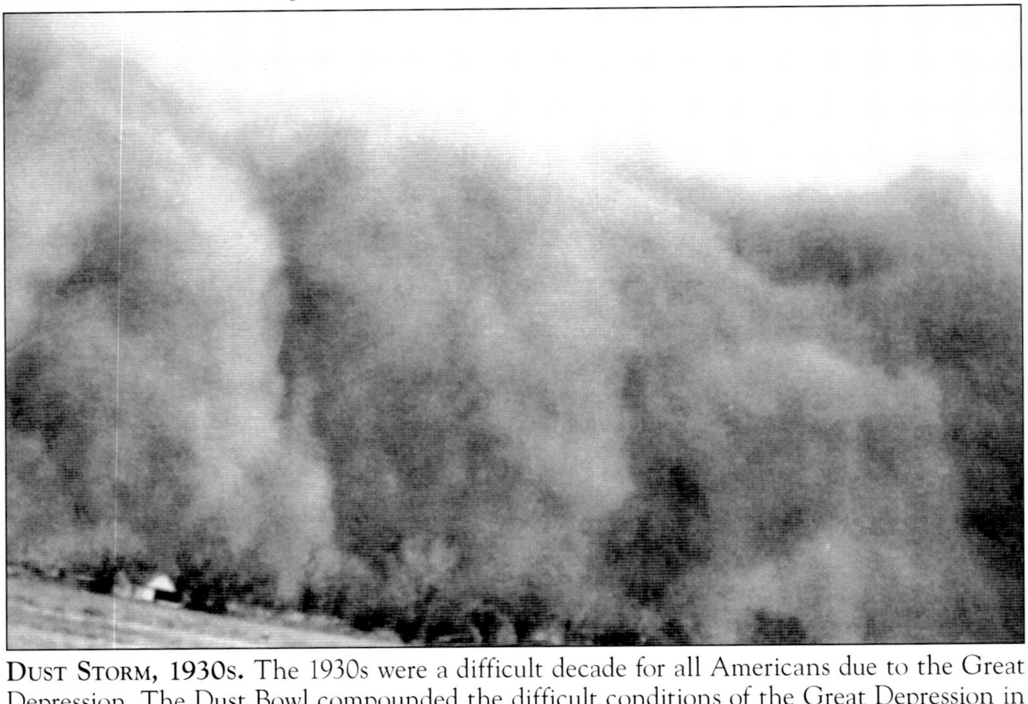

Dust Storm, 1930s. The 1930s were a difficult decade for all Americans due to the Great Depression. The Dust Bowl compounded the difficult conditions of the Great Depression in southeast Colorado's agricultural economy. The drought and wind caused massive "black blizzards," such as the one pictured here.

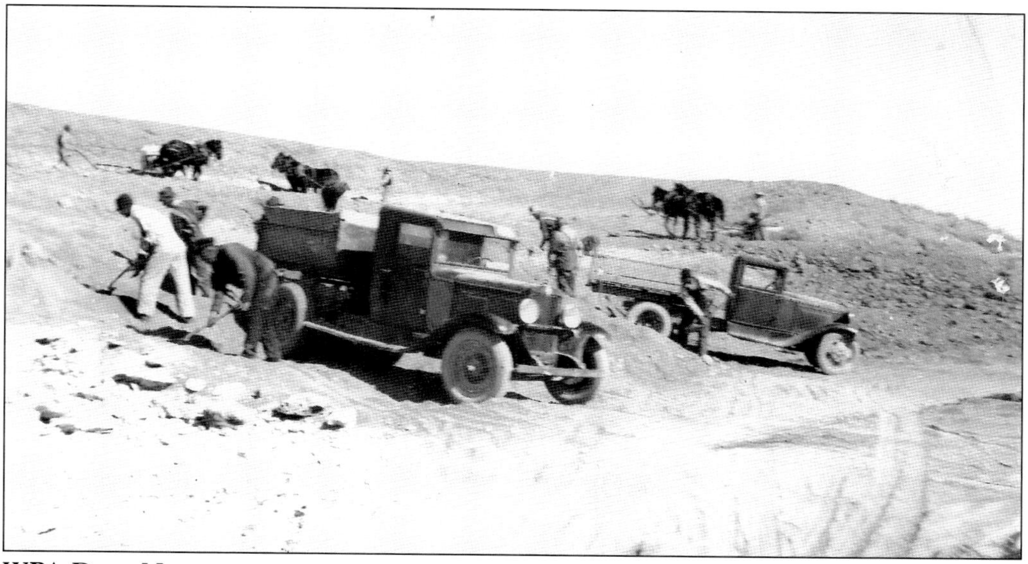

WPA Days, North of Eads, 1937. During the Great Depression of the 1930s, the Works Projects Administration provided many men in Kiowa County with a job. The WPA constructed many structures in Kiowa County. Harve W. Musselman, foreman of Kiowa County Road and Bridge, supervised many of the WPA's construction projects in the county.

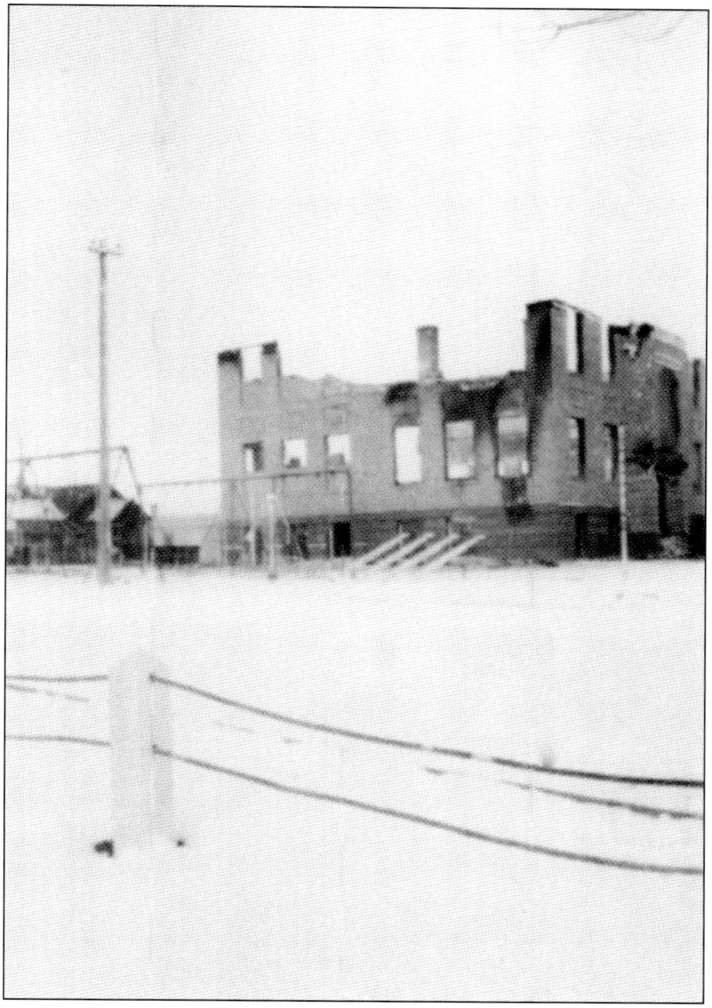

Eads School in Ashes, December 1, 1937. Constructed in 1916, the Eads School burned to the ground during the early morning hours of December 1, 1937, as a result of a boiler explosion. Fortunately, the explosion occurred in the middle of the night, so no one was hurt.

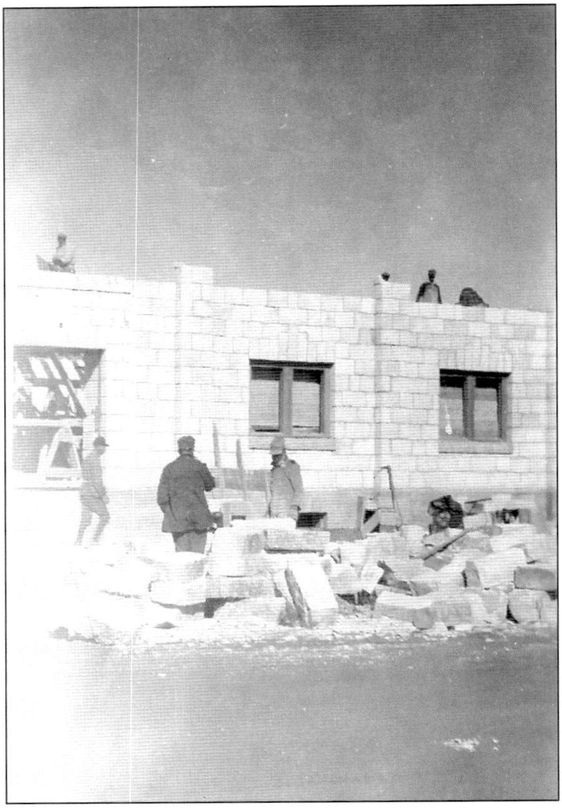

Eads City Hall Construction. WPA workers, under the supervision of H. W. Musselman, constructed the city hall in Eads from 1937 to 1939. The structure was built from limestone quarried in Bristol, Colorado, by Prowers County WPA workers.

City Hall. After the building's completion, the first floor became the home of Eads city offices, while the local Masonic Lodge used the second floor. The town hall was dedicated on October 7, 1938, the same day as two other WPA projects: the Weisbrod Memorial Hospital and the American Legion Hall.

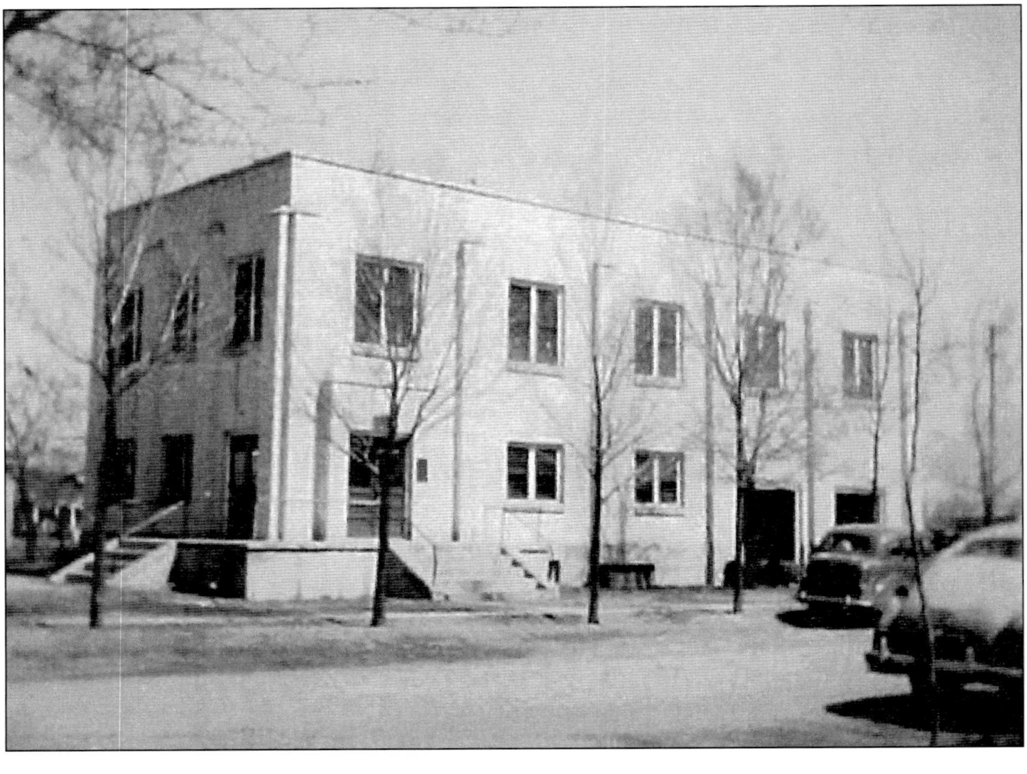

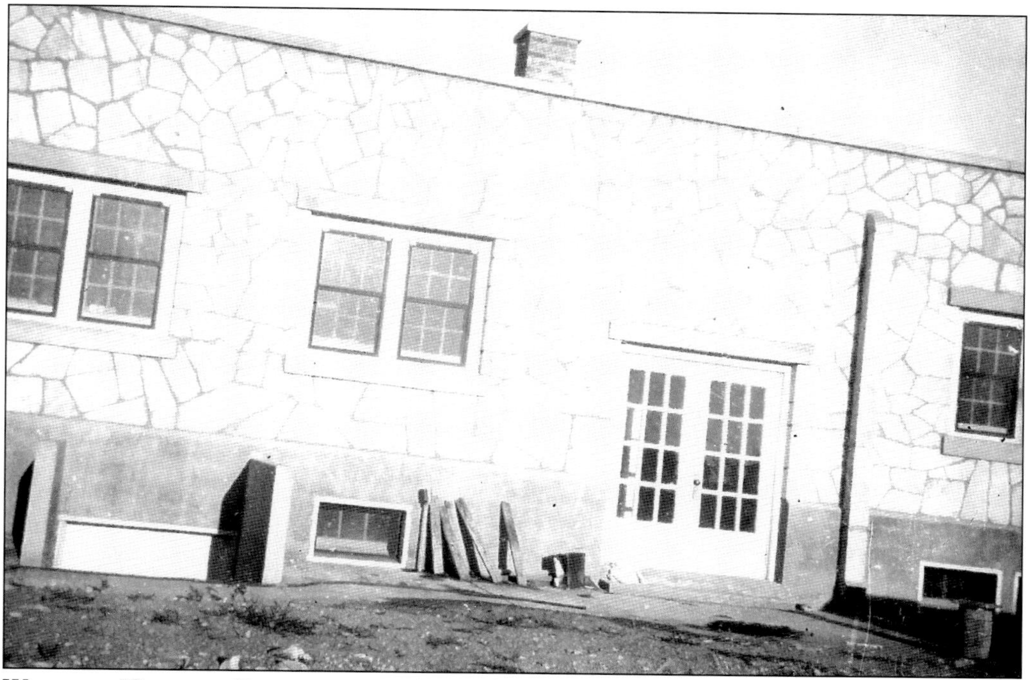

Weisbrod Hospital Construction. A member of the First National Bank Board of Directors from the bank's creation in 1906 until his death in 1924, George Weisbrod donated his estate, including Lots 10, 11, and 12 in Block 26, as well as an unspecified amount of money to build a hospital in Kiowa County. The construction of the hospital was accepted as a WPA project in 1937. The original sandstone building was completed in 1939 and has been in continuous use since that time.

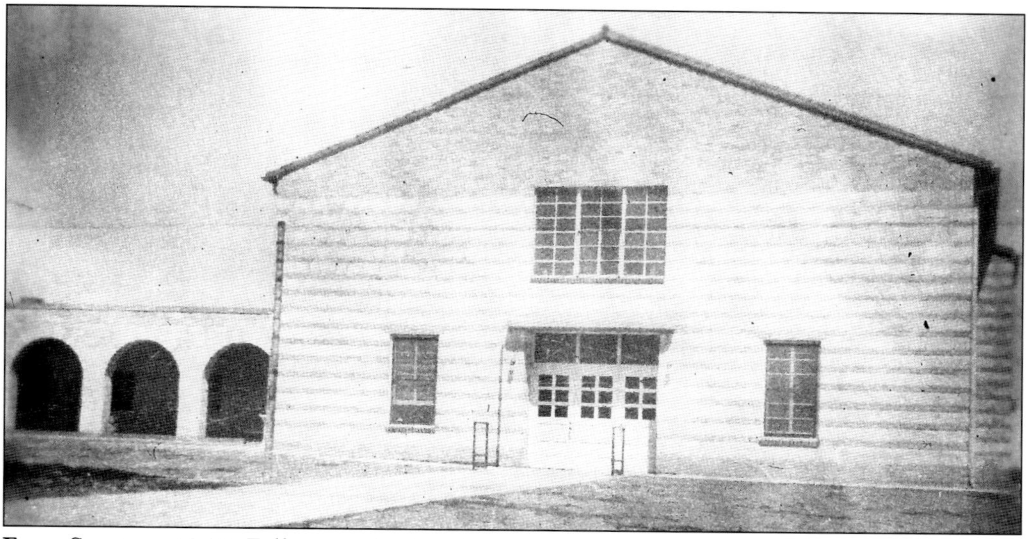

Eads School, 1940. Following the fire that destroyed the consolidated school in Eads, the school district discovered that the insurance coverage on the old building was inadequate for constructing a new school. In 1938, a WPA project application was submitted to clean up the school grounds and construct a new two-story school from limestone and salvaged brick from the old school. After several delays, the first through 12th grade school was completed on April 6, 1940. It has been used as the elementary school since 1964.

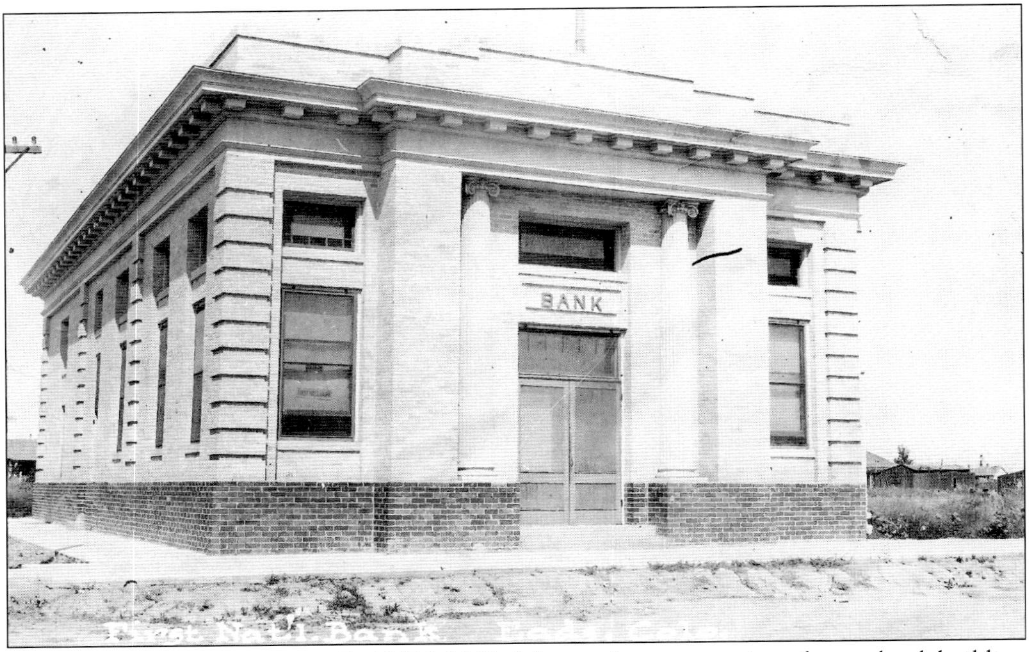

FIRST NATIONAL BANK, 1940s. In 1917, J. H. Peck began the construction of a new bank building in Eads. The structure was completed in 1918, and the bank moved into the new building. The bank survived the financial crisis of the Great Depression, and by 1938, the First National Bank of Eads was the only bank in Kiowa County. The exterior of the building was remodeled in the 1950s and 1970s; Kiowa County National Bank occupies the building today.

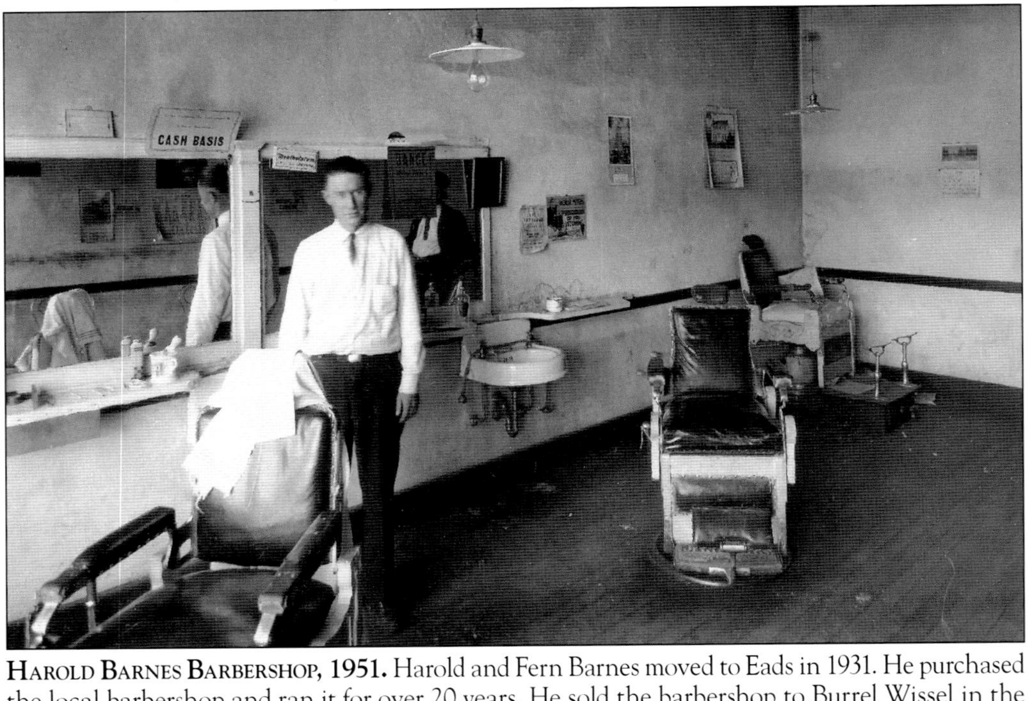

HAROLD BARNES BARBERSHOP, 1951. Harold and Fern Barnes moved to Eads in 1931. He purchased the local barbershop and ran it for over 20 years. He sold the barbershop to Burrel Wissel in the mid-1950s and became an insurance agent. Barnes loved to golf and was a founding member of the Eads Golf Club. He lived in Eads until his death in January 1983.

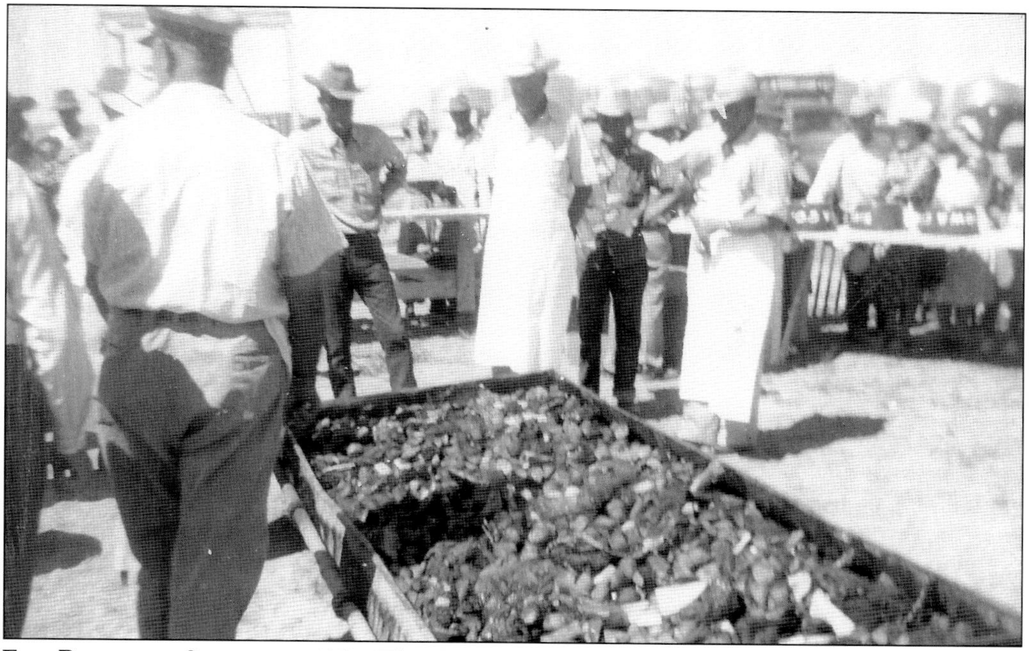

Fair Barbeque, September 1953. The Kiowa County Fair began as a Labor Day celebration in about 1910; it has been held at the fairgrounds since 1921 on land acquired by commissioners Wirt Bailey, C. C. Wolever, and John Rebel. George France started the free barbeque in 1916, and his son, Walter, took over in the 1920s when George's health began to fail. The free barbeque continues to be enjoyed by county residents at the fair.

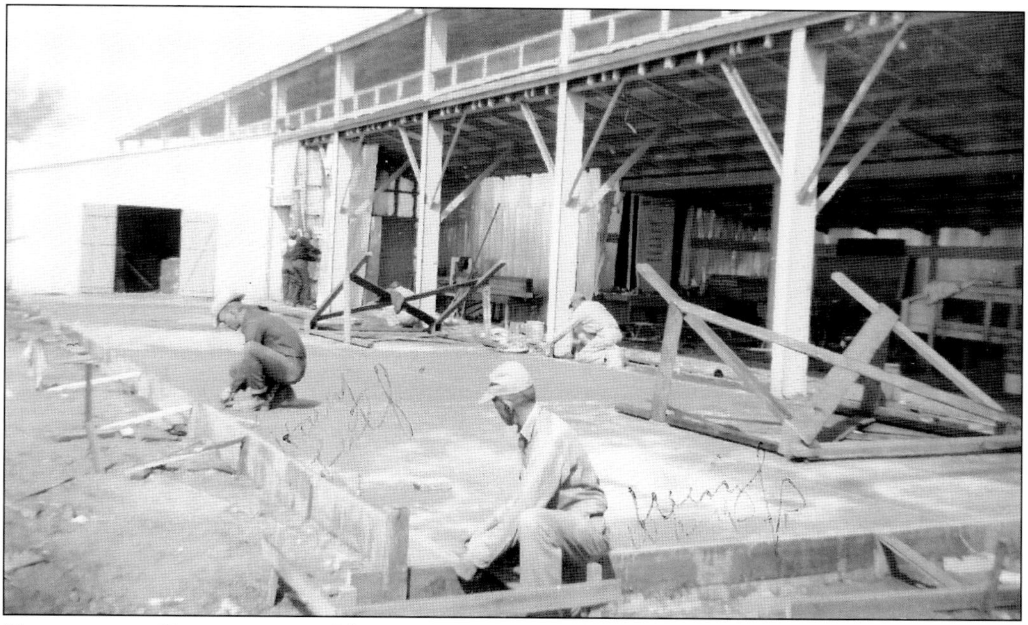

Grandstand Construction, March 1957. Responsible for the construction of many buildings and bridges in Kiowa County, Harve W. Musselman also constructed many buildings at the Kiowa County Fairgrounds. In the 1950s, he designed and drew plans for new grandstands with a capacity for 1,600 people to replace the original 300-seat wooden grandstand. Musselman also oversaw the construction of the grandstands, which still are in use today.

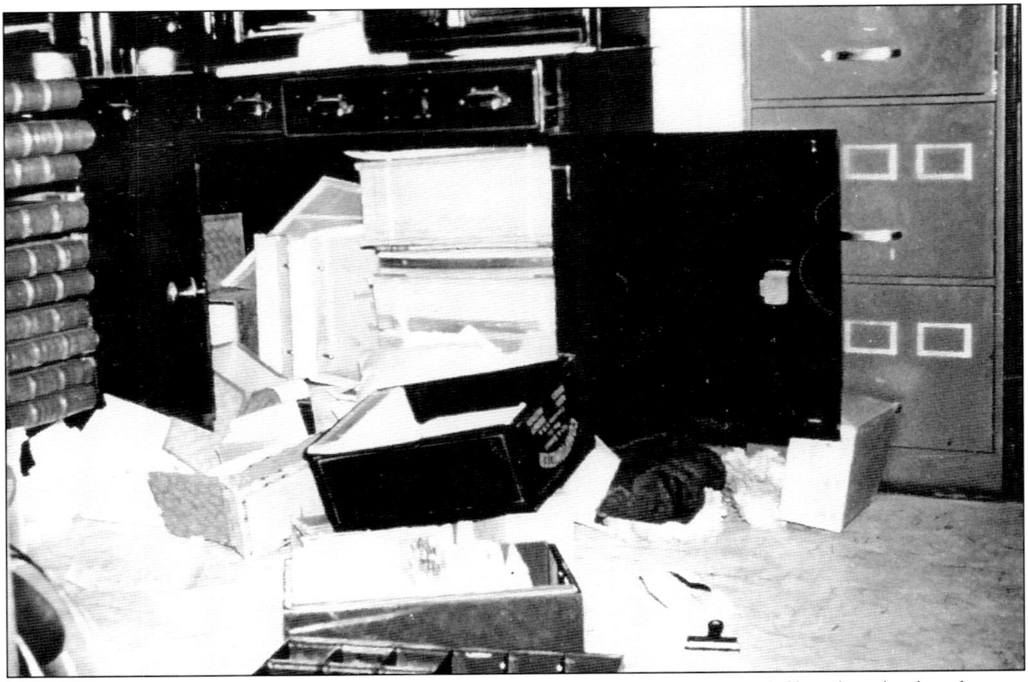

Treasurer's Office Robbery, 1957. The Kiowa County Treasurer's Office has had only one documented robbery in its history. On the morning of Friday, February 8, 1957, Mike Kasza, the custodian, discovered a robbery had taken place sometime the night before. A reported $1,524.80 was found to be missing. The investigation did not discover who was responsible, and the money was never recovered.

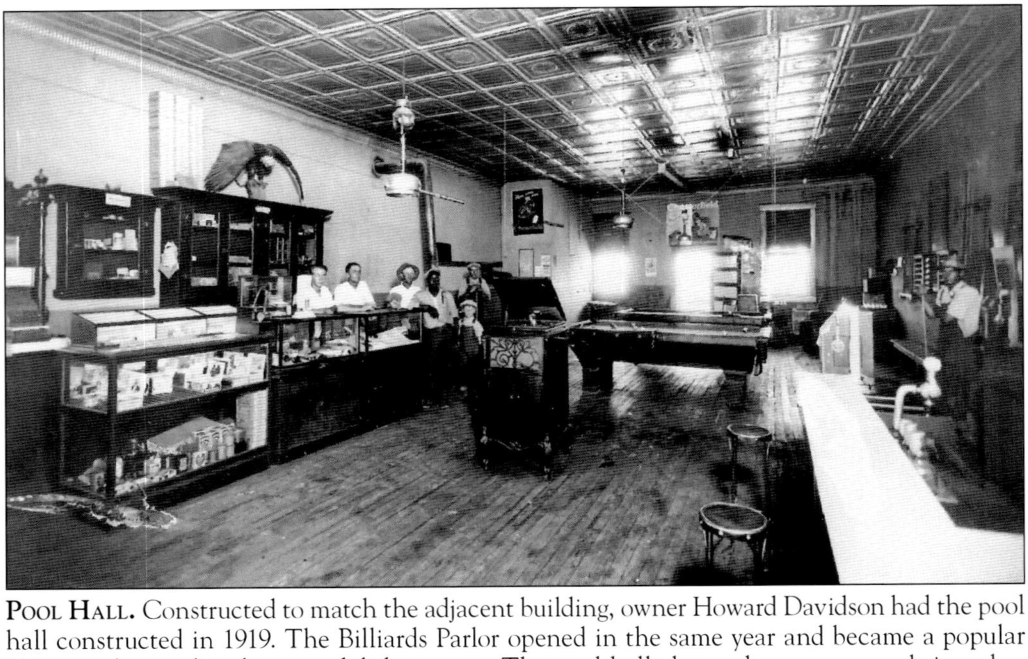

Pool Hall. Constructed to match the adjacent building, owner Howard Davidson had the pool hall constructed in 1919. The Billiards Parlor opened in the same year and became a popular place to play pool and enjoy adult beverages. The pool hall changed owners several times but remained a thriving business until it was sold in 1983. The business was never reopened, and the building has stood empty since that time.

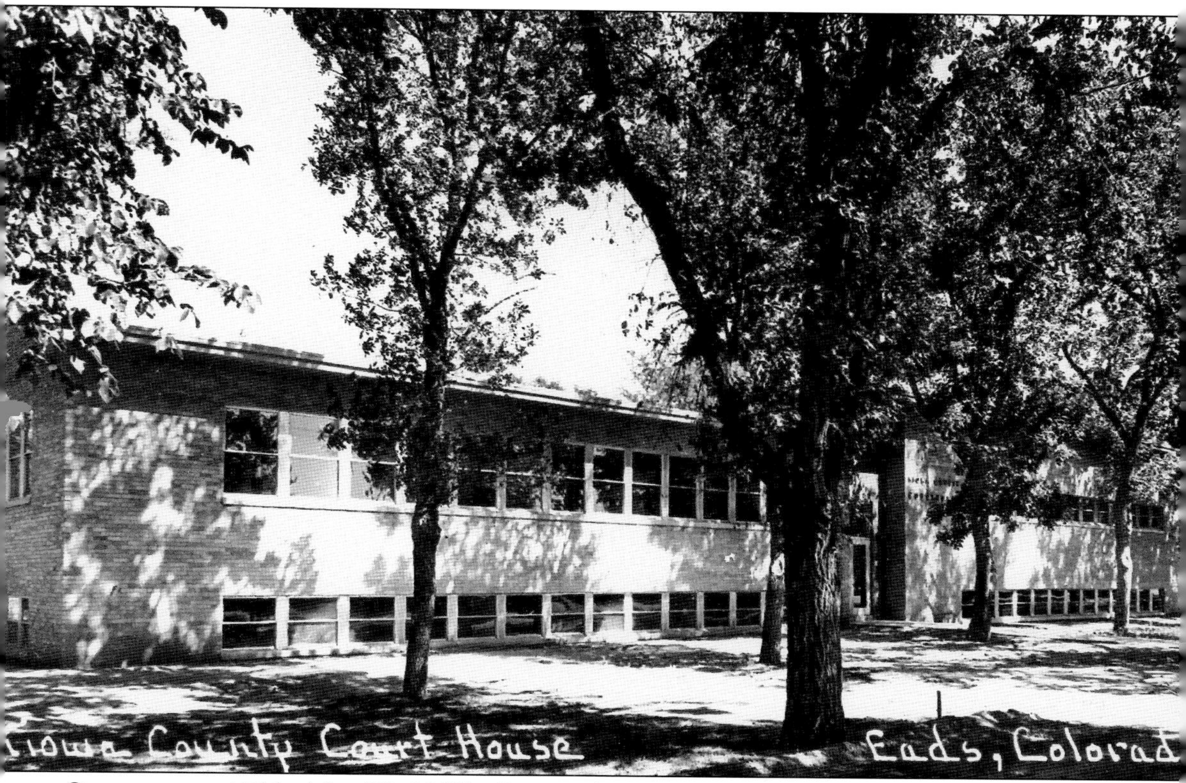

COURTHOUSE, 1956. After World War II, an eight-year mill levy was proposed to pay for the construction of a new, modern courthouse. The mill levy passed, and a $191,000 brick building was constructed just west of the old courthouse. The courthouse was dedicated on September 1, 1956; it houses all county offices and the Kiowa County Public Library.

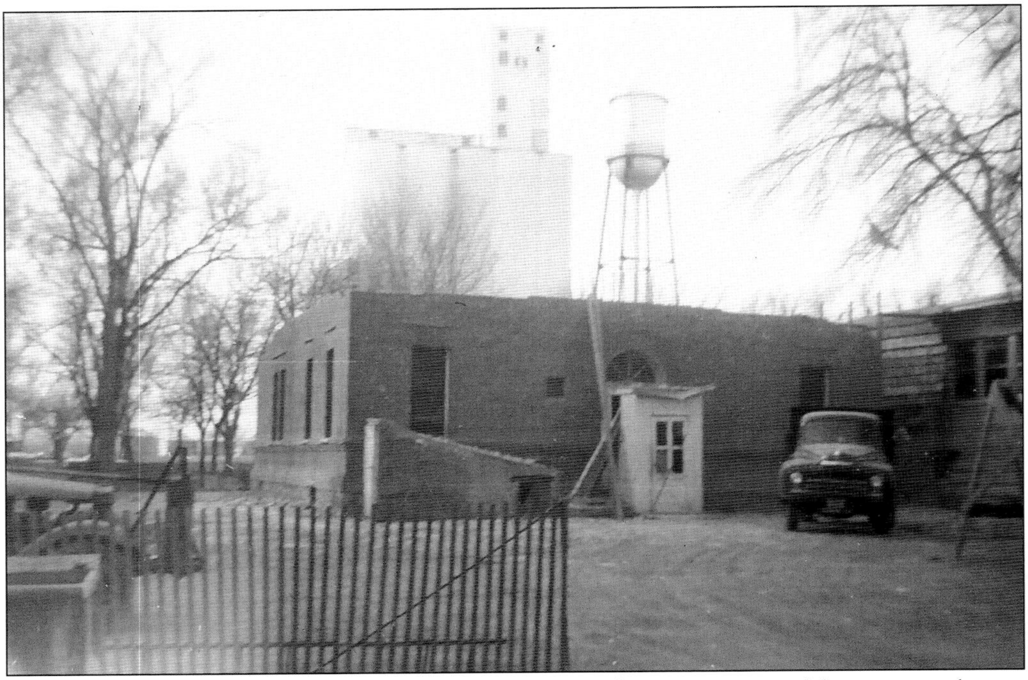

Old Courthouse Demolition, March 1957. Following the construction of the new courthouse, the old courthouse was torn down in 1957.

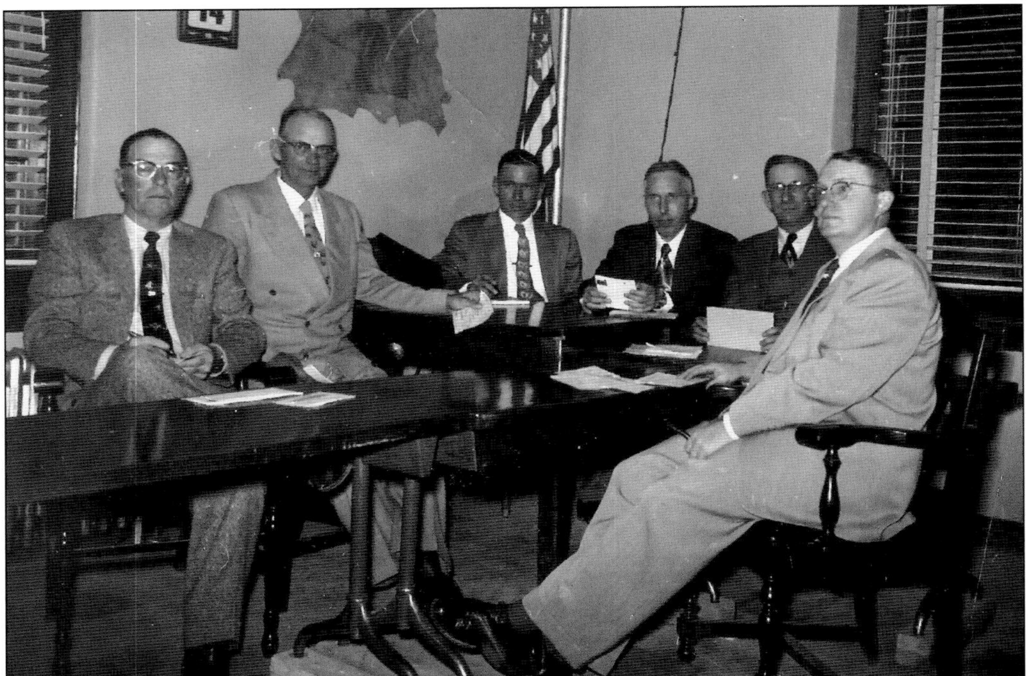

Eads School Board, 1962. In 1962, the Eads School Board approved the construction of a new high school. Pictured from left to right are school board members T. T. Teal, Earl Kelley, Ralph Koch, Robert Anderson (superintendent), Jimmy LaVelle, and Dr. Lyle Graham. The school was dedicated in 1964.

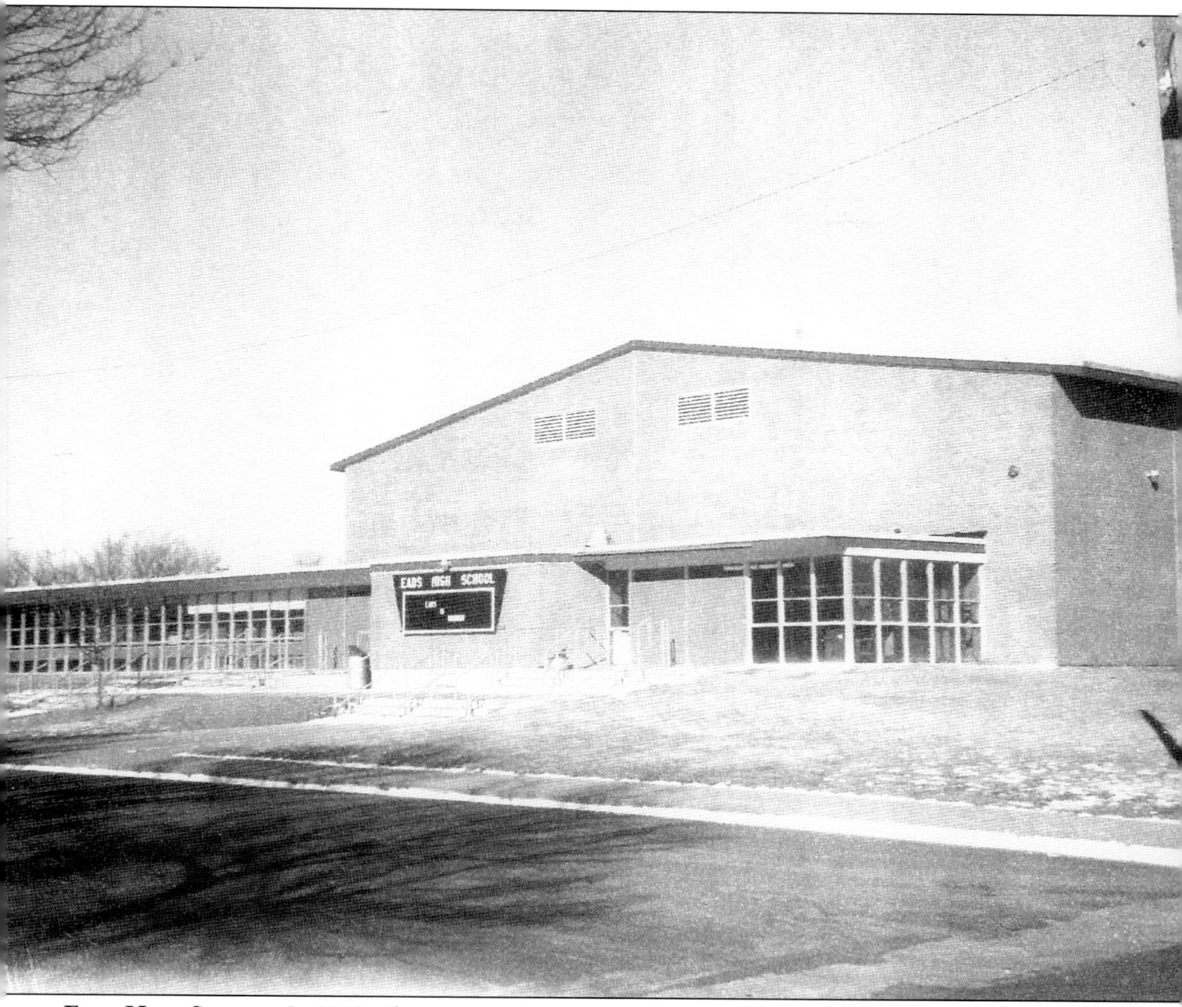

Eads High School. In 1963, after two previous proposals were voted down, Kiowa County voters passed a bond issue to construct a new high school and gymnasium in Eads at the cost of $438,000 and a new elementary school in Haswell for $133,400. The school districts were reorganized and consolidated at that time. The new high school was dedicated on February 9, 1964.

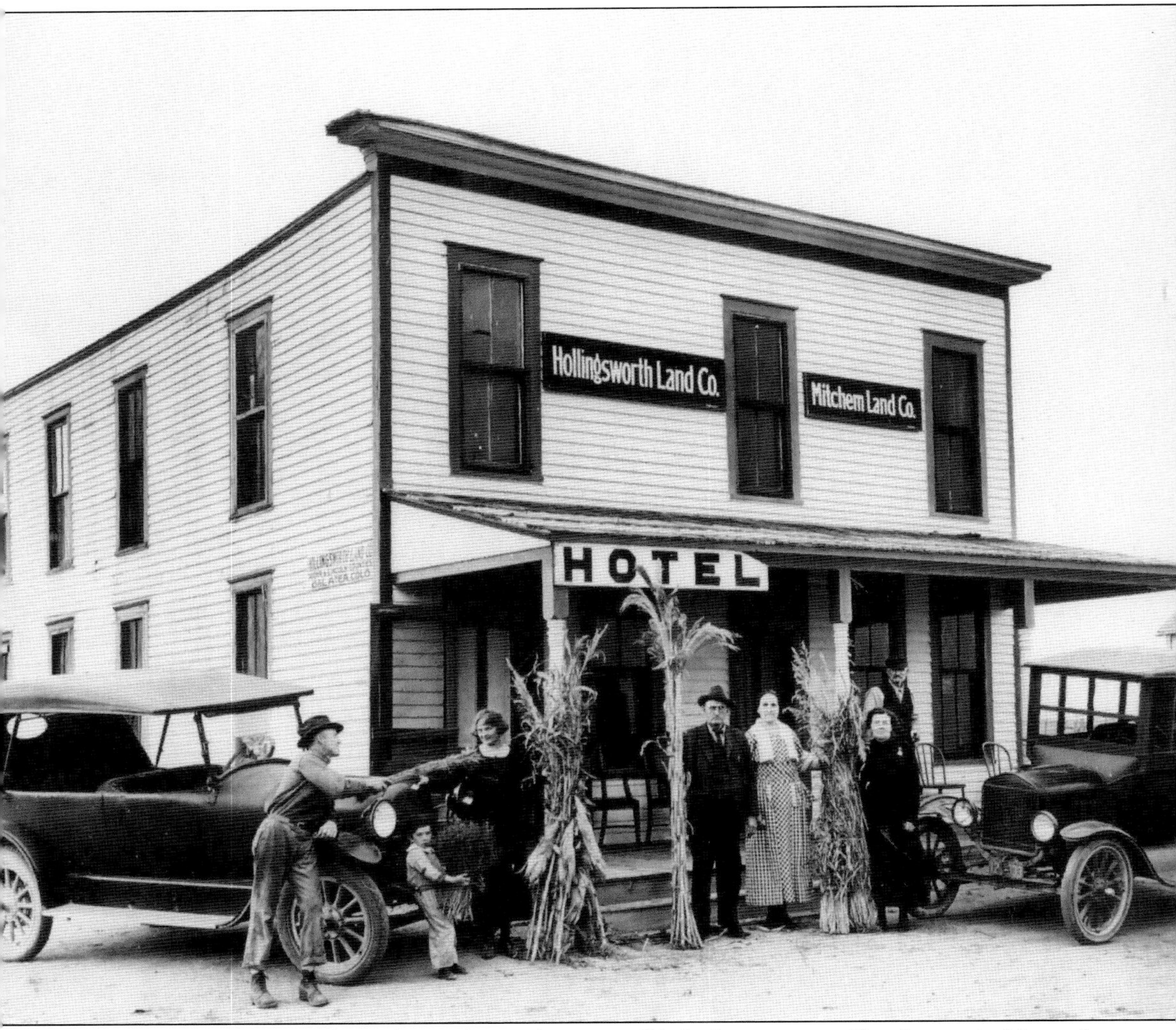

WINDSOR HOTEL. Galatea, located 14 miles west of Eads, became an official town in November 1887 and was plotted by the Pueblo and State Line Company. People who lived in Galatea depended on the train, as it transported many goods in and out of Galatea. By May 1888, Galatea reached its peak population of 330 people. The Windsor Hotel was owned and operated by the Glaspie family, who came to the area in 1887. Visitors could get a meal for 25¢ and a room for 50¢ a night.

MURIETT FAMILY. Pioneer Edith Glaspie Muriett moved to Galatea with her parents, who ran the Windsor Hotel, at age 14 in 1887. She attended school in Galatea and married C. E. Muriett in 1912. Muriett left in 1915, leaving Edith to run their business, Muriett General Merchandise, and raise their son, Boon Best, alone. Fondly known as "Galatea," Edith also ran a filling station, weighed for the elevator, and served as postmistress.

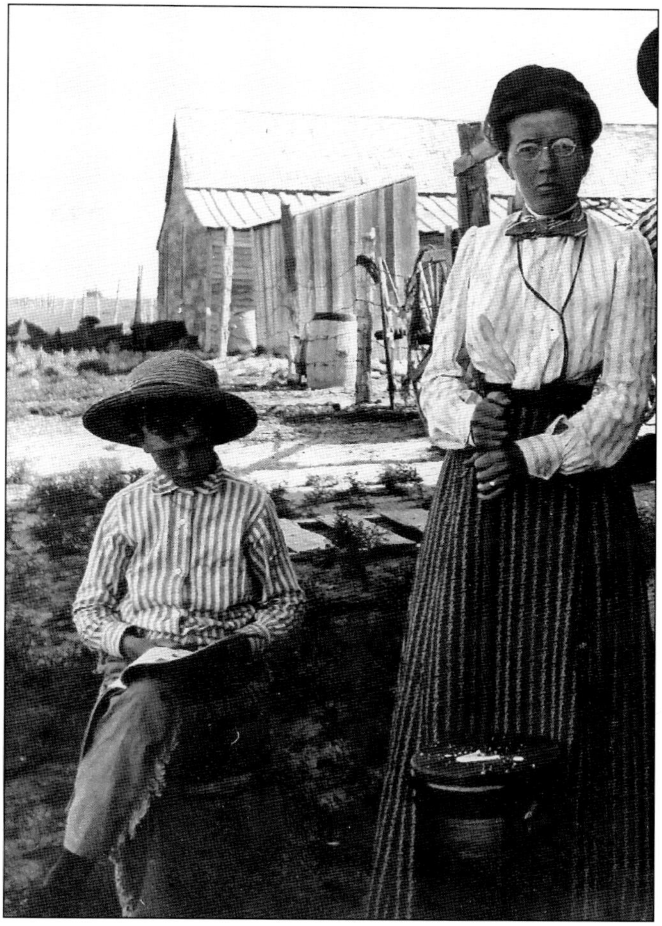

FIRST GALATEA SCHOOL. Kiowa County School District 6 was organized sometime in 1899; Galatea was the center point of this district. By 1917, there were eight schools in the district: Galatea, Buell, Prairie Queen, Blooding, Black Lake, Segregansett, Hide Out, and Weirich. The school in this photograph was destroyed by fire in January 1911.

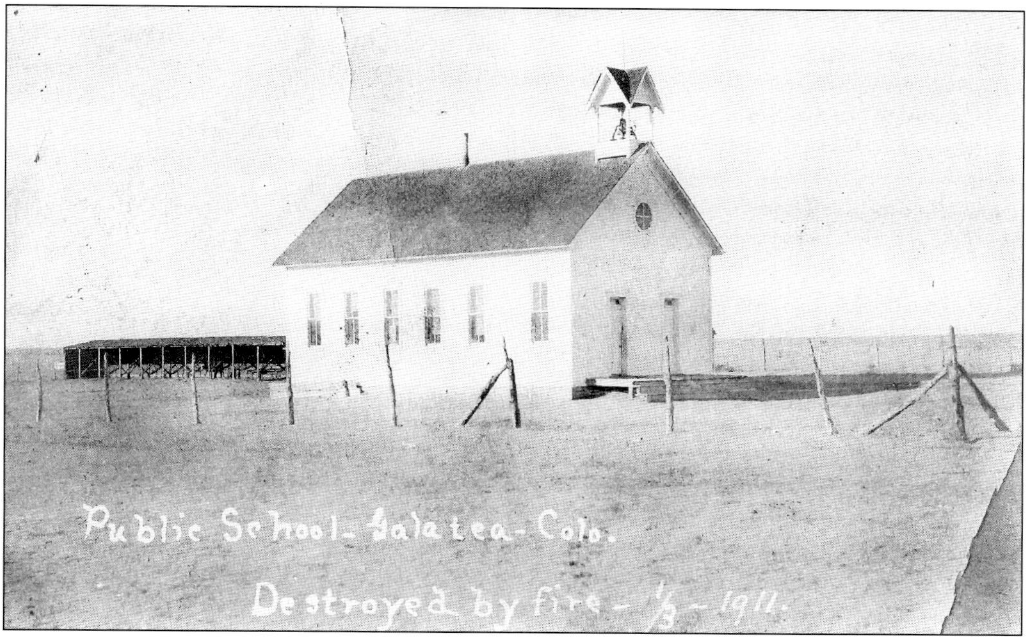

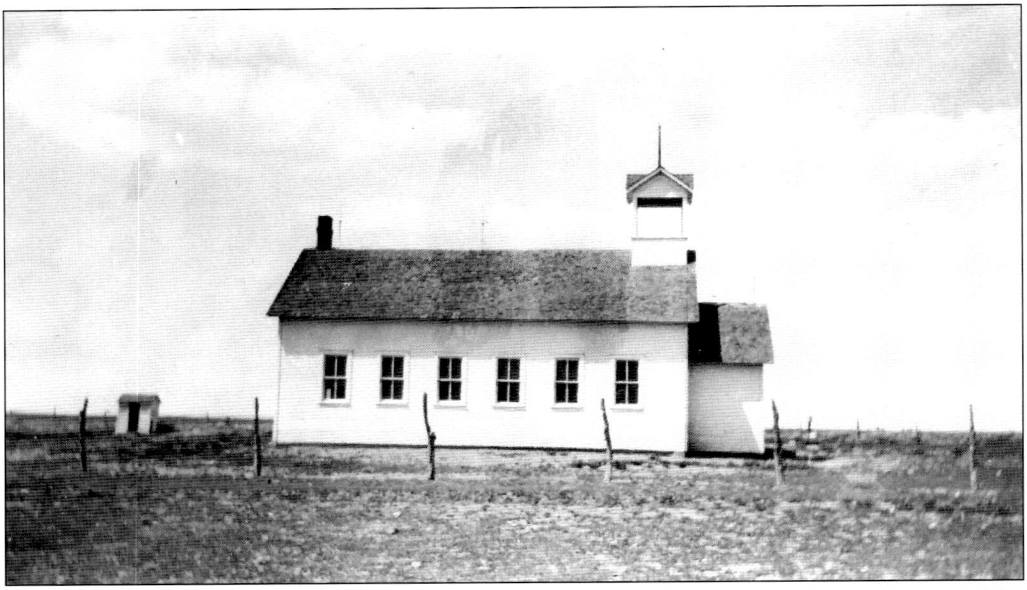

Galatea School. In 1911, a new school was constructed to replace the one that had burned. The two-room school had no water, so students took turns hauling water to school. Students could attend school in Galatea through 10th grade. The Galatea School closed in 1948 and was later moved to Eads for use as a classroom. When the new high school was built in Eads in 1964, the Eads Golf Club purchased the building for use as a clubhouse.

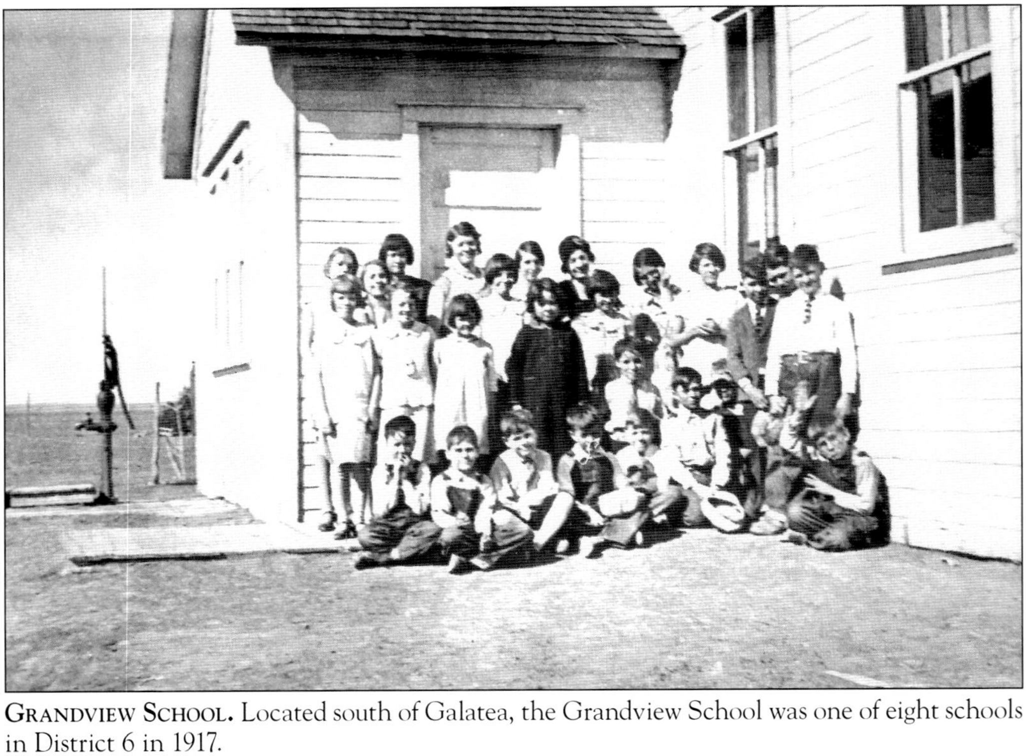

Grandview School. Located south of Galatea, the Grandview School was one of eight schools in District 6 in 1917.

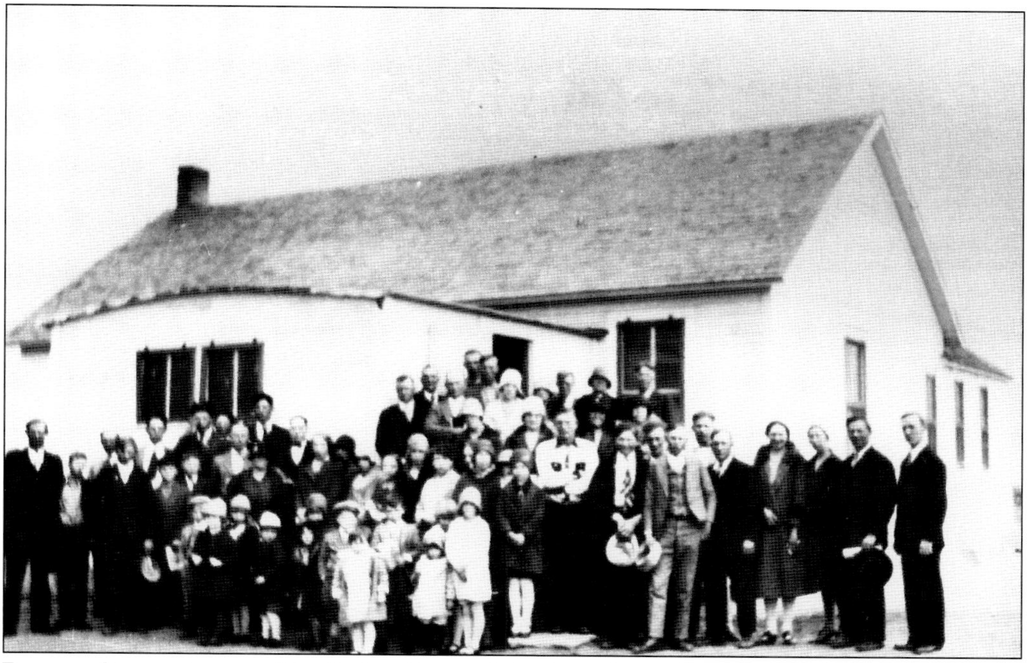

Prairie Queen School. The Prairie Queen School was located north of Galatea. In the 1920s, some of the schools in Kiowa County were centralized as a result of depopulation and lack of water. The Hideout School building was moved to the Prairie Queen site at this time. Belva McDaniel Berry (pictured back row, center) taught at Prairie Queen from 1930 to 1933 and again from 1937 to 1939. The school closed in 1948.

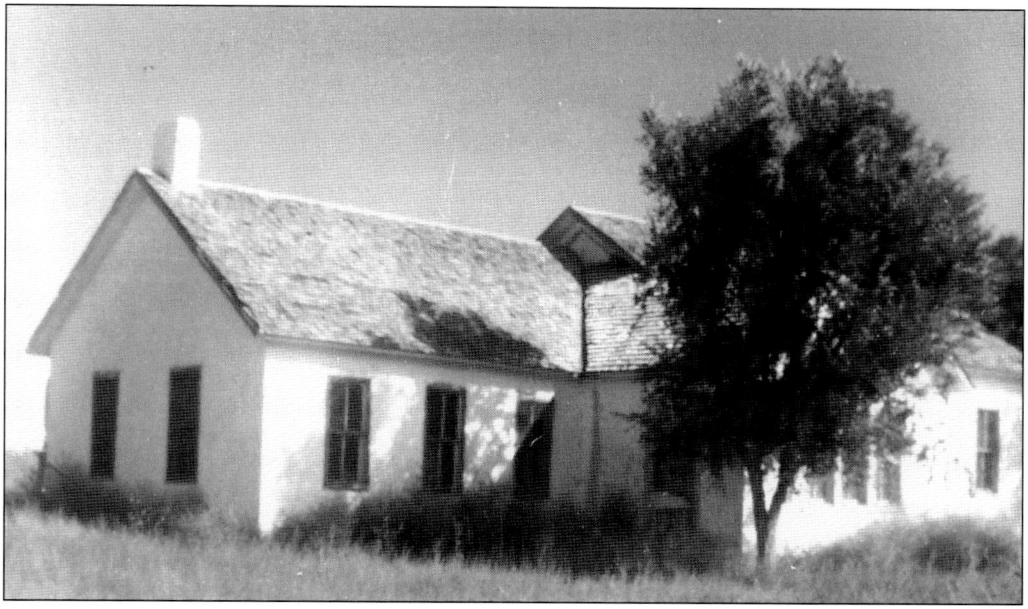

Prairie Center School. District 6 was gradually consolidated. The Segregansett Schoolhouse was renamed Grandview in 1944, and in 1945, it was moved and renamed Prairie Center. Serving as the consolidated school for District 6, students attended the Prairie Center school through eighth grade, until further district consolidation in 1961. In 1965, the school was used as the Prairie Center Community Club.

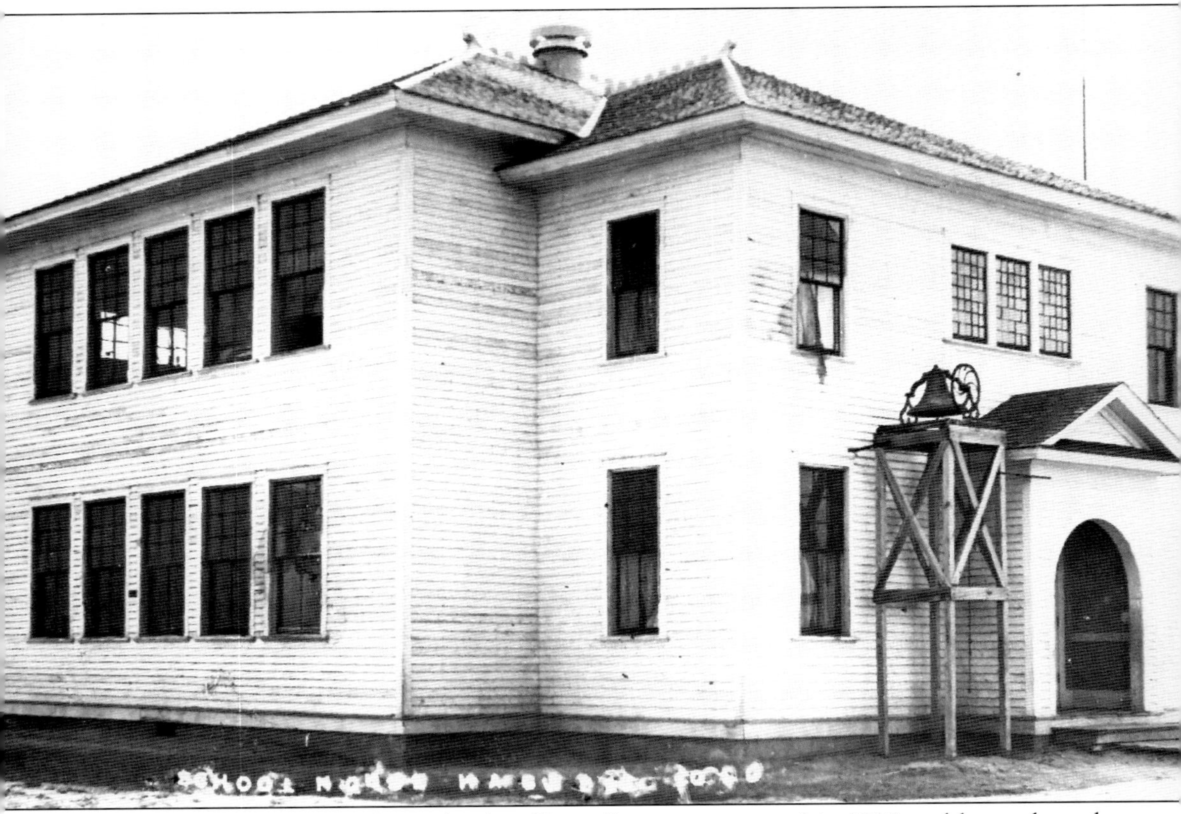

Haswell School. The first school in Haswell was constructed in 1908 and located on the southwest side of town. There was a baseball field in the pasture next to the school, and in the early 1900s, baseball was the most popular sport in Haswell and surrounding communities. The school was torn down in the 1960s when the new school in Haswell was constructed.

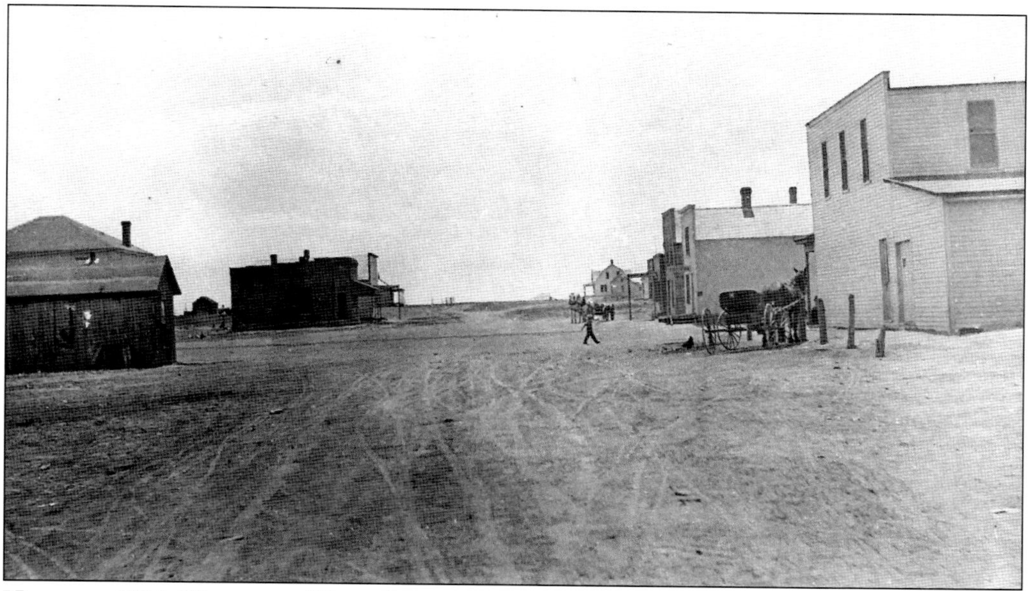

Haswell, 1910. The town of Haswell was not much more than a railroad stop until 1907. The first store was constructed at that time, and several other businesses followed in the next few years.

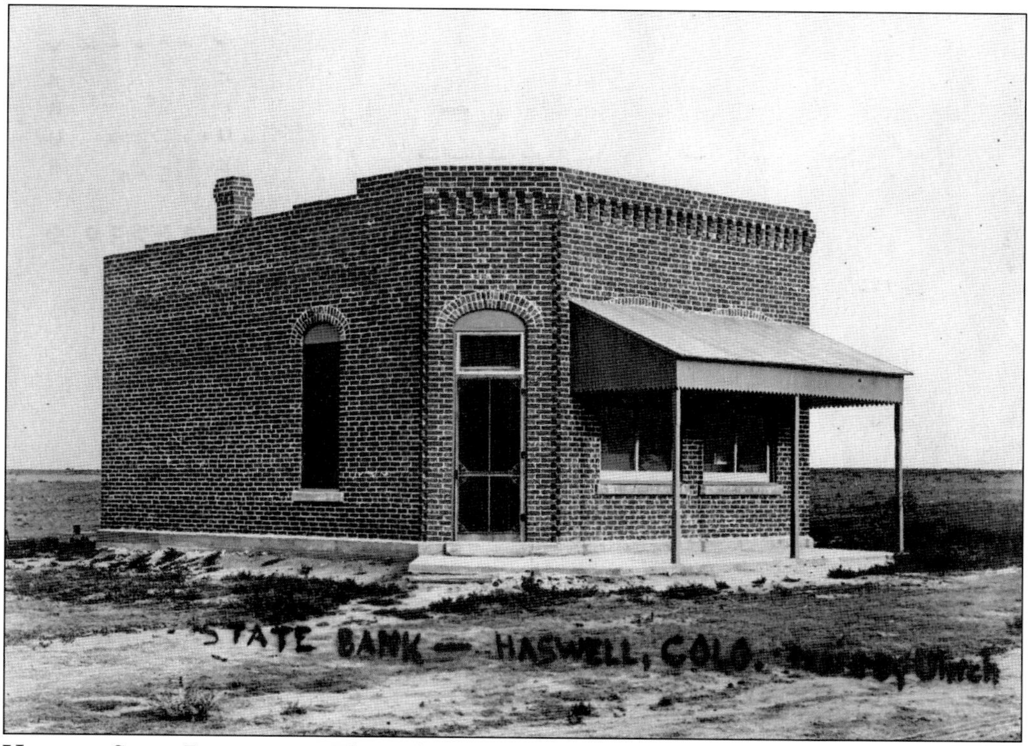

Haswell State Bank, 1909. The Colorado State Bank of Haswell opened in April 1909 with Sylvanus G. Hogue as president. The bank operated until April 15, 1929, when it closed its doors as a result of the difficult economy. John Rebel purchased the bank building, but it was vacant until 1963, when it was converted to a post office.

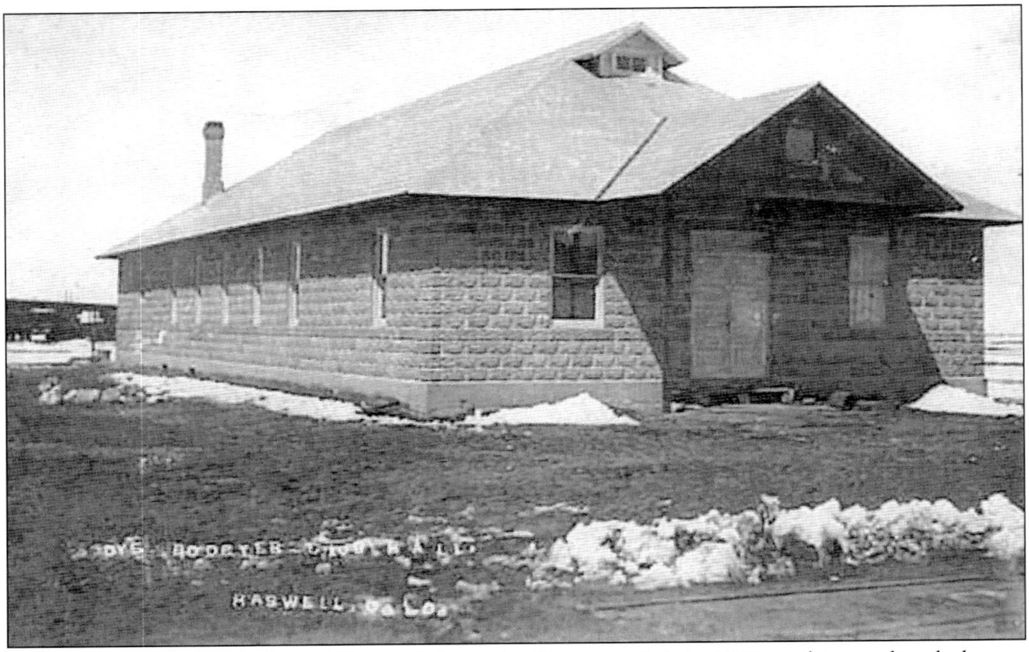

Booster Club. The ladies of Haswell formed a Booster Club in 1911 and immediately began fund-raising for a recreation building. The construction of the building was completed in 1915, and the Booster Club served the Haswell community into the 1980s. The Booster Club, a property listed on the Colorado State Register of Historic Places in 1996, was torn down in 2002.

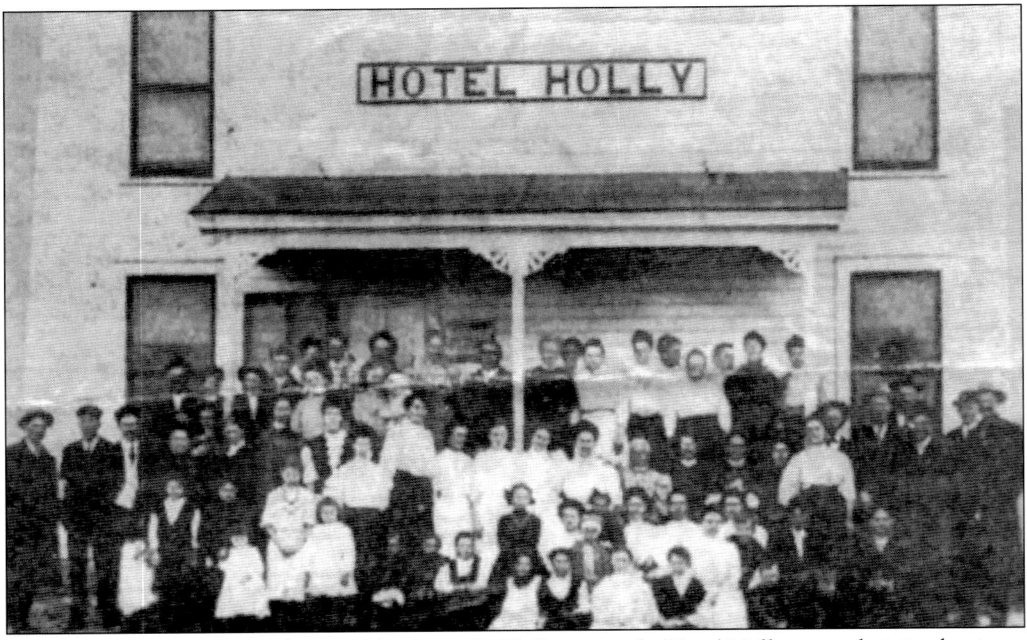

Hotel Holly. Constructed in 1907 by Acquilla Hollingsworth, Hotel Holly was a thriving business in Haswell for more than 60 years. Many members of the Haswell community operated the hotel throughout the years, including the Hogues, Rebels, and Covalts. The hotel was the center of social activities in town as well as a nice place for boarders, travelers, and teachers to stay.

Sands Building. Dr. G. M. Sands arrived in Haswell in 1911. He constructed a stone structure with the intention of opening a hospital in Haswell; however, he ended up using the building as a drugstore and doctor's office. The Sands family moved near Trinidad, Colorado, in 1916. The building was later used as a county shop in Haswell.

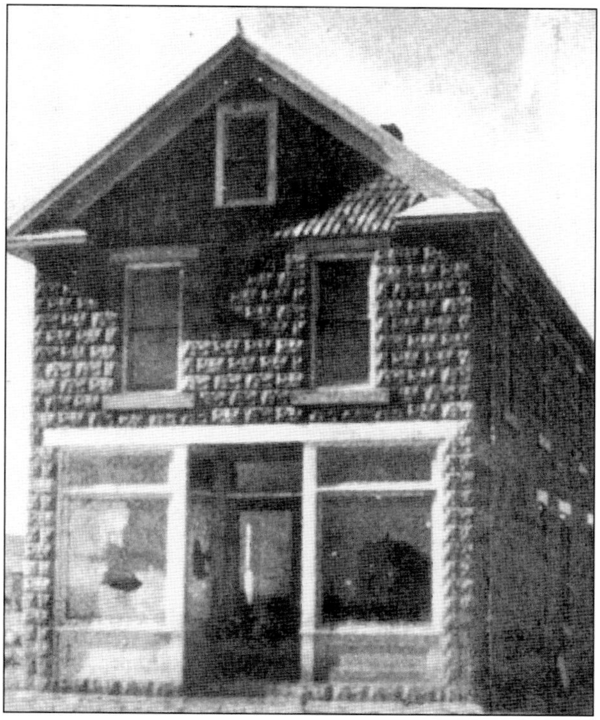

Haswell Jail. Constructed in 1921, the concrete Haswell jail is small—just 14 feet by 16 feet—and one of the few public buildings ever built in Haswell. Town marshal John Rebel occasionally used the "nation's smallest jail" in the 1920s, but by the 1940s, it had fallen out of use.

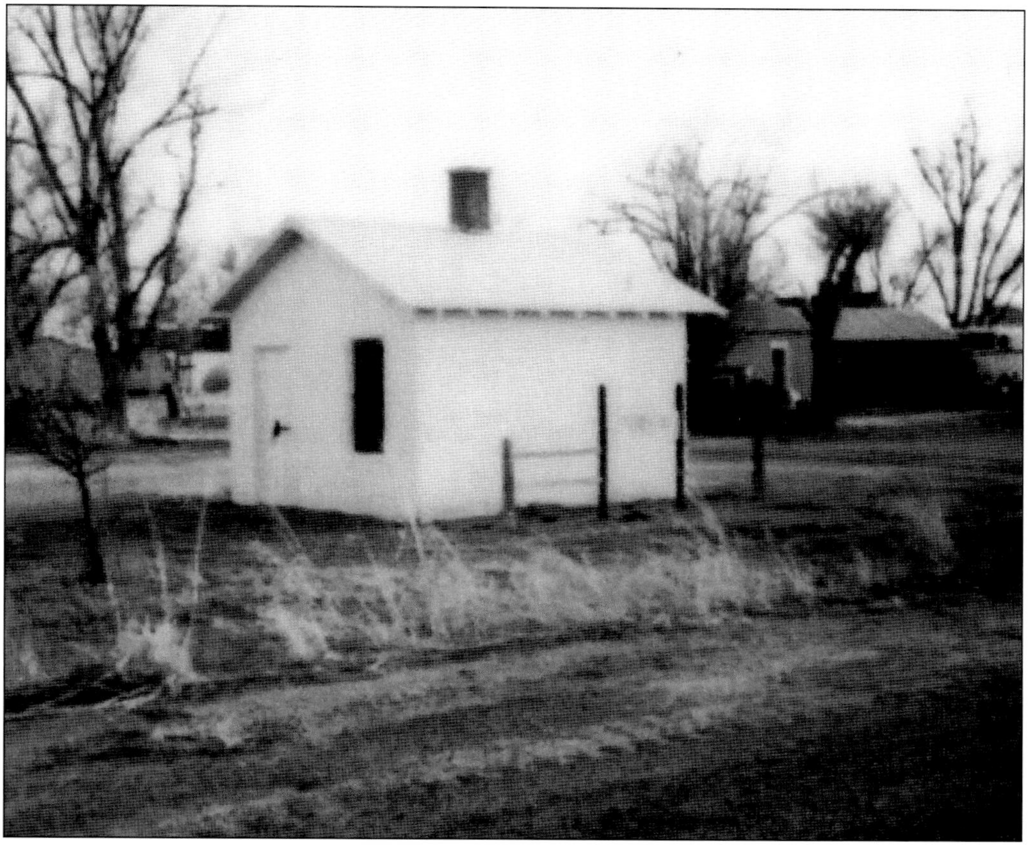

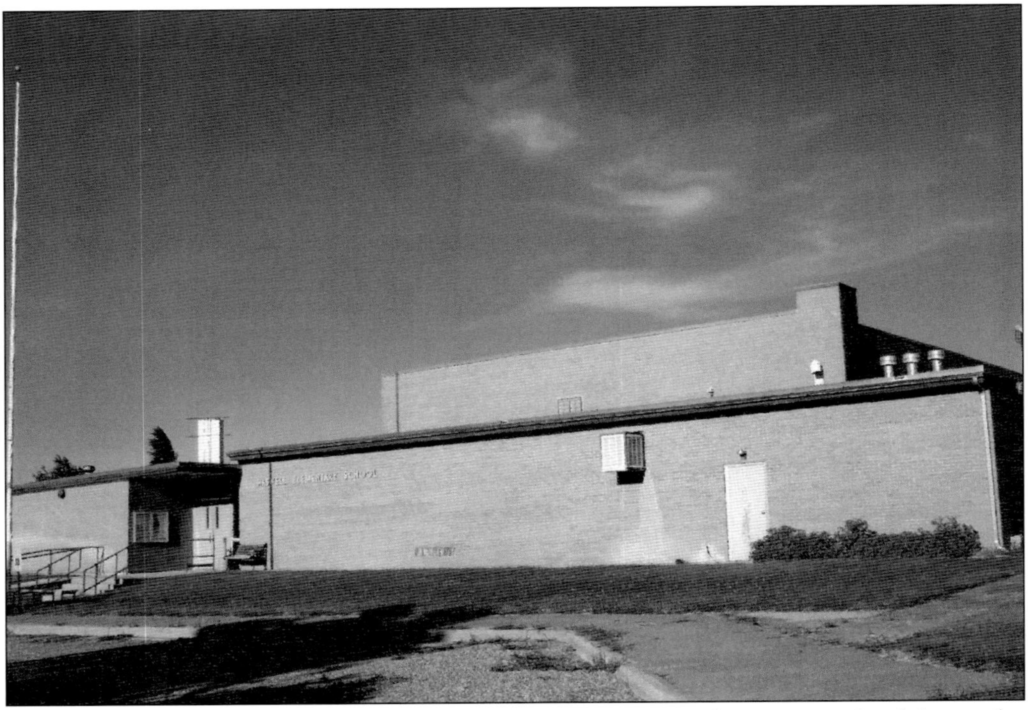

Haswell School. After a bond issue passed in 1963, a new elementary school for grades kindergarten through eight was constructed in Haswell. The school was dedicated on February 2, 1964, and consolidated the schools in Arlington, Prairie Center, and Haswell. The Haswell School closed in 1992 due to budget cuts; however, it continues to serve Haswell as a community center. (Photograph courtesy Tom Simmons, Front Range Research Associates, Inc.)

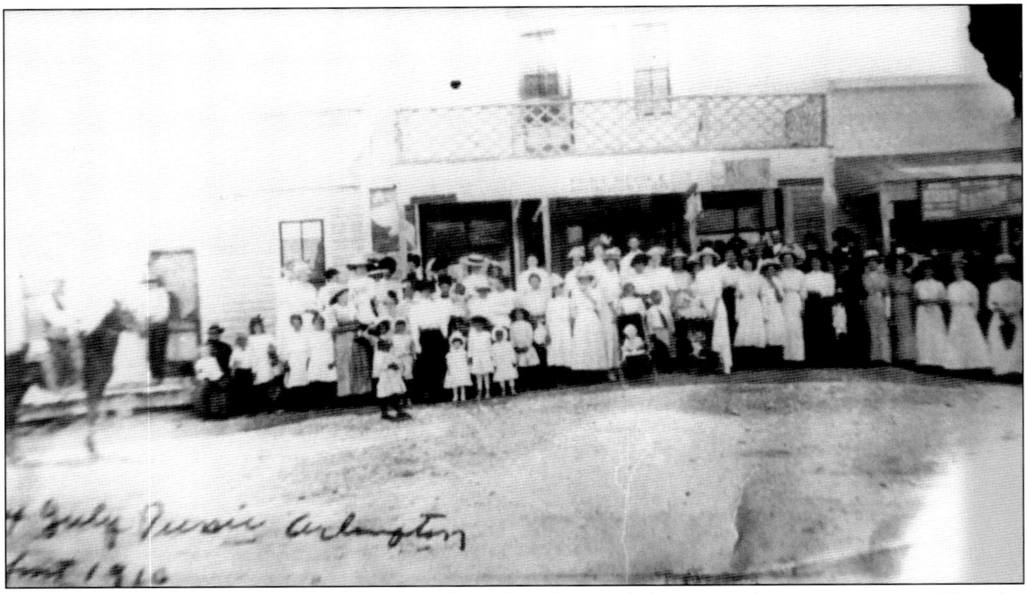

Arlington, 1910. Arlington citizens gathered in front of the general store and post office for this Fourth of July photograph in 1910. Several pioneers, including John S. Booher, founded Arlington Springs in 1887 before the railroad was built. The Pueblo and State Line Company founded Joliet, but the post office kept the name Arlington.

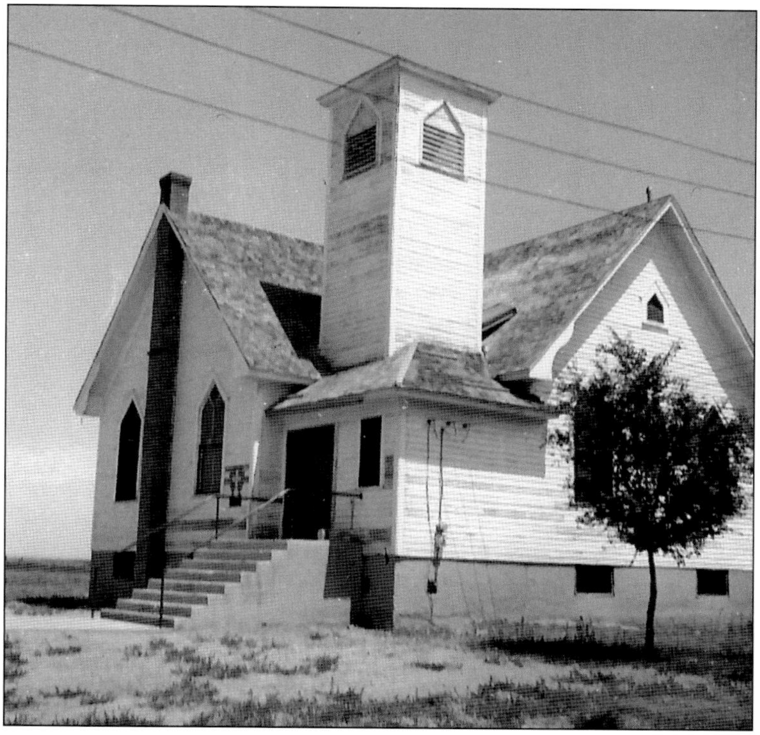

United Brethren Church. The United Brethren Church in Arlington was constructed in 1916. It was the only church ever built in the town. When the Evangelical and United Brethren Churches merged in 1951, the church was repaired and rededicated. In 1967, the church was relocated to the Colorado Boy's Ranch in La Junta, where it is still in use.

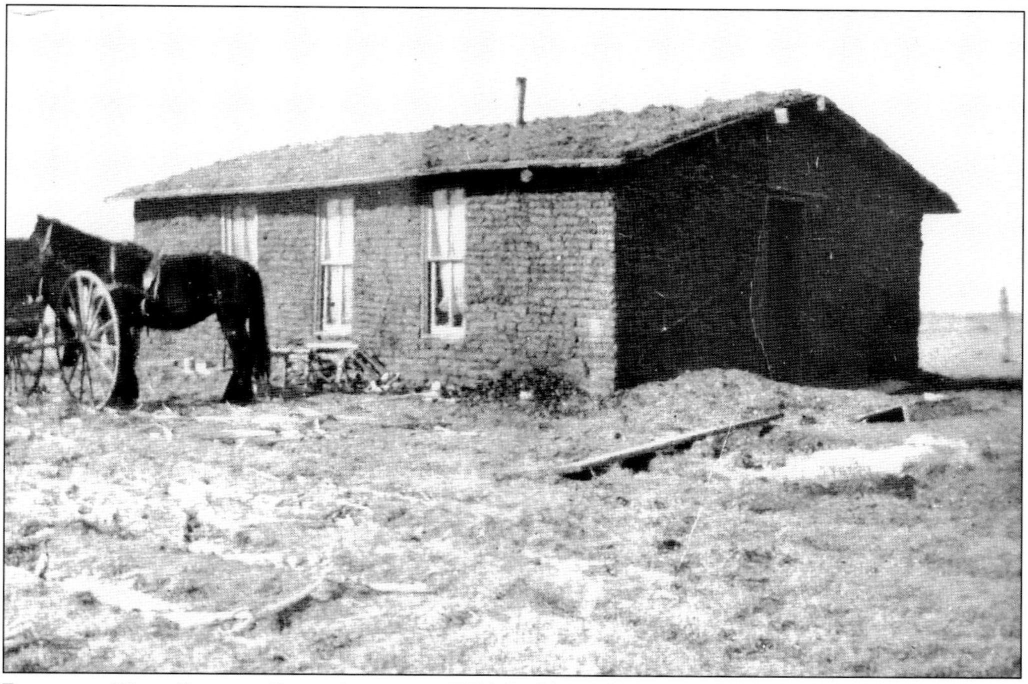

Pleasant View School. Better known as "Old Soddie," Pleasant View School was constructed by volunteer labor in 1914–1915. Located 9 miles north and 2.5 miles west of the town of Arlington, the school was also the center of community gathering: church, Sunday school, Literary Society, special parties, Red Cross meetings, and programs and other community activities. Alme Sires Johnston's horse, Old Faithful Polly, transported her to and from school.

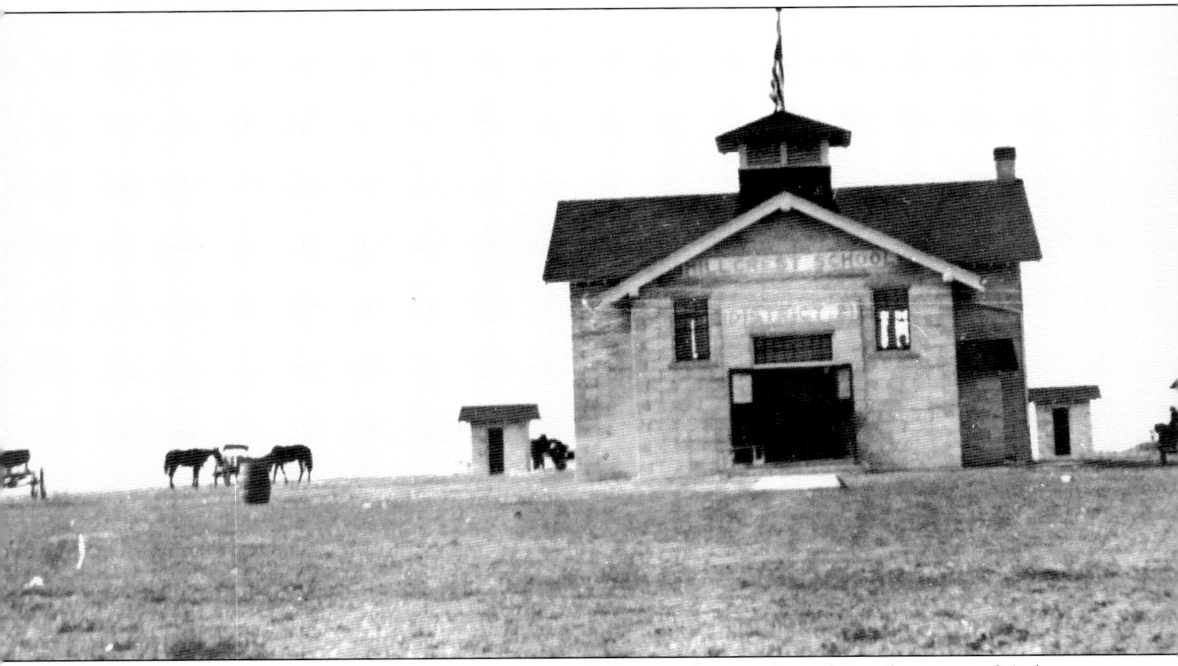

HILLCREST SCHOOL. Built in 1918 on top of a hill 10 miles north and 2 miles west of Arlington, the stone Hillcrest School replaced Old Soddie. Like its predecessor, the school was the center of community activities; it was one of seven schools in the Arlington area. It also had two outbuildings, a garage, and a set of swings for a playground.

Five

The Towner Bus Tragedy

On Thursday, March 26, 1931, snow fell softly in large flakes as the students of Pleasant Hill School awoke before dawn to perform chores. Carl Miller, the school bus driver, began picking up passengers as ominous clouds darkened the sky. The schoolteachers, Maude Moser and F. R. Freiday, decided to send the children back home. As the 20 pupils reboarded the bus, the snow and wind increased to blizzard conditions. Miller realized that time was of the essence, so he took a shortcut to get the children to safety.

The trail road soon disappeared beneath the snow, and Miller was unable to see. The bus became stuck in a ditch, and the engine died. Miller and the children spent the remainder of Thursday in the bus, moving to stay warm and burning their schoolbooks in a water pail. After keeping the children awake through the night to keep them warm, Miller went for help on Friday morning. The blizzard still raged as Miller clung to a barbed-wire fence, hoping it would lead him to a nearby home. The older students tried to keep the younger ones moving and alert, but by afternoon, three children had perished. The remaining 17 suffered from exhaustion and exposure.

On Friday morning, parents discovered their loved ones were on the bus rather than safe at school. A frantic search ensued, and worried fathers H. A. "Bud" Untiedt and Dave H. Stonebraker found the bus late Friday afternoon. They loaded the children into a wagon and took them to Andy and Fern Reinert's home half a mile away. Two children died soon after reaching the Reinert's. Parents and neighbors worked through the night to keep the survivors alive. Word spread, and a doctor battled through the snowdrifts from Holly. The children later were flown by airplane to Maxwell Hospital in Lamar, Colorado. Late Saturday afternoon, Miller's body was found 3.5 miles south of the bus, his frozen arms outstretched.

The Towner Bus Tragedy was a heartbreaking incident for the families and the surrounding communities. It gained national attention and resulted in reforms for school releases during inclement weather, bus upgrades, and the addition of two-way radios to all busses. The 15 survivors were honored for their courage, and a monument was erected at the Holly cemetery at the head of the graves of the deceased.

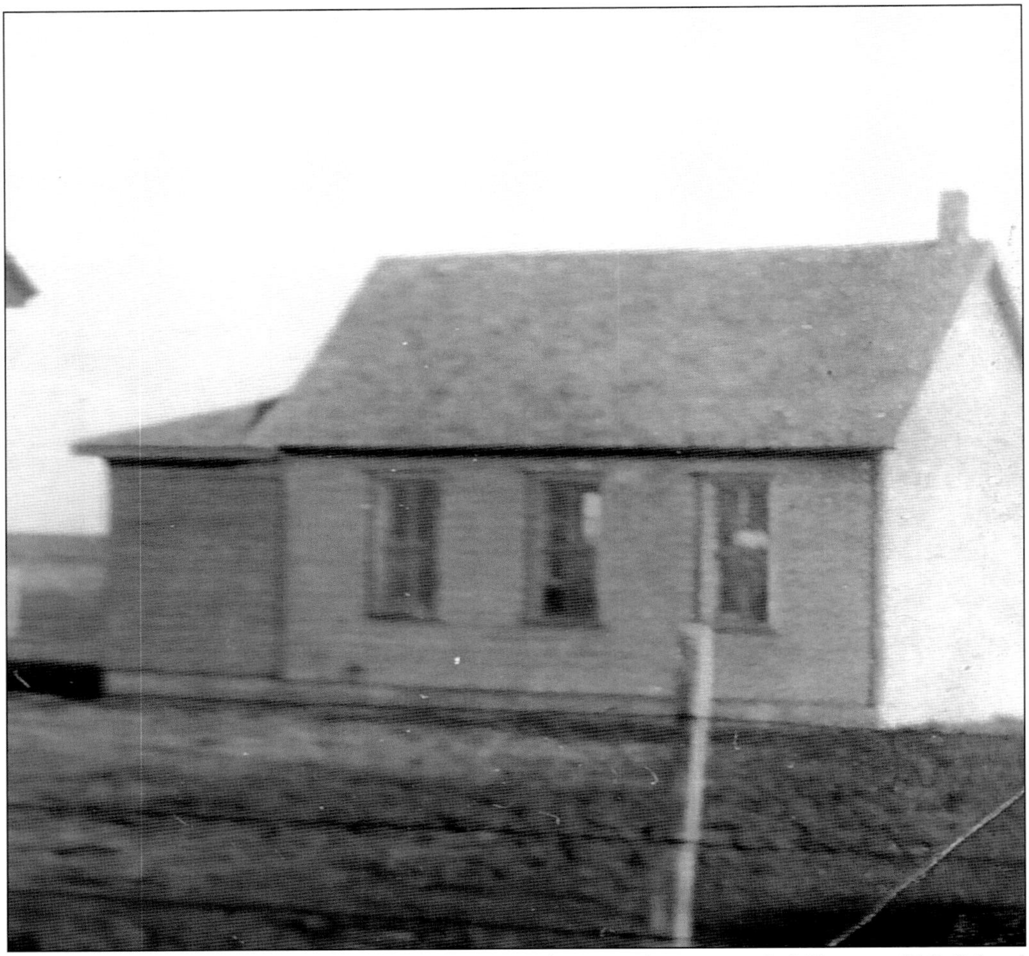

The Pleasant Hill Schoolhouse. Approximately 30 students attended Pleasant Hill School in 1931; grades one through six were in a one-room schoolhouse and grades seven through eight were in another one-room schoolhouse nearby. Maude Moser and F. R. Freiday taught arithmetic, English, history, geography, health, civics, and languages as well as honesty, independence, and integrity. Classes began at 9:00 a.m., and students were dismissed at 4:00 p.m. The school was also occasionally used for Sunday worship and community dinners and activities.

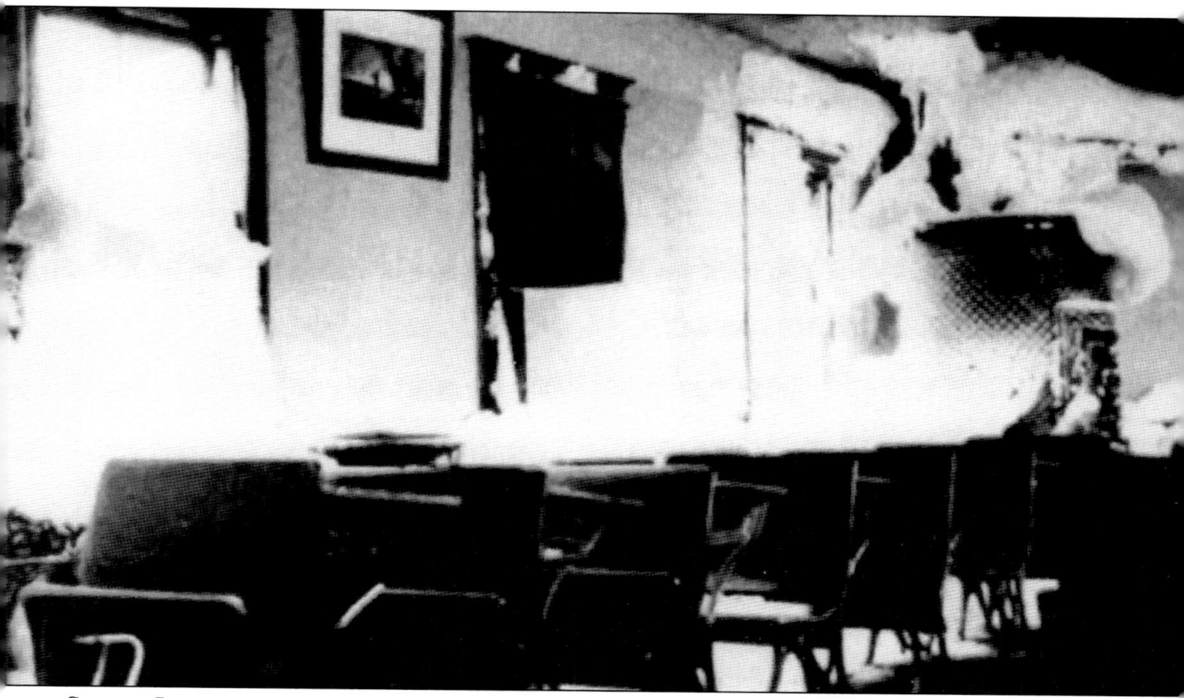

School Interior after Blizzard. During the blizzard, the fierce wind drove snow through small gaps in the wooden window frames and into the schoolhouse. Ernie Johnson, Dave Stonebraker, and Bud Untiedt discovered this scene when they went to the schoolhouse to get their children. Freiday was stranded at the school during the blizzard.

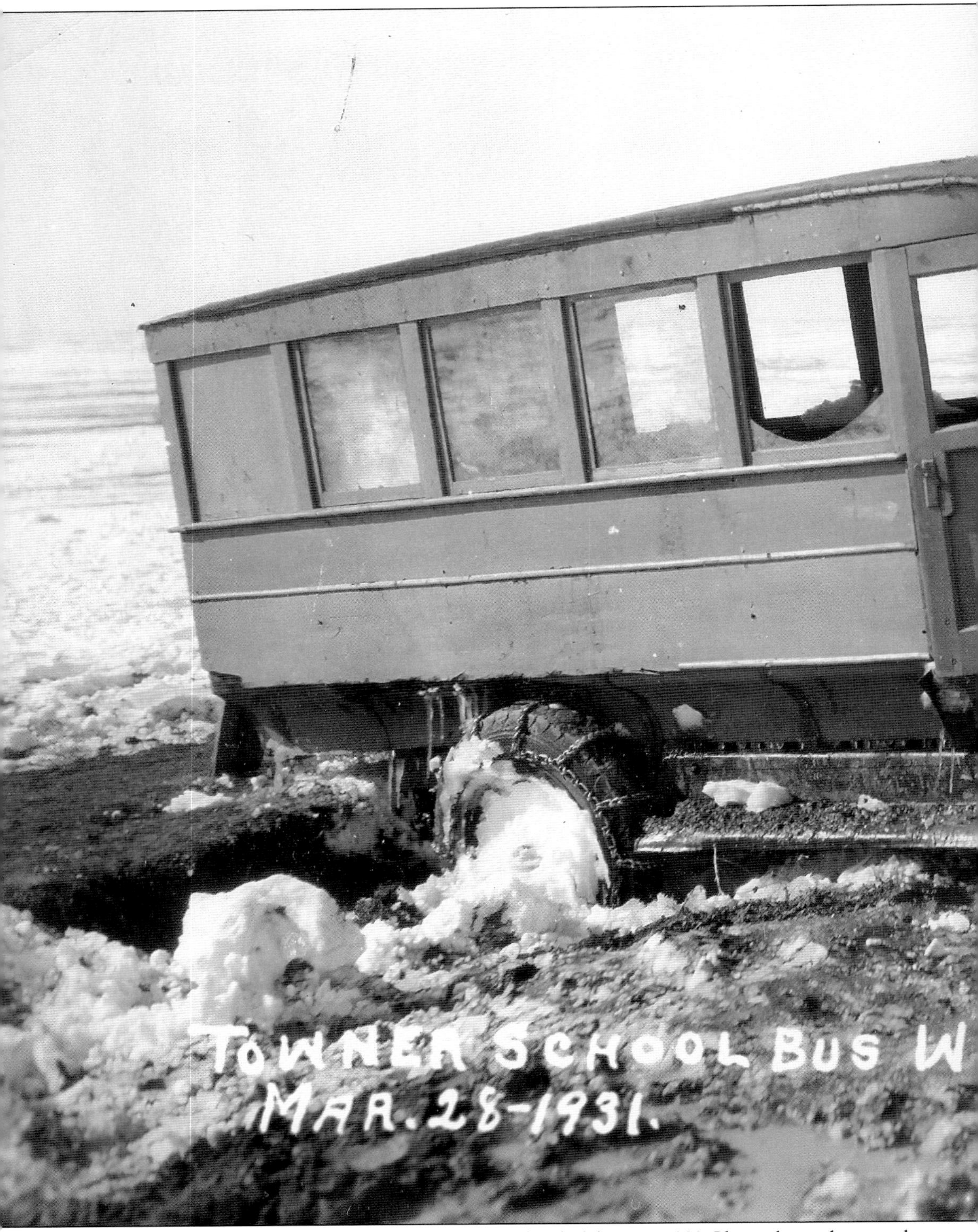

The Towner School Bus. Carl Miller drove a make-shift bus—a 1929 Chevrolet with a wooden frame with windows attached to the truck bed—to transport the children to and from school. The children pushed the wooden benches to the side to allow space for them to move around

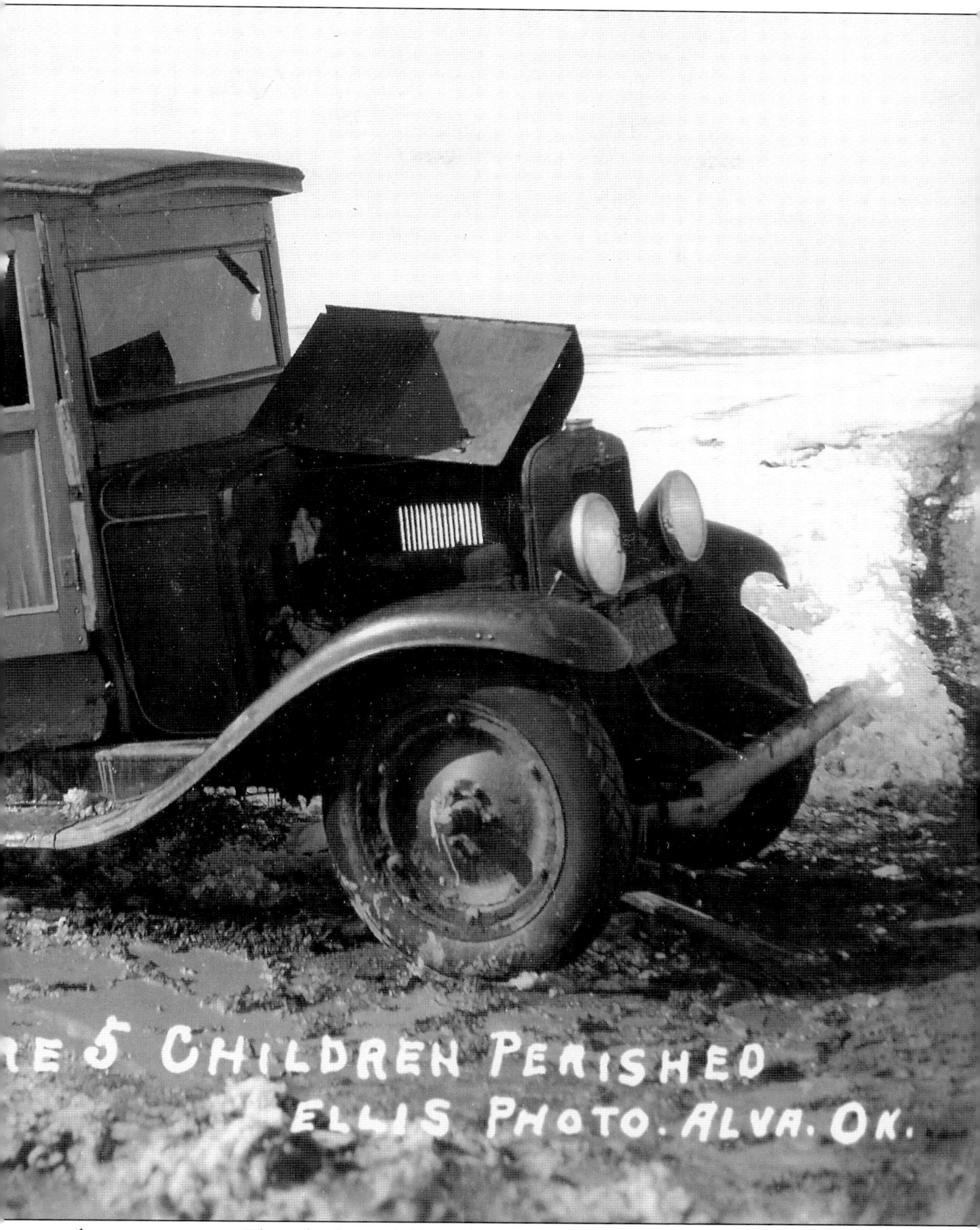

and try to stay warm. They also burned their schoolbooks in an effort to stay warm, but the bus filled with smoke. The children were trapped in the bus for 32 hours.

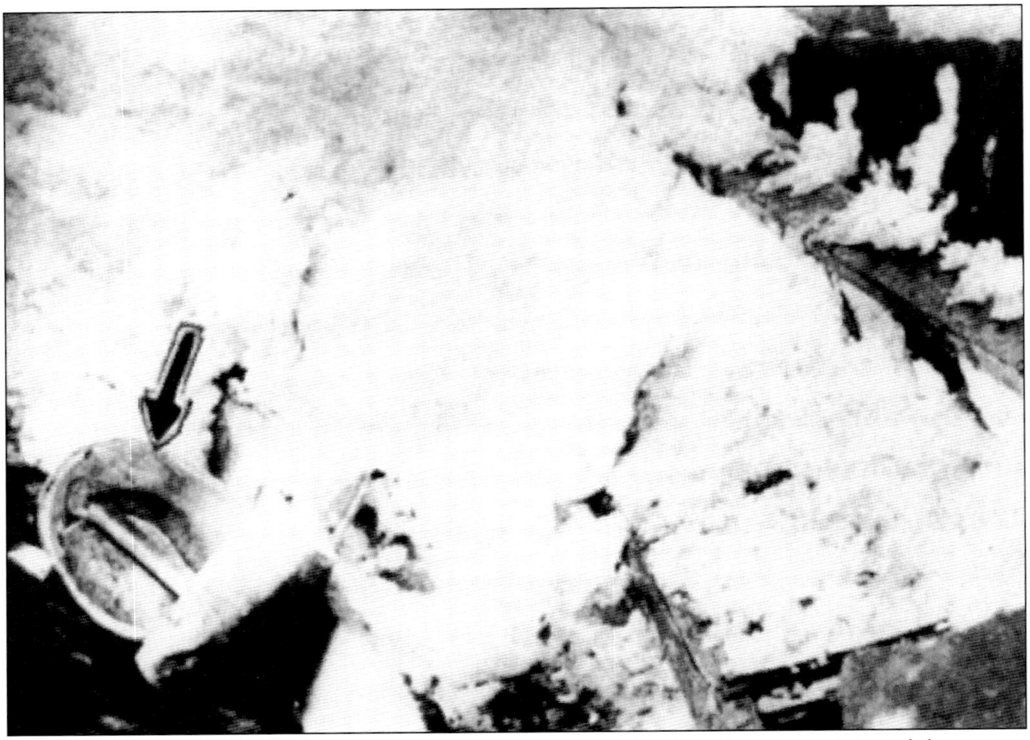

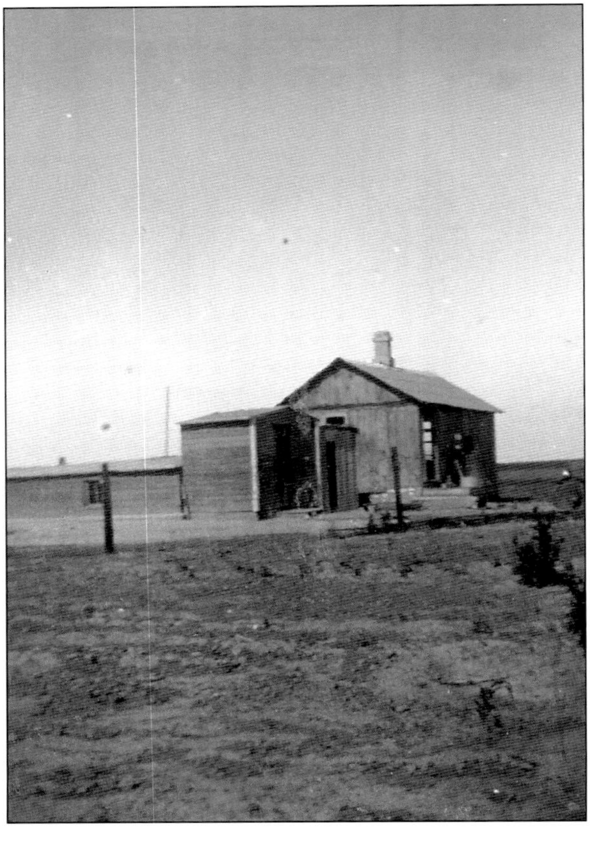

The Bus Interior. One of the back windows was broken and had been patched with cardboard; during the blizzard the cardboard blew out and caused the back of the bus to fill with snow.

Brown Home. The Browns were Carl Miller's first stop on his bus route. The children of Elmer and Margaret Brown were Rosemary, 13; Maxine, 8; and Robert, 11. While Rosemary and Maxine survived the tragedy, Bobbie perished on the bus. Rosemary Brown did not speak of the tragedy for years; however, she wrote her account of the event in the 1989 *Centennial History of Kiowa County*. She said, "Being children, as we were, we were not fully aware of the dangers we were facing, so we didn't panic as adults might have. Each of us did what we could, and by God's grace, some of us survived."

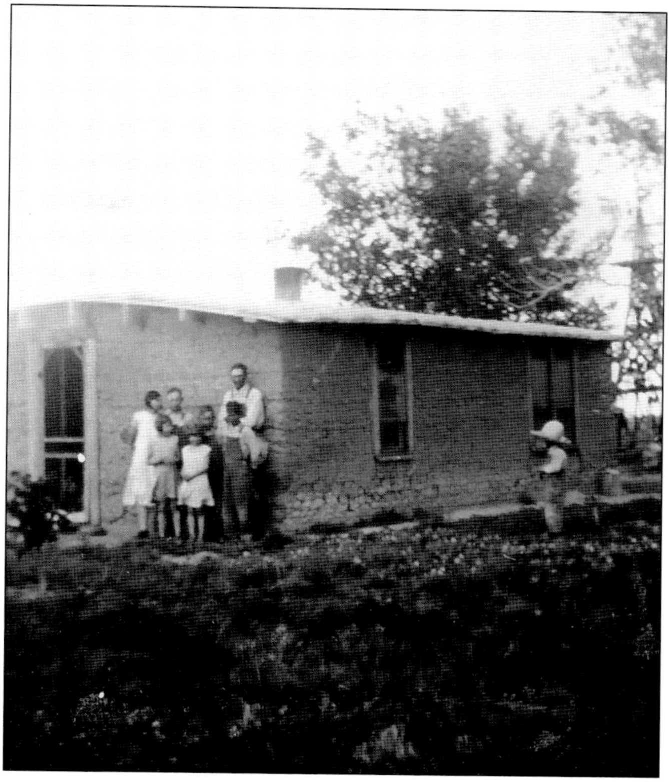

The Huffaker Family. In 1931, Reuben and Bessie Huffaker had nine children, but only six were school age. Their home was Carl Miller's second stop, and he picked up Alice, 14; Charles, 13; Carl, 11; Max, 10; Lena, 9; and Laura, 7. All six Huffaker children survived the blizzard, although Alice's hands were frostbitten. Looking back on the event, Charles Huffaker remarked that all of the children probably would have died in half an hour if H. A. "Bud" Untiedt and Dave Stonebraker had not arrived to rescue them. Exhausted and hungry, the children had decided to lie down and rest just before they were rescued.

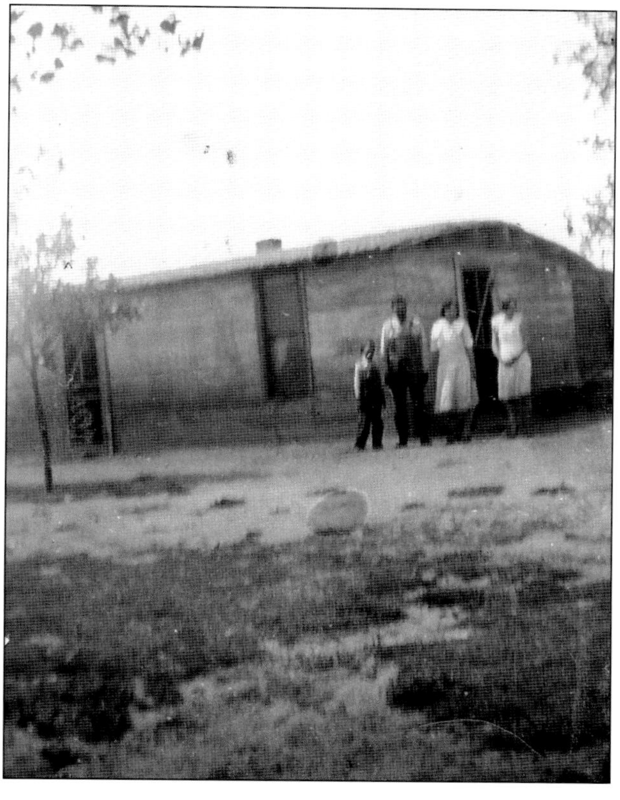

Frost Home. Miller picked up the Frost children, Eunice, 14, and Leland, 7, at his third stop. The Frost and Huffaker children were cousins, and Leland was the youngest child on the bus. Fern Reinert was the daughter of Claude and Mary Frost; she had a sister, brother, and six cousins on the bus. Both Eunice and Leland survived the tragedy. Leland fought in France during World War II; he was wounded on September 16, 1944, and died in England on October 6, 1944.

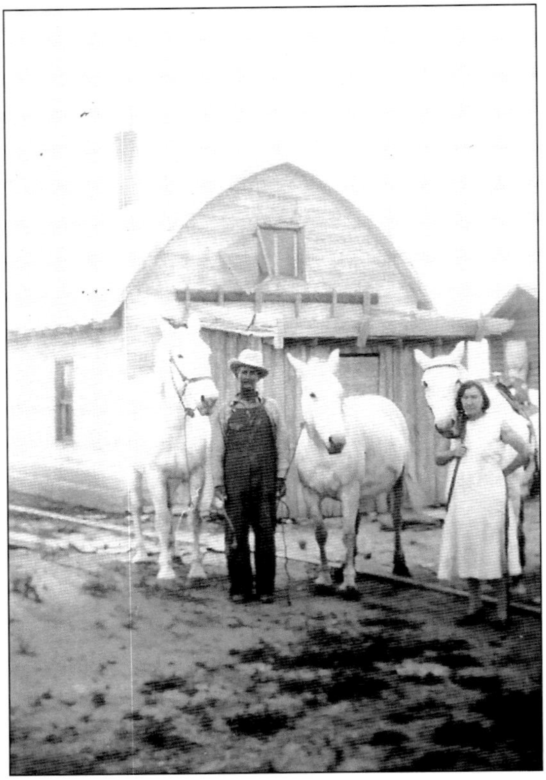

Johnson Home. Miller then got the Stonebraker girls, Louise, 13, and Blanche, 10. Kenneth Johnson, 7, was the adopted son and only child of Ernie and Florence Johnson and Miller's fifth stop. Eight-year-old Mary Louise Miller, Carl Miller's daughter was his next passenger. When Stonebraker and Johnson discovered that the children were not at the schoolhouse on Friday morning, they quickly spread word that the children were missing. Sadly, Louise Stonebraker and Kenneth Johnson perished on the bus before the children were rescued; Mary Louise Miller died at the Reinert house shortly after being rescued, despite the efforts of the adults at the home.

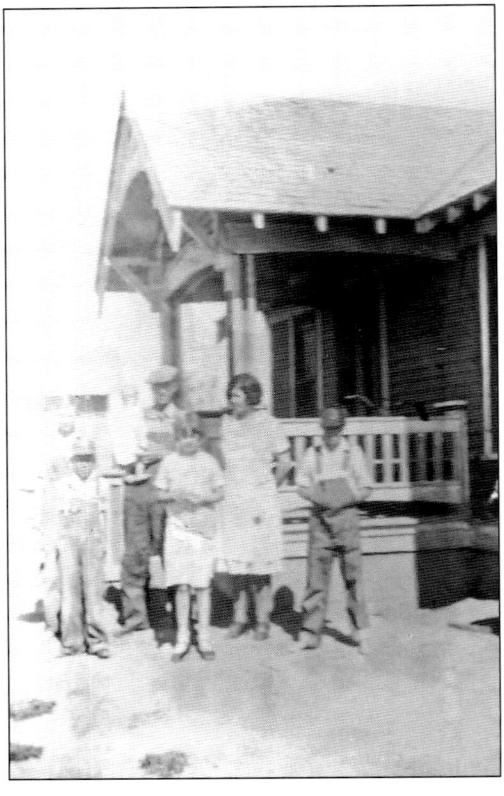

The Untiedt Family. Miller's last stop was at the Untiedt home. On March 26, he picked up Bryan, 13; Evelyn, 10; Ome, 9; and Arlo, 8. Their brother, Virgil, 11, stayed home sick that day. Clara Smith, 15, who helped Hazel Untiedt with household chores and the new baby, also got on the bus at the Untiedt's. Untiedt and Stonebraker found the children in the bus and carefully loaded them all into their wagon to transport them to the Reinert's. Both men lost a child. Like Mary Louise Miller, Arlo Untiedt passed shortly after reaching the Reinert home. Untiedt, Huffaker, Johnson, and Reinert fed the children, tried to treat their frostbite, and kept them awake yet another night, afraid if they went to sleep they would not wake.

Bryan Untiedt. After the children regained their health, they were taken to Denver, Colorado, to receive a medal for their courage, meet the mayor, and enjoy the city. They were treated to a five-course meal at the Brown Palace Hotel and then the next afternoon went shopping at Montgomery Ward and Company. The children later spent four days in Pueblo.

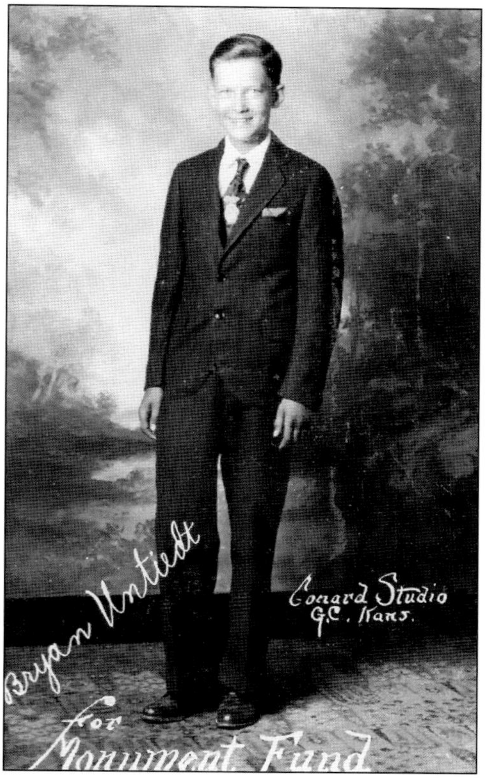

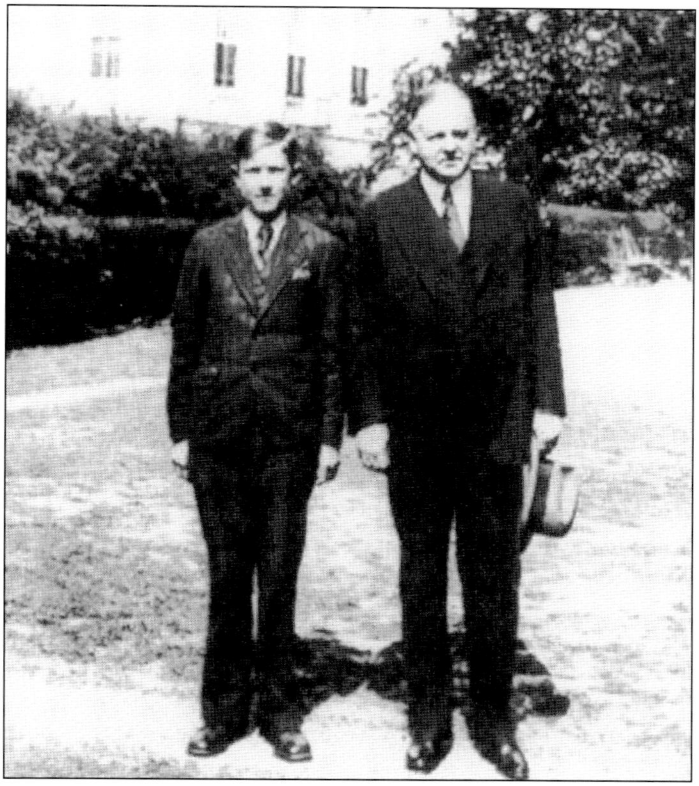

Bryan Untiedt and President Hoover. Although the survival of the 15 children was amazing, local newspapers dubbed Bryan Untiedt as the hero of the tragedy. Pres. Herbert Hoover invited Untiedt to visit him in Washington, D.C.; Untiedt toured the city just a month after the bus tragedy. Untiedt and the other survivors dealt with the unexpected publicity for much of the summer and periodically throughout their lives.

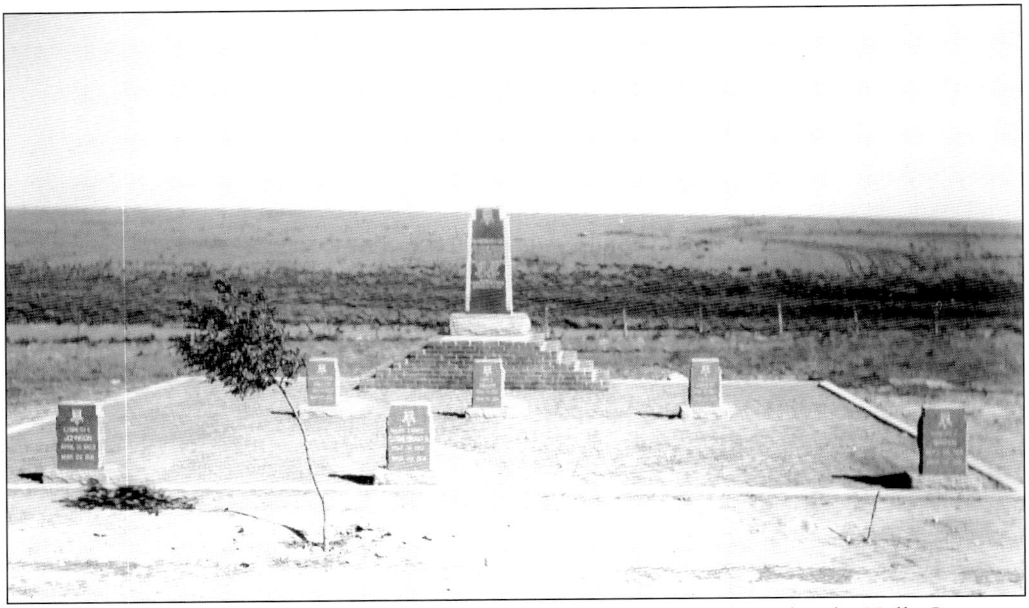

Monument in Holly. The six victims of the Towner Bus Tragedy were buried at the Holly Cemetery on March 31, 1931; the surviving children were not yet well enough to attend the service. It was a warm, sunny day, and it would have been Louise Stonebraker's 14th birthday. A few months later, on October 7, nearly 700 people, including the survivors and their families, attended a ceremony dedicating a stone monument to the victims and survivors of the Towner Bus Tragedy.

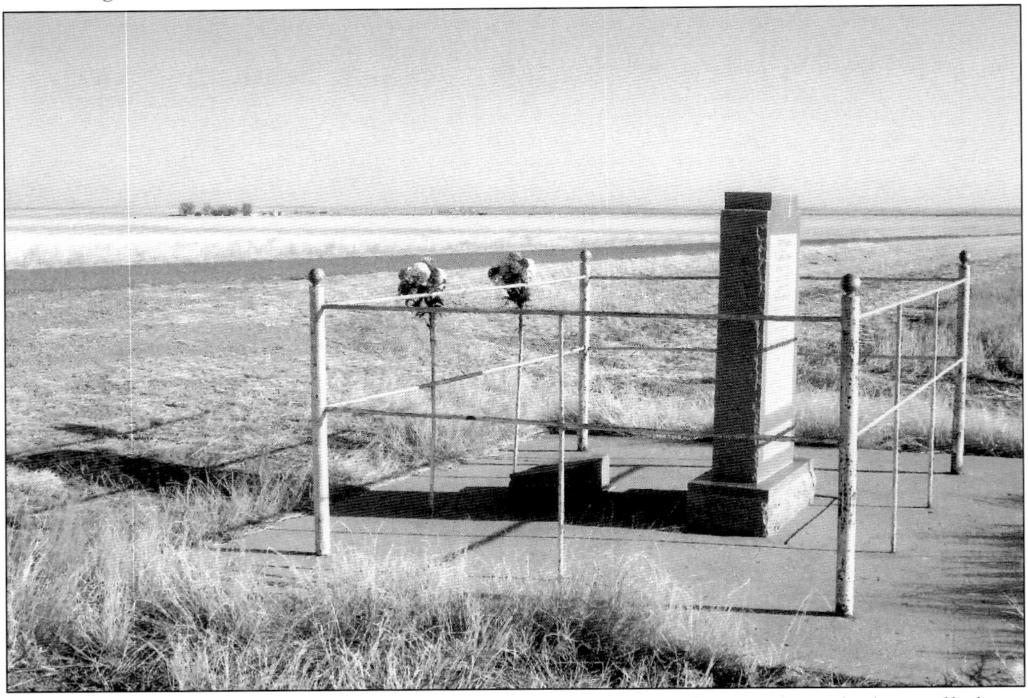

Stone monument at Site of Tragedy. In 1961, a monument at the site where the bus stalled was dedicated. It reads, "This marks the spot where the Towner-Holly School Bus and its 21 occupants were stalled in the blizzard of March 27, 1931. Six of the occupants lost their lives." The names of the six who died are also inscribed on the stone. (Photograph courtesy Jeff C. Campbell.)

Bibliography

Colorado Historic Newspapers. 30 November 2008: http://www.coloradohistoricnewspapers.org/Default/Skins/Colorado/Client.asp?Skin=Colorado&AW=1265301467535&AppName=2>. (Fall 2009).

Colorado Preservation, Inc. *The Legacy of the New Deal on Colorado's Eastern Plains*. Denver, CO: Colorado Preservation, 2008.

Harner, Ariana, and Clark Secrest. *Children of the Storm: The True Story of the Pleasant Hill School Bus Tragedy*. Golden, CO: Fulcrum, 2001.

Jacobs, Betty Lee, and Roleta D. Teal. *Kiowa County*. Boulder, CO: Johnson Publishing, 1976.

Jacobs, Ruthanna. *Kiowa County, Colorado: Centennial History*. Dallas, TX: Curtis Media, 1989.

Jenkins, Alyce. *Lost in a Blizzard*. Logan, IA: Perfection Learning, 2001.

Kiowa County Public Library. *Biographies of Pioneer Women*. Holly, CO: Holly Publishing, 1983.

Kiowa County Public Library. *Railroad in the Development of Kiowa County*. Holly, CO: Holly Publishing, 1983.

Kiowa County at the Dawn of a New Millennium. 1999–2000. http://eadseagles.com/projects.htm (Fall 2009).

McKean, Karlene, Roleta Teal, Betty Jacobs, and Mary Owen. *Tri-County History*. Limon, CO: The Eastern Colorado Printery, 1989.

Pearson, Georgene. *A Light in the Window*. Tulsa, OK: Logos to Rhema, 1995.

"The Sand Creek Massacre Timeline." 10 February 2010. http://www.kclonewolf.com/History/Sand Creek/sctime-05-1864-fall.html

www.arcadiapublishing.com

Discover books about the town where you grew up, the cities where your friends and families live, the town where your parents met, or even that retirement spot you've been dreaming about. Our Web site provides history lovers with exclusive deals, advanced notification about new titles, e-mail alerts of author events, and much more.

MADE IN THE USA

Arcadia Publishing, the leading local history publisher in the United States, is committed to making history accessible and meaningful through publishing books that celebrate and preserve the heritage of America's people and places. Consistent with our mission to preserve history on a local level, this book was printed in South Carolina on American-made paper and manufactured entirely in the United States.

This book carries the accredited Forest Stewardship Council (FSC) label and is printed on 100 percent FSC-certified paper. Products carrying the FSC label are independently certified to assure consumers that they come from forests that are managed to meet the social, economic, and ecological needs of present and future generations.

FSC
Mixed Sources
Product group from well-managed forests and other controlled sources

Cert no. SW-COC-001530
www.fsc.org